IRAQ: ISSUES, HISTORICAL BACKGROUND, BIBLIOGRAPHY

IRAQ: ISSUES, HISTORICAL BACKGROUND, BIBLIOGRAPHY

LEON M. JEFFRIES (EDITOR)

Nova Science Publishers, Inc.
New York

Senior Editors: Susan Boriotti and Donna Dennis
Coordinating Editor: Tatiana Shohov
Office Manager: Annette Hellinger
Graphics: Wanda Serrano
Editorial Production: Vladimir Klestov, Matthew Kozlowski and Maya Columbus
Circulation: Ave Maria Gonzalez, Vera Popovic, Luis Aviles, Raymond Davis, Melissa Diaz and Jeannie Pappas
Communications and Acquisitions: Serge P. Shohov
Marketing: Cathy DeGregory

Library of Congress Cataloging-in-Publication Data
Available Upon Request

ISBN: 1-59033-292-X.

400 Oser Ave, Suite 1600
Hauppauge, New York 11788-3619
Tele. 631-231-7269 Fax 631-231-8175
e-mail: Novascience@earthlink.net
Web Site: http://www.novapublishers.com

Printed in the United States of America

CONTENTS

PREFACE

Iraq has been in the center of world attention for the latter part of the 20th century and hasn't budged from there in the 21st. The country seems to be on its best international behavior as America utilizes its vast military machine and strikes out in either revenge or prevention at what it considers its enemies, whether real or imagined. And Iraq may be both – it might indeed be harboring terrorists with their sights on America and may not be, but as long as Saddam Hassan is at the helm, many in the Bush Administration apparently feel that it is their unfinished business to finish the business with Iraq and bring it to heel. But Iraq is not Afghanistan. Iraq has a long and rich history and is a geopolitical plum not to mention oil rich. This book brings together the current issues within the historical background and presents an extensive bibliography with access by subject, author and title indexes.

PART 1: CURRENT ISSUES

Chapter 1

IRAQ'S OPPOSITION MOVEMENTS

Kenneth Katzman

SUMMARY

Many in Congress and the Administration agree that the only way to blunt the long-term threat from Iraq is to remove Saddam Husayn from power. The Iraq Liberation Act (H.R. 4655, P.L: 105-338), signed October 31, 1998, gives the President authority to provide up to $97 million worth of defense articles to support an insurgency against Saddam. However, there are disagreements over the viability of the opposition and over how aggressively the United States should support the opposition groups. This report will be updated to reflect legislative and other developments.

INTRODUCTION[1]

Since October 1997, in the course of repeated crises over Iraqi non-cooperation with U.N. weapons inspections, a number of foreign policy experts and Members of Congress have been calling for a long-term U.S. effort to overthrow Iraq's President Saddam Husayn. In November 1998, amid one such crisis, the Administration adopted that recommendation as official policy. In January 1999, the Administration named senior diplomat Frank Ricciardone as Coordinator for the Transition in Iraq.

PAST ATTEMPTS TO OUST SADDAM

Prior to Desert Storm, which began January 16, 1991, President Bush called on the Iraqi people to overthrow Saddam. Within days of the end of the Gulf war (February 28, 1991),

[1] Much of the information in this paper is derived from press accounts of U.S. covert operations. CRS has no way to independently confirm the information contained in these press reports.

opposition Shiite Muslims in southern Iraq and Kurdish factions in northern Iraq, heartened by the U.S. call and the regime's postwar weakness, launched rebellions against Saddam and his Sunni Muslim-dominated regime.[2] The rebellion in southern Iraq reached the suburbs of Baghdad, but enough Republican Guard forces survived the war to defeat the rebels by mid-March 1991. The Kurds, benefiting from a U.S.-led no fly zone established in April 1991, were able to carve out an enclave in northern Iraq, free of Iraqi troops and governmental presence. However, Iraq is an Arab state that would not accept Kurdish political leadership or independence.

According to press reports, in May 1991, about two months after the failure of the Shiite and Kurdish uprisings, President Bush forwarded to Congress an intelligence finding justifying new U.S. efforts to topple Saddam Husayn. Press accounts indicate that about $15 - $20 million were allocated to efforts to cultivate ties to Iraqi military and security officials in the hopes of fomenting a coup.[3] The Bush Administration believed — and this view apparently still is shared by many in and outside the Clinton Administration - that a coup could produce a more favorable regime without risking the fragmentation of Iraq. Many observers maintain that Shiite and Kurdish groups, if they succeed in ousting Saddam, would divide the country into warring ethnic and tribal groups, and open Iraq to political and military influence from neighboring Iran, Turkey, and Syria.

An Opposition Coalition Emerges

Although reports in July 1992 of a serious but failed military rebellion suggested that the "coup strategy" might ultimately succeed, in its last months the Bush Administration appeared to shift toward backing the diverse opposition groups that had led the postwar rebellions. The Kurdish, Shiite, and other opposition elements were coalescing into a broad and diverse movement that appeared to be gaining support internationally. Congress more than doubled the budget (to about $40 million for FY1993) for covert support to the opposition and to maintain clandestine anti-Saddam radio stations.[4]

The Iraqi National Congress

The Iraqi National Congress (INC) served as the vehicle for U.S. support. The INC was formed when the two main Kurdish militias—the KDP, headed by Masud Barzani, and the PUK, headed by Jalal Talabani — decided to participate in a June 1992 meeting in Vienna of dozens of opposition groups. In October 1992, the major Shiite groups came into the coalition and the INC held a pivotal meeting in Kurdish-controlled northern Iraq. Selected to chair the Executive Committee was Ahmad Chalabi, a secular Iraqi Shiite Muslim and U.S.-trained mathematician. In the late 1950s, before the Ba'th Party came to power in Iraq (July 1968), Chalabi had fled Iraq to work in Jordan, eventually chairing the Petra Bank there.

---

[2] Shiites constitute about *65%* of Iraq's -population but have historically been repressed and underrepresented in governing bodies by the members of the Sunni Muslim sect. Kurds are about 20% of the population of about 20 million.

[3] Tyler, Patrick. "Plan On Iraq Coup Told To Congress." *New York Times,* February 9, 1992.

[4] Sciolino, Elaine. "Greater U.S. Effort Backed To Oust Iraqi." *New York Times,* June 2, 1992.

The INC appeared viable because it brought under one banner not only varying Iraqi ethnicities but also diverse political ideologies, including nationalists, ex-military officers, and defectors from the ruling Iraqi Ba'th Party. The INC also had a source of armed force (the Kurdish militias) and a presence on Iraqi territory (the northern enclave). Its constituent groups nominally united around a platform that appeared to match U.S. values and U.S. interests, including establishment of "human rights and rule of law within a constitutional, democratic, and pluralistic Iraq;" preservation of Iraq's territorial integrity; and compliance with U.N. resolutions on Iraq.[5] However, many observers have noted that the INC might not act as a democratic body if it came to power, because most of its groups have an authoritarian internal structure.

Some observers believe the Kurds would seek independence or full autonomy from an INC-dominated Iraq. Iraq's Kurds have been fighting for autonomy since the 1920s, shortly after their region was incorporated into the newly formed Iraqi state after World War I. In 1961, the Kurdistan Democratic Party (KDP), now led by Masud Barzani, son of KDP founder Mullah Mustafa Barzani, began an insurgency that has continued until today, albeit interrupted by periods of negotiations with Baghdad for Kurdish autonomy. The Patriotic Union of Kurdistan (PUK), led by Jalal Talabani, split off from the KDP in the 1960s. Together, the two Kurdish parties have about 35,000 fighters, which initially formed the backbone of the INC's military threat to Saddam Husayn. A small Islamic faction, the Islamic Movement of Iraqi Kurdistan (MIK), is headed by Shaykh Ali Abd-al Aziz. Based in Halabja, Iraq, the IMIK has been publicizing the effects of Baghdad's March 1988 chemical attack on Halabja.

Several outside experts have concerns about the alliance between Iran and another INC component, the Iraqi Shiite Islamic fundamentalist group called the Supreme Council for the Islamic Revolution in Iraq (SCIRI). SCIRI was set up in 1982 to increase Iranian control over Shiite opposition groups in Iraq and the Persian Gulf monarchies. SCIRI has about 4,000-8,000 fighters in an organization called the Badr Brigade operating against the Iraqi military in southern Iraq. Although Iran has improved relations with Iraq over the past few years, Iran's Revolutionary Guard reportedly continues to provide the Badr Brigade with weapons and training. SCIRI's close ties to Iran contributed to the failure of the Shiite uprising in southern Iraq after the 1991 Gulf war; most Iraqis do not want an Islamic government or to be controlled by Iran. SCIRI's leader, Ayatollah Muhammad Baqr al-Hakim, was the late Ayatollah Khomeini's choice to head an Islamic Republic of Iraq. "SCIRI has periodically distanced itself from the INC and has publicly refused to attend.opposition meetings in the United States or accept U.S. assistance.

THE FRAGMENTATION OF THE OPPOSITION

The differences within the INC eventually led to its virtual collapse as a viable challenge to Saddam Husayn. In May 1994, the two main Kurdish parties began fighting with each other over territory, revenues from duties levied at the Iraq-Turkey border, and control over the Kurdish regional government based in Irbil. To bolster their positions against each other,

[5] The Iraqi National Congress and the International Community. Document provided by INC representatives, February 1993.

the PUK obtained a measure of support from Iran while the KDP, always somewhat amenable to negotiations with Baghdad, sought and received countervailing backing from Saddam. The infighting contributed to the failure of an INC offensive against Iraqi troops in March 1995; the KDP refused, at the last minute, to participate in the offensive.

As a result of the growing difficulties within the INC, the United States began seeking out other Iraqi opposition groups.[6] One group, the Iraqi National Accord (INA), consisted primarily of military and security officers who had defected from Iraq and who were perceived to have some residual influence in Baghdad. The INA had received U.S. and Saudi backing in 1991 and 1992, before the INC came into favor in Washington. Its prospects appeared to brighten in August 1995 when Saddam's son-in-law Husayn Kamil al-Majid — architect of Iraq's weapons of mass destruction programs — defected to Jordan. The defection suggested to many in the region that Saddam's grip on power was weakening and Jordan's King Hussein agreed to allow the INA to operate from Jordan.

However, the INA became penetrated by Iraq's intelligence services and, in June 1996, Baghdad broke the back of the INA by arresting 100 military officers linked to it and executing 30 others. The leader of the INA, Dr. lyad Alawi, claims that INA sympathizers continue to operate throughout Iraq.

Iraq's counteroffensive against the opposition was completed two months after the INA arrests. In late August 1996, the KDP asked Baghdad to provide armed support for its capture of Irbil from the rival PUK. Iraq took advantage of the request to strike against the INC base in Salahuddin, northern Iraq, as well as remaining INA operatives in the north. Iraq executed two hundred oppositionists and arrested as many as 2,000. The United States evacuated and eventually resettled in the United States 650 oppositionists (mostly INC).

REBUILDING AN OPPOSITION STRATEGY

For the two years after the collapse of the opposition in northern Iraq, the Administration had little contact with the INC or other groups. Secretary of State Albright said on February 26, 1998, in testimony before a Senate Appropriations subcommittee, that the opposition is fragmented and that it would be "wrong to create false or unsustainable expectations" about what U.S. support for the opposition can accomplish. However, Iraq's deteriorating cooperation with UNSCOM throughout 1998, coupled with growing congressional calls for overthrowing Saddam, contributed to the Administration decision in November 1998 to formally adopt a policy of overthrow of Saddam Husayn.

Congressional pressure for a policy of regime began in early 1998 with an FY1998 supplemental appropriation (P.L. 105-174, signed May 1, 1998). Among other provisions, the law appropriated $5 million in aid (Economic Support Funds, ESF) to the opposition and $5 million for a Radio Free Iraq, under the direction of Radio Free Europe/Radio Liberty (RFE/RL).[7] The State Department received approval from Congress to use $3 million of the ESF for an overt program to coordinate the diverse participating groups, promote comity among the various opposition leaders, and highlight Iraqi violations of U.N. resolutions. The remaining $2 million was used to translate, analyze, and publicize the regime's alleged war

---

[6] An account of this shift in U.S. strategy is essayed in Hoagland, Jim. "How CIA's Secret War On Saddam Collapsed." *Washington Post,* June 26, 1997

[7] RFE/RL began broadcasting on October 30, 1998, from its headquarters in Prague.

crimes — including material retrieved from the Kurdish north and contained on 176 CD-ROM diskettes - an issue on which virtually all the opposition groups agree.

Perhaps reflecting congressional concern about the diffuse nature and external focus of the State Department plan, a provision of the FY1999 omnibus appropriation (Section 590 of H.R. 4328, P.L. 105-277), provided $8 million in FY1999 aid to the opposition. The provision made the INC the focus of U.S. assistance and stipulated that at least $3 million in ESF be given directly to the INC and at least another $2 million be used for opposition activities inside Iraq itself. As stipulated in that law, another $3 million went to the opposition-led INDICT (the International Campaign to Indict Iraqi War Criminals) organization for war crimes issues. All the FY1998 and FY1999 funds have been spent, according to the State Department, and the obligations included the first direct payment to the INC - a March 2000 grant of $267,000 to help it organize and open new offices. The $2 million in funds for opposition activities inside Iraq were used for humanitarian projects mainly in the Kurdish north, according to the State Department. Another $10 million in ESF for the opposition was appropriated in the FY2000 foreign aid law, passed by reference in P.L. 106-113. Of that amount, $2 million is to be spent on war crimes issues. No FY2000 funds for the opposition have been obligated as of late June 2000.

Iraq Liberation Act (ILA)

Apparently seeking a more assertive U.S. policy, another bill was introduced in 1998, authorizing funds to provide U.S. defense articles and services to the opposition. The Iraq Liberation Act (H.R. 4655), which passed the House on October 5, 1998 (360-38) and the Senate on October 7, 1998 (unanimous consent), gives the President the discretion to provide up to $97 million in defense articles (and $2 million in broadcasting funds) to opposition organizations to be designated by the Administration. The Act appeared to support the concept, advocated by Ahmad Chalabi and some U.S. policy experts, to promote an insurgency by using U.S. airpower to protect opposition-controlled enclaves. The Administration briefed several Members on the difficulty and risks of promoting an insurgency in Iraq,[8] but the President signed the bill (P.L. 105-338) on October 31, 1998, in the course of a crisis with Iraq over U.N. weapons inspections. On February 5, 1999, after consultations with Congress, the Administration designated (Presidential Determination 99-13) the following organizations as eligible to receive U.S. military assistance under the ILA: the INC; the INA; the Islamic Movement of Iraqi Kurdistan (IMIK); the KDP; the PUK; the Movement for Constitutional Monarch (MCM); and SCIRI. The IMIK and the MCM, in particular, are considered small movements that cannot contribute much to an overthrow effort.

In May 1999, in concert with an opposition visit to Washington, the Administration announced it would draw down $5 million worth of training and "non-lethal" defense equipment under the ILA. In late 1999, three opposition members began civil administration training at Hurlburt air base in Florida. As of June 2000, that training and some drawdown of non-lethal U.S. equipment amounted to $20,000. In concert with another opposition visit to Washington in June 2000 and a meeting on June 26 with Vice President Gore, the

[8] Pincus, Walter. "Bill Tries to Shift U.S. Policy on Iraq." *Washington Post,* October 1, 1998.

Administration announced that another 145 oppositionists would undergo similar training. The Defense Department-run courses will teach them skills in field medicine, logistics, computers, communications, broadcasting, and power generation. No combat training will be provided.

CONTINUED DEBATE OVER POLICY

The U.S. efforts during 1999 and 2000 to rebuild and train the opposition has not silenced the debate over the viability of the opposition or the contribution of this effort toward overall U.S. policy toward Iraq. Some in Congress believe the Administration should move more forcefully to aid the opposition with ILA drawdowns and appropriated funds. In a reflection of that view, a provision of the Senate version of the FY2001 foreign aid bill (S. 2522) provides for the INC to distribute $15 million in humanitarian aid to the Iraqi people and use another $10 million for broadcasting inside Iraq. Administration officials say they generally support the concept of opposition distribution of aid inside Iraq but question whether the INC has the capability to perform that mission.

Some Administration statements suggest a pessimistic view of the opposition and a hint of disagreement within the Administration on some aspects of the policy. Since the ILA was passed, outgoing Commander of the U.S. Central Command Gen. Anthony Zinni, has openly opposed implementing the Chalabi insurgency plan on the grounds that the INC or other groups are not sufficiently strong to challenge Saddam's grip on power. The United States, Zinni believes, would probably be drawn into a direct military effort to support or rescue the opposition forces.[9] In testimony before the Senate Foreign Relations Committee in February 2000, Secretary of State Albright said the opposition has "a long way to go" before it could pose a major threat to Iraq's regime. On the other hand, in his June 26, 2000 statement after meeting with the opposition, Vice President Gore appeared to suggest that the Administration would strongly pursue an opposition-based overthrow strategy. He reaffirmed the Administration's "strong commitment to the objective of removing Saddam Husayn from power..."

Some outside experts say that strong U.S. backing will give the Iraqi opposition legitimacy inside Iraq and could spark a broad revolt against Saddam Husayn's rule. Other experts, however, say that there is no evidence of broad support for the opposition inside Iraq. Many have noted that virtually none of Iraq's neighbors is willing to host an armed insurgent opposition effort against Saddam Husayn. Others note that the two main Kurdish parties are increasingly reluctant to host other opposition groups or to participate in a renewed effort to change the regime. Some believe that pursuing a strategy of overthrow conflicts, to some extent, with the goals of the United Nations' "oil-for-food program" to alleviate human suffering and with U.N. efforts to obtain Iraqi cooperation with a restart of weapons inspections, suspended since December 1998.

Perhaps in an attempt to develop an alternative to the ILA strategy, in 1998 the Administration reportedly tried to obtain congressional approval of and funding for an unspecified CIA plan to oust Saddam through covert operations.[10] However, press reports in

[9] Richter, Paul. Top Military Commander Questions Plan to Topple Hussein. Los Angeles Times. October 22, 1998.

[10] Rogers, David. Congress Passes $250 Billion Budget for Pentagon With Anti-Iraq Funds. Wall Street Journal, September 30, 1998.

January 1999 said that the Senate Select Committee on Intelligence rejected the Administration plan.[11] It is possible that the Administration's covert plan represented a attempt to return to the "coup strategy" pursued earlier, in which the United States would attempt to find sympathetic Iraqi military or security chiefs who might mount a rebellion against Saddam. It is also possible that the plan was rejected by the Senate committee because it might have involved sabotage against humanitarian targets, such as power grids, that are needed to alleviate the suffering of the Iraqi people. Some observers privately speculate that some covert operations, combined with opposition funding authorized by the DLA, could form a cohesive strategy intended to provoke a coup against Saddam or force him to make key concessions on weapons inspections or other outstanding issues.

[11] Wright, Robin. U.S. Dispute Holds Up Covert Iraq Operation. Los Angeles Times, January 5, 1999.

Chapter 2

IRAQ-U.S. CONFRONTATION

Alfred B. Prados and Kenneth Katzman

SUMMARY

Efforts by Iraq to impede U.N. weapons inspections since late 1997 and to challenge the allied-imposed no-fly zones over northern and southern Iraq have resulted in further confrontations with the United States and its allies. A decision by Iraq to ban almost all U.N. inspections on October 3l, 1998, led the United States arid Britain to conduct a 4-day air operation against Iraq on December 16-20, 1998 (Operation Desert Fox). The two allies launched approximately 415 missiles and dropped more than 600 bombs targeted at Iraqi military and logistical facilities.

Since the December 1998 operation, the United States and Britain have carried out air strikes against Iraqi air defense units and installations on a frequent basis, in response to Iraqi attempts to target allied aircraft enforcing no-fly zones over northern and southern Iraq. On October 7, 2001, following the September 11 terrorist attacks on the United States, the U.S. Ambassador to the United Nations warned Iraq not to move against Iraqi opposition groups or attack its neighbors while the United States was involved in its campaign against terrorism.

According to the U.S. Defense Department as of late November 1998, expanded military operations and crisis build-ups in the Gulf since the 1991 war had cost a total of $6.9 billion.

Incremental costs of these operations amounted to approximately $1.6 billion in FY1998, 1.3 billion in FY1999, $1.1 billion in FY2000, and $1.1 billion estimated in FY2001. These figures do not include costs resulting from operations in Afghanistan.

Erosion of the former allied coalition and U.S. force constraints limit some military options. Although some Arab states, notably Kuwait and Saudi Arabia, host U.S. aircraft enforcing no-fly zones, no Arab states with the exception of Kuwait have publicly supported allied air strikes against Iraq. At an Arab summit conference on March 27-28, 2002, the attendees welcomed Iraqi assurances that it would respect the independence of Kuwait, called for respecting the integrity of Iraq, and announced its "categorical rejection" of attacking Iraq.

Some officials and analysts have called for expansion of no-fly zones over Iraq. Others support covert operations to inflict damage on key Iraqi facilities and build a viable opposition to the regime. According to press articles, some U.S. officials favor more strikes against Iraq even in the absence of evidence linking it to the September attacks, in view of its efforts to acquire mass destruction weapons, refusal to readmit U.N. weapons inspectors, and long-standing support for terrorism.

Most Recent Developments

On January 29, 2002, in his State of the Union address, President Bush described Iraq, Iran, and North Korea as constituting "an axis of evil. " Secretary of State Colin Powell told a Senate committee on February 5 that Iraq "remains a significant threat to the [Middle East] region's stability." He added that "we have not ruled out other options " with respect to Iraq and went on to say that "we believe strongly in regime change in Iraq. " Speaking of Iraqi President Saddam Hussein, President Bush told reporters on March 13, 2002, that "he is a problem. And we 're going to deal with him. "

At a summit conference in Beirut, Lebanon on March 27-28, 2002, Arab leaders adopted a resolution that contained several clauses dealing with Iraq. The resolution welcomed assurances by Iraq that it will respect "the independence, sovereignty, and security of the state of Kuwait"; it called on Iraq to cooperate with Kuwait in identifying and returning missing Kuwaiti persons and property; it called for lifting economic sanctions on Iraq; it rejected "threats of aggression against some Arab states, particularly Iraq "; and it reiterated a "categorical rejection" of attacking Iraq or threatening any Arab state. After subsequent talks between President Bush and Saudi Crown Prince Abdullah on April 25, Saudi Foreign Minister Prince Saud al-Faysal told reporters that "we see no need for any military or other action" against Iraq, inasmuch as Iraq and U.N. representatives are discussing the issue of re-admitting weapons inspectors.

Background and Analysis

This issue brief covers the most recent U.S.-Iraqi confrontations, which began in the fell of 1998. It summarizes events that led to the crisis, the allied military build-up, military strikes against Iraq, international reactions, costs, and options for U.S. policy makers. It does not cover developments in the war in Afghanistan, except insofar as they may relate to the U.S.-Iraqi confrontation.

Since the cease-fire of March 3, 1991, that ended the Persian Gulf war (Operation Desert Storm), the United States has resorted on several occasions to the use or threat of force against Iraq. Some of these incidents resulted from Iraqi challenges to U.N. cease-fire terms that followed the war. Others resulted from bilateral issues between Iraq and the United States and its allies.

A principal factor in the most recent confrontation was Iraq's failure to cooperate fully with U.N. weapons inspectors. The inspection regime, established by U.N. Security Council Resolution 687 adopted on April 3, 1991, is designed to identify and dismantle Iraq's programs to develop weapons of mass destruction, including chemical, biological, and nuclear warfare systems as well as missiles capable of delivering them. Two agencies are charged with conducting these inspections: the U.N. Special Commission on Iraq

(UNSCOM), which deals with chemical, biological, and missile systems; and the International Atomic Energy Agency (IAEA), which deals with Iraqi nuclear weapons programs. Since the inception of the inspection regime, Iraq has obstructed its work in various ways:

- False, misleading, or incomplete responses to questions posed by inspectors;
- Interference by Iraqi escorts with the conduct of inspections;
- Denial of access to "sensitive" sites on grounds of national security;
- Removal of or tampering with material evidence of weapons programs; and
- Attempts to exclude U.S. personnel from inspection teams.

On seven occasions between 1991 and 1993, the U.N. Security Council found Iraq in "material breach of cease-fire terms"; however, the Council has not issued a finding of "material breach" since June 17, 1993, despite subsequent Iraqi provocations. According to news reports, some Council members are reluctant to agree to another such finding, which they think might provide, the basis for an attack on Iraq.

Another factor contributing to the recent confrontation was Iraqi violation of the no-fly zones imposed by the United States and its allies over portions of northern and southern Iraq. U.S. and British aircraft (and formerly French aircraft) have conducted overflights of northern and southern Iraq since 1991 and 1992, respectively, to enforce the bans on Iraqi aircraft in these zones. The allied overflights are known as Operation Northern Watch and Operation Southern Watch and are designed to exclude Iraqi aircraft from flying north of the 36th parallel and south of the 33rd parallel, respectively. The southern zone, covering 227,277 square kilometers (87,729 square miles) is larger than the northern zone, which covers 43,707 square kilometers (16,871 square miles), but Iraqi air defenses reportedly are thicker in the northern zone. Together, these zones cover 270,985 square kilometers (104,600 square miles), or 62% of Iraqi territory.

U.S. officials base the no-fly zones primarily on U.N. Security Council Resolution 688 of April 5, 1991, which demands that Iraq end repression of its population (notably Kurds in the north and Shi'ite Muslims in the south), and on the military cease-fire agreements after the Gulf war (the Safwan Accords), which forbid *Iraq* to interfere with allied air operations over Iraq. Some countries question this interpretation, arguing mat Resolution 688 was not passed under Chapter VH provisions (peace and security) and does not by itself permit military action to enforce its terms. Iraq maintains mat the no-fly zones constitute an illegal infringement on its sovereignty and has occasionally fired on allied planes conducting overflights to enforce these zones.

Events of the Crisis

Forerunner Episodes

Between mid-1993 and 1996, UNSCOM personnel were able to carry out their inspections of Iraqi weapons programs with relatively little interference by the government of Iraq. Increasing attempts by Iraq in 1997 to impede U.N. weapons inspections and to exclude U.S. personnel from UNSCOM teams prompted demands by the U.N. Security Council mat

Iraq cease its interference or face further sanctions. A Russian undertaking in November 1997 to seek "balanced representation" in UNSCOM membership temporarily averted a crisis; however, tensions mounted again in January 1998, as Iraq once more barred U.S.-led teams from conducting inspections and declared several "sensitive sites" off limits to U.N. inspectors. After a month of intensive diplomacy and a continuing build-up of U.S. forces in the Persian Gulf region, the Iraqi Deputy Prime Minister and the UN. Secretary-General signed an agreement with the following provisions:

- Reconfirmation by Iraq that it accepts relevant U.N. resolutions
- Commitment of U.N. member states to "respect the sovereignty and territorial integrity of Iraq"
- 'Immediate, unconditional, and unrestricted access" by UNSCOM and IAEA within Iraq, with respect for Iraqi concerns relating to "national security, sovereignty, and dignity"
- Special procedures to apply to inspections at eight "presidential sites" defined in an annex to the agreement
- Efforts to accelerate fee inspection process, and an undertaking by the Secretary-General to bring to U.N. Security Council members the concerns of Iraq over economic sanctions.

On March 3, the U.N. Security Council unanimously passed Resolutionl 1154, co-sponsored by Britain and Japan, which commended the initiative of the Secretary-General in security these commitments from Iraq, stressed that Iraq must comply with its obligations, and warned that any violation of these terms or other Security Council resolutions "would have the severest consequences for Iraq." Although inspections during the spring of 1998 proceeded relatively smoothly, many questions concerning Iraq's weapons programs remained unresolved. Also, Iraqi spokesmen continued periodically to warn of a new crisis if economic sanctions were not quickly removed.

December 1998 Air Strikes

After a lull of several months, tensions mounted in August 1998, as Iraq began to challenge U.N. operations once more. On August 5, Iraq announced that it would no longer allow UNSCOM to inspect new facilities, and followed with a ban on all remaining UNSCOM activities on October 31. U.S. officials described Iraq's actions as unacceptable, as did some other members of the Security Council. Resolution 1205 of November 5, which demanded that Iraq rescind its bans on U.N. weapons inspection activities and resume full cooperation with UNSCOM, did not specifically mentioned use of force; however, U.S. officials emphasized again that all options are open including military force to compel Iraqi compliance. On November 11, the United Nations evacuated more than 230 staff personnel from Baghdad, including all weapons inspectors, as the United States warned of possible retaliatory strikes against Iraq.

As U.S. forces were on the verge of conducting air and missile strikes against Iraq on November 14, the Clinton Administration delayed them for 24 hours upon learning that Iraq had agreed to resume cooperation with UNSCOM. After further negotiations, Iraq agreed in a letter to the Security Council on November 15 to provide unconditional cooperation to UNSCOM and rescind its ban on UNSCOM activities. The Administration men canceled the planned strikes; however, the President warned that Iraq must fulfill its obligations. Specifically, in a news conference on November 15, he listed five conditions Iraq must fulfill to meet the criteria of unconditional cooperation;

- Resolution of all outstanding issues raised by UNSCOM and the IAEA.
- Unfettered access for inspectors with no restrictions, consistent with the February 23 memorandum signed by Iraq.
- Turnover by Iraq of all relevant documents.
- Acceptance by Iraq of all U.N. resolutions related to mass destructions weapons.
- No interference with the independence or professional expertise of weapons inspectors.

Despite its pledges on November 14-15, Iraq began to impede the work of U.N. weapons inspectors once more, according to statements by UNSCOM Chief Butler on December 8. On December 15, Butler submitted a report in which he concluded that 'Iraq did not provide the full cooperation it promised on 14 November 1998" and "initiated new forms of restrictions upon the Commission's work." On December 15, Butler withdrew remaining UNSCOM inspectors from Iraq, saying that they could no longer perform their mission. On the following day, then President Clinton directed U.S. forces to strike military and security targets in Iraq. He described the mission as "to attack Iraq's nuclear, chemical and biological weapons programs and its military capacity to threaten its neighbors."

Attacks began on December 16, 1998, at 5:06 p.m. EST (December 17 at 1:06 a.m. Baghdad time) in an operation known as Desert Fox, as U.S. forces launched over 200 cruise missiles (officials declined to give an exact number) at over 50 targets in Iraq, from the aircraft carrier *U.S.S. Enterprise,* other Navy ships in the region, and some 70 Navy and Marine Corps aircraft According to some media reports, B-52 bombers based in the Indian Ocean island of Diego Garcia took part as well. British forces also joined in the attacks. A second wave of attacks took place on the evening of December 17-18, involving approximately 100 cruise missiles (but with larger warheads than those used in the first wave of attacks) and B-52 bombers, again with British participation. B-l bombers joined the attack during the third wave (evening of December 18-19), marking the first combat operations for this aircraft. After the fourth wave of attacks (evening of December 19-20), President Clinton halted the 72-hour operation (code named Operation Desert Fox) on December 20. Senior U.S. officials warned that the United States would repeat its attacks as often as necessary to prevent Iraq from continuing programs to develop mass destruction weapons.

During Operation Desert Fox, U.S. and British forces launched approximately 415 cruise missiles (325 Tomahawks fired by Navy ships and 90 air launched cruise missiles mainly by B-52s) and dropped more than 600 bombs. According to reports by the U.S. Department of Defense, the 97 targets of allied attacks included lethal weapons production or storage facilities (11), security facilities for weapons (18), Iraqi Republican Guards and other military facilities (9), government command, control, and communications facilities (20), air defense systems (32), airfields (6), and one oil refinery. According to preliminary Defense Department assessments on December 20, 10 targets were destroyed, 18 severely damaged,

18 moderately damaged, 18 lightly damaged, and 23 not yet assessed. A second assessment on December 21 cited a total of 98 targets, of which 43 were severely damaged or destroyed, 30 moderately damaged, 12 lightly damaged, and 13 not damaged. The U.S. theater commander described the estimates as conservative, pointing out that even lightly damaged facilities can be rendered unusable: There were no U.S. or British casualties. According to the Iraqi Deputy Prime Minister, the allied action killed 62 Iraqi military personnel (including 38 Republican Guards) and wounded 180; there have been no estimates of Iraqi civilian casualties. Chairman of the Joint Chiefs of Staff General Harry Shelton told the Senate on January 5, 1999, however, that allied strikes killed or wounded an estimated 1,400 members of Iraq's elite military and security forces (600 from the Special Republican Guard and 800 from the Republican Guard).

Further Actions

A series of follow-on military actions have occurred since December 28, 1998, as Iraqi air defenses have tried to target U.S. and British aircraft patrolling the no-fly zones and Iraqi aircraft have made brief intrusions into the zones. U.S. Air Force and Navy aircraft, as well as British aircraft, have responded to Iraqi challenges with anti-radiation missile strikes directed against Iraq air defense and command and control installations and have fired at intruding Iraqi aircraft. Before Operation Desert Fox, U.S. responses to Iraqi violations of the no-fly zones were usually confined to the immediate source of the violation, i.e., an air defense battery or an intruding Iraqi aircraft. On January 27, 1999, authorities expanded rules of engagement to allow U.S. aircraft to target a wider range of Iraqi air defense systems and related installations in response to Iraqi violations of the no-fly zones. In congressional testimony on March 23, 2000, a Defense Department official said operational commanders have been given additional flexibility in responding to Iraqi provocations; under the current rules of engagement, pilots may respond not only by defending themselves but also by acting to reduce the overall Iraqi air defense threat to coalition aircraft.

Official Iraqi media reported on January 3, 1999 that President Saddam Hussein condemned the no-fly zones as illegal and said his people would resist them with "bravery and courage." The Iraqi President followed up by offering a $14,000 bounty to any unit that succeeded in shooting down an allied plane and an additional $2,800 reward for capturing an allied pilot. In an NBC interview carried on June 17, 2001, the Iraqi Ambassador to the United Nations said Iraq would do "anything possible to down American planes" and confirmed that the government had offered a reward to Iraqi military personnel who succeeded in doing so.

In a May 8, 2000 interview, the U.S. commander of Operation Northern Watch said Iraqi air defense weapons, which can reach altitudes of 40,000 feet, have the capability to hit U.S. aircraft. According to a July 24 press report, however, the newly designated commander responsible for file Southern Watch operation told the Senate Armed Services Committee that Iraqi air defense missiles are largely ineffective because they do not use their radar systems (which allied pilots can target) and because they must move frequently (approximately every 12 hours). On June 15, the commander of Iraqi air defense forces asserted that Iraq had succeeded in shooting down or intercepting 100 U.S. high-speed anti-radar missiles (HARM) used by allies to target Iraqi radar; however, allied sources dismissed the Iraqi claim.

Similarly, allied officials state that no U.S. or British planes have been lost, despite Iraqi claims to the contrary. (On September 13, 2000, an Iraqi air defense spokesman asserted that Iraqi air defense units had shot down 10 allied aircraft since December 17, 1998.)

Iraq has claimed that allied air strikes have killed a number of Iraqi civilians. In a note to the U.N. Human Rights Commission released by U.N. officials on March 26, 2001, the Iraqi government protested that allied air strikes had killed 315 and wounded 965 Iraqis, all civilians; the note described the allied overflights as a violation of international law. Subsequently, the Iraqi government claimed that a U.S.-British air strike on June 20, 2001 killed 23 Iraqis and injured 11 others participating in a soccer game near the city of Mosul in northern Iraqi.

U.S. and British officials have denied some Iraqi reports of civilian casualties and have attributed others to the Iraqi practice of placing air defense weapons in close proximity to populated areas, thus using nearby residents as human shields. For example, on August 18, 1999, U.S. Defense Department officials said reconnaissance photographs showed two Iraqi missile launchers located 115 feet from homes in the northern city of Mosul. On at least one occasion, in May 1999, U.S. authorities reportedly acknowledged the likelihood that allied units had erroneously identified a civilian target as an air defense installation. Allied officials have dismissed some Iraqi complaints as distortions or fabrications; with regard to the alleged soccer casualties, for example, allied spokesmen said their aircraft had not carried out any air strikes on June 20 and suggested that any casualties or injuries that occurred may have been caused by misdirected Iraqi groundfire...

The year 2001 has seen what appears to be a more aggressive effort by Iraq to bring down an allied aircraft by upgrading its air defense capabilities and mounting more challenges against allied overflights. Iraq reportedly has succeeded in extending the range of some of its older model air defense missiles and has made its communications less vulnerable by installing fiber optic cable, reportedly with Chinese assistance. On July 31, 2001, U.S. Defense Department spokesman Rear Admiral Quigley told reporters that Iraq has shown "a considerably more aggressive stance in trying to bring down a coalition aircraft." He noted continuing provocations by Iraq against allied aircraft over the two no-fly zones, especially in the southern zone, and allied retaliations (number of days on which allied aircraft have struck Iraqi targets in response):

- Southern Watch: 221 provocations in 2000 (18.4 per month); 370 in the first seven months of 2001 (30.8 per month).
- Northern Watch: 145 provocations in 2000 (12.1 per month); 62 in the first seven months of 2001 (8.9 per month).

In response, allied forces conducted strikes on Iraqi targets in the Southern Watch area on 32 days in 2000 and 19 days during the first 7 months of 2001; in the Northern Watch area, on 48 days in 2000 and 7 days during the first 7 months of 2001.

U.S. officials have acknowledged increased risks to allied pilots posed by Iraqi challenges and have made further efforts to counteract them. On June 4, 2001, U.S. Secretary of Defense Donald Rumsfeld told reporters that "there is a risk to pilots mat fly in areas that are dangerous and defended." He added that "[t]he risk grows to the extent that other nations assist Iraq in strengthening its military capability, its air defense capability and its ability to proceed with its clear and unambiguous desire to have increasingly powerful weapons and military capabilities." On August 3, he said: "[i]t does appear that Iraq has been successful in quantitatively and qualitatively improving their air defenses." According to news reports, allied strikes have been increasingly designed to set back recent improvements in Iraqi air defense capabilities.

The February 2001 Strikes

On February 16, between the hours of 11:20 a.m. and 1:40 p.m. Washington, D.C. time, 24 U.S. and British combat aircraft struck five Iraqi air defense command-and-control installations, using precision guided munitions. According to a U.S. Department spokesman, four of the five installations struck by the allied aircraft were located north of the 33rd parallel (the northern limit of the southern no-fly zone), but the aircraft themselves did not go north of the 33ri parallel. The spokesman noted that this was the first time since Operation Desert Fox that allied aircraft had hit targets outside the southern no-fly zone, although targets outside the northern zone had been struck during the fell of 1999.

According to press reports, one goal of the allied strikes was to destroy a fiber optic cable network that Chinese are reportedly installing to upgrade the effectiveness of Iraqi air defense radars. On March 6, China's foreign minister said relevant agencies had investigated these allegations and found no evidence that Chinese companies had assisted Iraq in installing fiber optic cables for Iraqi air defenses. A March 17 *Washington Post* article, citing U.N. documents and unidentified diplomats, reported that a Chinese company, Huawei Technologies, has been seeking U.N. approval to sell Iraq telecommunications equipment and switching systems.

Subsequent press reports indicated that many of the munitions fired by allied units had missed their targets; according to these reports, a majority of the AGM-154A Joint Stand-Off Weapons (JSOWs) dropped by U.S. aircraft went astray, although two other types of "smart weapons" (AGM-130 guided missiles and Stand-Off Land Attack missiles) achieved somewhat more success. These alleged problems have been attributed by press sources to several possible factors: human error in programming, heavy wind, software defects, mechanical failure, or jamming of signals by Iraqis; officials reportedly believe the first two explanations are the most likely. Defense spokesmen have declined to identify the munitions used in the strikes.

Additional Strikes and Provocations

Since February, allied forces have carried out several significant strikes against Iraqi air defense installations, including an Iraqi mobile early warning radar in southern Iraq on April 19, an air defense site in northern Iraq on April 20, an air defense installation 180 miles southeast of Baghdad on May 18, and an air defense site in northern Iraq on August 7. On August 10, in the largest air strike since February, U.S. and British aircraft hit three installations: a surface-to-air missile battery 170 miles southeast of Baghdad, an associated long-range mobile radar system, and a fiber optic communications station 70 miles southeast of Baghdad Before this strike, on July 29, U.S. National Security Advisor Condoleeza Rice told CNN that the Administration is contemplating the use of "military force in a more resolute manner" and said that "Saddam Hussein is on the radar screen for the Administration."

Meanwhile, some observers believe Iraqi air defense forces may be improving their ability to target allied aircraft. On July 24, Iraqi forces fired a surface-to-air missile at a U.S.

high altitude U-2 reconnaissance aircraft, and Defense Department sources reportedly said the missile came close to hitting the plane. On August 27, according to the U.S. Defense Department, a U.S. Air Force RQ- IB Predator - an unmanned aerial vehicle (UAV or "drone") - was reported missing over southern Iraq while on a routine mission in support of Operation Southern Watch. A Defense Department statement described the Predator as "one of many systems used for reconnaissance and surveillance to monitor Iraqi compliance with United Nations Security Council Resolutions." Iraqi media claimed that Iraq's air defense units successfully hit the UAV, while the U.S. Defense Department statement said the aircraft may have crashed or may have been shot down. According to the U.S. Defense Department, no sensitive technology was compromised by the loss of the aircraft. Press reports have noted, however, that if the Iraqi claim is correct, it would be the first time that a U.S. aircraft involved in enforcing the Northern or Southern Watch Operations has been brought down by enemy fire. A second RQ-1B was lost over southern Iraq on September 11 and a third on October 10. Again, Iraqi media claimed responsibility for both losses but U.S. military spokesmen said they had not confirmed the cause. According to a-U.S. military spokesman commenting on the first incident, U.S. officials are aware of efforts by Iraq to bring down a manned allied aircraft. Press articles on April 23, 2002, reported that Iraq had significantly reinforced its surface-to-air missiles in the no-fly zones; however, Chairman of the Joint Chiefs of Staff General Richard B. Myers said Iraq frequently moves anti-aircraft systems in and out of these zones.

Aftermath of the Terrorist Attacks

The Iraqi government was the only Middle East regime that did not send condolences to the United States after the September 11 attacks, although Iraq officials did express sympathy to several U.S. non-government organizations known to oppose U.S. containment policies toward Iraq. According to numerous press reports, U.S. officials have found no hard evidence of an Iraqi hand in the attacks or subsequent cases of anthrax, although some U.S. officials suspect Iraqi involvement. Some commentators have pointed to several alleged meetings, in recent years between Iraqi intelligence officials and members of Osama bin Laden's, Al Qaeda organization and speculated that Iraq could provide Al Qaeda with money and expertise on chemical and biological warfare. Other commentators counter that Saddam and bin Laden have different views and ideologies and note that Iraq has been trying recently to cultivate better relations with western countries in an effort to gain support for terminating economic sanctions imposed after Iraq invaded Kuwait in 1990. In testimony before the Senate Armed Services Committee on March 19, 2002, Director of Central Intelligence George Tenet said "the jury's out" regarding any Iraqi involvement in the September 11 attacks but added that "it would be a mistake to dismiss the possibility of state sponsorship, whether Iranian or Iraqi, and we'll see where the evidence takes us."

On October 11, U.S. Defense Department spokesmen were quoted as saying that there had been no significant increase in skirmishes between allied forces and Iraqi forces since the September 11 attacks. According to a November 19 press article, however, even in the absence of evidence linking Iraq to the attacks, some U.S. officials are in favor of more strikes against Iraq because of its efforts to acquire mass destruction weapons, its refusal to readmit U.N. weapons inspectors, and its long-standing support for terrorism. In a press interview on October 28, Iraqi Deputy Prime Minister Tariq Azaz accused the United States and Britain of trying to overthrow the Iraq regime under the guise of fighting terrorism and charged that the two governments had plans to strike 300 targets in Iraq with 1,000 missiles. According to a February 15, 2002 press report, Aziz said Iraq would consider readmitting U.N. weapons inspectors, but only if other countries in the region were subject to the same inspection process.

On January 29, 2002, in his State of the Union address, President Bush described Iraq, Iran, and North Korea as constituting "an axis of evil." Secretary of State Colin Powell told a Senate committee on February 5 that Iraq "remains a significant threat to the [Middle East] region's stability." He added that "we have not ruled out other options" with respect to Iraq and went on to say that "we believe strongly in regime change in Iraq." On February 19, National Security Adviser Condoleezza Rice was quoted by the press as saying that "[w]e're pursuing a range of policy options, including, for instance, trying to change the nature of the sanctions with Iraq." President Bush, speaking of Saddam Hussein, told reporters on March 13, said "he is a problem. And we're going to deal with him."

Force Deployments and Costs

The 1998 Build-Up

U.S. force levels have fluctuated somewhat since the latest series of confrontations that began in the fell of 1997. During the mid-1990s, U.S. forces in the Persian Gulf region on an average comprised 15,000 to 20,000 personnel (many of them Navy and Marine Corps personnel embarked on ships), together with up to 200 aircraft and 20 ships, usually but not always including an aircraft carrier. The first phase of the crisis saw U.S. force levels increase to more than 40,000 personnel in late February and March, reinforced with British and other allied contingents. As the crisis receded later in the spring, forces were briefly drawn back down to their pre-1997 levels.

As the crisis worsened again in the fall of 1998, U.S. force levels in the Gulf began to climb once more. Additional deployments begun on November 11 were briefly halted after November 16, following cancellation of planned allied strikes in response to a last-minute understanding reached with Iraq. As Iraq failed to honor its November commitments, Secretary Cohen announced "a sharp increase in our forces in me Gulf' (approximately 24,100 personnel as of December 15). Cohen and General Shelton announced the deployment of a "crisis response force" consisting of nearly 60 additional Air Force and Marine jet fighters (including 10 F-l 17A radar-evading stealth fighters), additional Patriot missiles, elements of an Army brigade (some 2,700 troops), and a second aircraft carrier, the *U.S.S. Carl Vinson* with up to 60 Navy jet fighters, to the Gulf region. According to subsequent reports, up to 15,000 additional military personnel were deployed or ordered to the region. During Operation Desert Fox, Defense Department officials said U.S. force strength in the Gulf reached 29,900 on December 19, together with 37 ships and 348 aircraft.

After Desert Fox

These forces were once more reduced after Operation Desert Fox was over, even though smaller scale military action continued. U.S. commanders pointed out that the lack of an effective Iraqi response to Desert Fox made the reinforcements unnecessary at the time, and said the United States would return to a normal continuous presence in the Gulf. Most U.S. personnel in the region, including those conducting Operation Southern Watch, are assigned to the U.S. Central Command (CENTCOM), whose area of responsibility covers large parts of the Middle East, southern and central Asia, and northeast Africa. U.S. forces conducting Operation Northern Watch are based in Turkey and assigned to U.S. European Command (EUCOM). The task forces responsible for enforcing the two no-fly zones are linked by a hot line and coordinate many of their operations. On September 12, 2000, a Defense Department official said that at any given time the United States has between 20,000 and 25,000 personnel in the region, most of them afloat. The total number of U.S. military aircraft (Navy and Air Force) in the Gulf region has generally averaged about 200 in recent years. Ship totals have varied; as of June 2001, the U.S. Navy had 20 ships (including one aircraft carrier and eight other combatants) in the Gulf region

U.S. and other allied forces in the region have increased significantly since the September 11 attacks. Recent official figures are not available; however, according to a February 24, 2002 *Washington Post* article, Defense Department officials said there are 60,000 U.S. troops in the CENTCOM area of operations, of which 4,000 are on the ground in Afghanistan. Many other troops in the CENTCOM area are involved in supporting allied operations Afghanistan.

Costs

A Defense Department spokesman told reporters on November 17, 1998 that expanded military operations and crisis build-ups in the Gulf since the war in 1991 had cost a total of $6.9 billion. Much of this figure represents the costs of enforcing the no-fly zones over northern and southern Iraq. Following are costs estimates for several other crisis build-ups and retaliatory operations undertaken by the United States between 1991 and 1997.

- Troop movements and retaliatory strikes against Iraq, December 1992-January 1993: $400 million
- Troop deployments to counter Iraqi force movements, October 1994 (Operation Vigilant Warrior): $257 million (partially defrayed by Kuwait and Saudi Arabia)
- Retaliatory strikes following Iraqi incursion into protected northern zone, August-September 1996 (Operation Desert Strike): $102.7 million.

Incremental costs of U.S. operations in the Persian Gulf since FY1997 appear in **Table 1,** below. Cost figures since FY2001 are not available.

Britain, according to an August 23, 1999 *London Times* report, is spending approximately 4.5 million pounds ($7.19 million at exchange rate of U.K. 1 pound = U.S. $1.5974) per month on its deployments in the Gulf. Current figures are not available.

Table 1. Costs of Persian Gulf Operations (in U.S. $ millions)

Operation	FY1998	FY1999	FY2000	FY2001*
Southern Watch	1,497.2	933.2	755.4	678.0
Northern Watch	136.0	156.4	143.7	138.7
Desert Spring (Kuwait training)**	5.6	13.8	239.8	241.8
Desert Thunder (Nov. 1998 build-up)	n/a	43.5	n/a	n/a
Desert Fox (Dec. 1998 air strikes)	n/a	92.9	n/a	n/a
Totals	1,638.8	1,239.8	1,138.9	1,058.5

Source: Department of Defense, Comptroller.
*Estimate.
**Known as Intrinsic Action until FY2000.

U.S. AND INTERNATIONAL REACTIONS

Administration Position on Use of Force

U.S. administrations have taken the position that they already have sufficient authority to use military force to compel Iraqi compliance. On February 3, 1998, during an earlier phase of the present confrontation, Clinton Administration officials reportedly cited the joint resolution passed by Congress on the eve of the 1991 Gulf war (P.L. 102-1) as the basis for this authority. PJL 102-1 has no expiration date, and some specialists in international law agree that this law provides sufficient authority to U.S. administrations to use force against Iraq.

In the international context, the United States believes that two previous U.N. Security Council resolutions provide sufficient authority to use force against Iraq: Resolution 678 (November 29, 1990), which authorized military action after Iraq's invasion of Kuwait, and Resolution 687 (April 3, 1991), which made a cease-fire conditional on Iraqi compliance with various specified terms, including the inspection and dismantling of Iraq's lethal weapons programs. U.N. Security Council Resolution 1154 of March 2, 1998 (see above) does not specifically mention the use of force, but warns Iraq of "severest consequences" for violation. In a news conference on March 11, President Clinton said "We believe that the resolution gives us the authority to take whatever actions are necessary. But, of course, we would consult [with other Security Council members]." Subsequently, U.N. Security Council Resolution 1205 of November 5, 1998 condemned Iraq's refusal to cooperate with UNSCOM as a "flagrant violation" of Resolution 687 and other relevant agreements, and expressed full support for efforts by the Secretary-General to seek full implementation of the February 23 agreement. Other members of the Security Council, however, with the notable exception of Britain, do not believe that the wording of recent U.N. Security Council resolutions provides an automatic trigger authorizing military force.

Congressional Reactions

Congress has been largely supportive of Administration efforts to compel Iraqi compliance with U.N. resolutions. Some Members have argued for even stronger measures against Iraq, although others believe the Administration should seek farther congressional authorization before engaging in any significant escalation of hostilities. Congress has also appropriated funds to defray the cost of increased U.S. force deployments to the Gulf since 1997.

Some Republican Members of Congress questioned the timing of the Clinton Administration's decision to launch the strikes in December 1998, noting that the decision coincided with the floor debates in the House on impeachment of then President Clinton. The President denied that issue of impeachment was related to his decision to launch air strikes, and said the timing was dictated by the need for surprise, along with his desire to avoid starting hostilities during the month of Ramadan. On December 17, 1998, the House of Representatives passed H.Res. 612, expressing unequivocal support for the men and women of our Armed Forces carrying out missions in the Persian Gulf region, and supporting efforts to remove Saddam Hussein from power, by 417 to 5, with one voting "present" (Roll No. 539).

Some Members of Congress have expressed support for expanding the campaign against terrorism to Iraq, in the aftermath of the September 11 terrorist attacks on the United States. On December 20, 2001, the House of Representatives passed H.J.Res. 75, entitled "Regarding inspection and monitoring to prevent the development of weapons of mass destruction in Iraq", by 392 to 12, with 7 present, Roll no. 511. Among other things, this resolution stated that Iraq "remains immaterial and unacceptable breach of its international obligations" and that Iraq's refusal to allow U.N. weapons inspectors "immediate, unconditional, and unrestricted access ... presents a mounting threat to the United States, its friends and allies, and international peace and security." President Bush has also demanded that Iraq agree to a resumption of U.N. weapons inspections.

International Reactions

International reactions to U.S. reprisals against Iraq have been mixed and have varied according to the nature of the crisis that precipitated a U.S. military response. On the whole, altered international conditions have caused some erosion since 1991 in international support for the use of force against Iraq. Contributing factors include U.S.-Russian tensions, Arab disillusionment with broader U.S. Middle East policies, diminished Arab concerns over a potential threat from Iraq, and increasing sympathy for the sufferings of the Iraqi people.

Most European allies supported Desert Fox, as did Japan, South Korea, Australia, and Canada. Britain, on its part, has continued to participate in U.S. military actions against Iraq and, along with the United States, takes the position that existing U.N. resolutions provide the necessary legal basis for such action. France, on the other hand, regretted the air strikes and China and Russia condemned them. France also suspended its participation in the allied overflights of southern Iraq. The latter three countries have continued to criticize the U.S.-British retaliatory responses to Iraqi challenges in the no-fly zones since December 1998. Criticism increased after the February 16, 2001 allied strikes on Iraq's air defense installations. According to the Kremlin, Russian President Vladimir Putin described the strikes as "counter-productive for the process of a political settlement" and the French Foreign Minister said there was "no legal basis for this type of bombardment." Turkey's Prime Minister said "[t]he U.S. Administration should have informed us beforehand" of the strikes. In east Asia, Japan declined either to endorse or to criticize the strikes, but South Korea's national news agency warned that the "policy of strangling Iraq" has failed to achieve its goals. Meanwhile, according to a U.S. official, the U.S. State Department has been in touch with China about reports of Chinese assistance in upgrading Iraqi air defense units.

Most Arab leaders were restrained in their comments on the December 1998 strikes, but hostile demonstrations took place in several countries including Egypt, Jordan, Yemen, Palestinian areas, and Syria (where they briefly turned violent). The 55-member Islamic Conference Organization appealed for a halt to the attacks on Iraq. Kuwait and Oman, alone among the six pro-western Gulf states, allowed U.S. and British combat aircraft to launch strikes from bases on their territory. The other four, Saudi Arabia, Bahrain, Qatar, and the United Arab Emirates (UAE), allowed support operations and including air space clearance and take-off by refueling planes. Saudi Arabia expressed hopes that the strikes would end quickly, and the UAE Defense Minister went so far as to say "the option of force should not even have been considered, as the only ones who suffer are the Iraqi people." On December 30, 1998, Saudi Defense Minister Prince Sultan reaffirmed that Saudi Arabia would not agree to air strikes from its territory, but called on Iraq to implement U.N. Security Council resolutions.

Arab countries have reacted ambivalently to follow-on allied military operations against Iraq during 1999 and 2000. Gulf states have not publicly endorsed U.S. responses to Iraqi challenges in the no-fly zones and Qatar's foreign minister expressed concern during a joint news conference with then Secretary of Defense Cohen on March 9, 1999, commenting that "We do not wish to see Iraq bombed daily or these attacks which are being made in the no-fly zones." An Arab League foreign ministers' meeting on March 18 called for an end to all operations against Iraq not backed by the U.N. Security Council, but urged all countries to abide by Security Council resolutions in "spirit and letter." A year later, on April 9, 2000, Saudi Minister of Defense Prince Sultan made the following statement in a news conference:

> ... the [U.S.] troops which have been in Saudi Arabia since the end of Desert Storm are within the frame of United Nations assignments and directions to continue the surveillance of southern Iraq, and also the border of Kuwait and Saudi Arabia, as well as the other GCC countries. And these troops are doing their duties to protect peace only, and not for aggression.

Saudi officials continue to cite provocations by Iraq. On June 4, 2001, the Saudi Ambassador to the United Nations charged that Iraq had staged 11 raids on Saudi border outposts during recent months.

Arab governments, including those friendly to the United States, denounced the allied strikes conducted against Iraqi air defense installations on February 16, 2001. The Secretary-General of the Arab League stated that the raid "has no justification, violates international law, and has provoked anger and resentment in the Arab world." Egypt's Foreign Minister called the raid "a serious negative step that we cannot accept," while his Jordanian counterpart said Jordan "never condones the use of military force against Iraq." Saudi Arabia initially withheld official comment and a senior Saudi official said his country was not previously informed of the strikes. On February 21, 2001, however, Saudi Foreign Minister Prince Saud al-Faysal during a visit to Damascus issued a joint statement with the Syrian Foreign Minister that "[b]oth sides expressed feelings of denunciation and anxiety over the recent escalation against south Baghdad." In nearby Oman, the Minister of State for Foreign Affairs commented that "[t]hose attacks will not benefit regional security or negotiations and discussions."

Since the September 11, 2001 attacks, friendly Arab leaders have urged the United States not to expand the current war against terrorism to target Iraq or other Arab countries. At a summit conference in Beirut, Lebanon on March 27-28, 2002, Arab leaders adopted a resolution that contained several clauses dealing with Iraq. The resolution welcomed assurances by Iraq that it would respect "the independence, sovereignty, and security of the state of Kuwait"; it called on Iraq to cooperate with Kuwait in identifying and returning missing Kuwaiti persons and property; it called for lifting economic sanctions on Iraq; it rejected "threats of aggression against some Arab states, particularly Iraq"; and it reiterated a "categorical rejection" of attacking Iraq or threatening any Arab state. After subsequent talks between President Bush and Saudi Crown Prince Abdullah on April 25, Saudi Foreign Minister Prince Saud al-Faysal told reporters that "we see no need for any military or other action" against Iraq, inasmuch as Iraq and U.N. representatives are discussing the issue of re-admitting weapons inspectors.

Some U.S. officials and commentators believe Arab leaders would secretly welcome the overthrow of the Saddam Hussein regime, notwithstanding public statements to me contrary. On his return from a trip to the Middle East, Vice President Dick Cheney told reporters on March 21 that he had found regional leaders "uniformly concerned about the situation in Iraq, in particular about Saddam Hussein's failure to live up to the U.N. Security Council resolutions, especially number 687, that he pledged to at the end of the war, that said he'd get rid of all of his weapons of mass destruction." But news reports indicated that the Vice President's hosts expressed more concern over mounting Israeli-Palestinian tensions in the Israeli-occupied West Bank territory than with issues related to Iraq.

PLANS AND ALTERNATIVES

Military options present various challenges. Ship-borne missile strikes against selected Iraqi targets incur relatively few risks and have the added advantage of not requiring overflight permission or logistical support from Gulf allies; however, missile strikes by themselves have had only limited effects in the past. Supplementing missile strikes with a more massive bombing campaign could succeed in destroying some key military organizations, weapons production facilities, and command and logistical installations, as in the 1998 Desert Fox operation. A bombing campaign, however, entails risks to U.S. pilots and aircrews, inflicts more civilian casualties, and elicits significant opposition within the Arab world. A further limiting factor is the reluctance of Saudi Arabia and some other Gulf states to permit air strikes from their territory. Similarly, ground action would be difficult without more widespread allied support than currently exists; it is doubtful that Saudi Arabia or other neighboring states would allow the United States to stage a ground invasion of Iraq from their territory.

Since the attacks of September 11, 2001, however, reports that the Bush Administration is considering expanding the war on terrorism to Iraq have prompted further discussion in news media over the nature, timing, and military feasibility of an attack against that country. According to a *New York Times* article of April 28, 2002, for example, the Administration is developing plans for a potential combined air and ground invasion that would deploy between 70,000 and 250,000 U.S. troops, depending on the mission and force mix. Another report alleges that planners are studying two broad options: a heavy invasion force with a strong ground force component, perhaps on the order of 200,000 troops; and a smaller force with the main emphasis on air power and special operations forces, somewhat more akin to the Afghanistan model. Administration spokesmen have said the President has not made a decision on launching such an attack. In congressional testimony on May 1, Secretary of State Colin Powell said "the President does not have a military plan on his desk now of the kind described in the *[New York Times]* press story."

Availability of weaponry could affect decisions on scope and timing of a military operation. According to a *Washington Post* article of February 24, 2002, depletion of arms stocks during operations in Afghanistan, coupled with severe strains on U.S. active and reserve forces, could compel the United States could delay a coordinated assault on Iraq for some months. Analysts cited in particular the need to produce additional precision bombs such as the Joint Direct Attack Munitions (JDAM) used in Afghanistan. According to a *USA Today* article of February 25, however, U.S. Defense Department officials do not believe temporarily depleted stocks of munitions would necessarily deter the United States from launching an attack on Iraq in a shorter time frame. Defense officials reportedly said that production of JD AMs has been accelerated and that the munitions themselves are relatively cheap, at approximately $20,000 each as compared with $1 million for a cruise missile.

U.S. officials and analysts have suggested various other options that could be used in conjunction with or as a substitute for a conventional military attack. These options include further curtailments on Iraqi military activity, more emphasis on unconventional warfare, or more active support for anti-government militia or other opposition groups in their efforts to topple the regime of Saddam Hussein. For example, the United States could consider extending the two no-fly zones imposed by the allies over northern and southern Iraq to cover the entire country, coupled with a ban on helicopter flights and imposition of "no-drive" zones forbidding movement of Iraqi armored forces in designated areas. To enforce such measures, however, the United States and its allies would have to allocate more assets, incur greater risks, and deal with further challenges by Iraq. Another approach would-involve covert action against the Iraqi regime, combined with an expanded program to buttress the efforts of opposition groups. Many analysts believe the opposition is too fragmented and lacking in support within the Iraqi heartland to be effective, and cite the failure of previous efforts to build a viable opposition in Iraq. Others maintain that the United States has provided insufficient support to opposition groups and missed key opportunities to further their efforts.

Table 2. Comparative Military Strengths and Inventories: Gulf States

Country	Military Personnel	Tanks	Other Armored Vehicles	Field Artillery		Attack Heli-copters	Combat Aircraft	Naval Units	
				Towed	Self-Propelled			Surface Combat-ants	Sub-marines
Saudi Arabia.	205,500	910	5,017	160	200	33	348	8	0
United Arab Emirates	65,000	411	1,360	80	181	49	101	2	0
Oman	43,400	117	290	96	24	0	40	0	0
Kuwait	15,500	293	556	0	68	20	82	0	0
Qatar	12,330	35	302	12	28	19	18	0	0
Bahrain	11,000	106	306	22	62	40	34	1	0
Total: Allies	*348,730*	*1,872*	*7,831*	370	563	*161*	*623*	*11*	*0*
Iraq	424,000	2,200	3,700	1,900	150	100	316	0	0
Iran	513,000	1,565	1,455	2,085	330	104	288*	3	5

Source: International Institute for Strategic Studies, *The Military Balance 2001-2002.* (Note: Figures shown here do not include materiel believed to be in storage and inoperable.)

* Includes aircraft flown from Iraq to Iran during 1991 Gulf war.

Chapter 3

IRAQ: COMPENSATION AND ASSETS ISSUES

Kenneth Katzman

THE U.N. COMPENSATION PROCESS

U.N. Security Council Resolution 674 (October 29, 1990) reminded Iraq that, "under international law, it is liable for any loss, damage, or injury arising in regard to Kuwait and third States, and their nationals and corporations, as a result of the invasion and illegal occupation of Kuwait by Iraq." Security Council Resolution 687 (April 3, 1991) reaffirmed Iraqi liability for compensation to the victims of its invasion and authorized creation of a unique mechanism to adjudicate and pay invasion-related claims. A May 2, 1991 report by the U.N. Secretary General, accepted by the Security Council in Resolution 692 (May 20, 1991), established a Compensation Fund, in which monies for compensation would be deposited and held. The plan also set up a Compensation Commission (UNCC), run by a 15-member Governing Council composed of the representatives of the current members of the Security Council at any given time. Security Council Resolution 705 (August 15, 1991) determined that the compensation effort would be funded by deducting 30% of *Iraq's future* oil revenues. (Iraqi oil exports were banned immediately after the August 2, 1990 invasion of Kuwait.) Iraq grudgingly accepted these conditions.

Decisions of the UNCC's Governing Council are taken by a majority vote of its members, with no veto permitted. The Council is assisted by an undetermined number of commissioncrs — experts in finance, law, accounting, insurance, and environmental damage assessment — and by a secretariat to do administrative work. These experts evaluate the claims submitted, verify their validity, and recommend final judgments. The expenses of the UNCC are paid out of the Compensation Fund.

Claims Processing and Payment

The U.N. Secretary-General and the UNCC deemed it unworkable to process all claims individually. Governments file claims and distribute payments on their own behalf and on behalf of their nationals and corporations. Claims are categorized as those of individuals (Category A,B,C, and D claims) corporations (Category E), and governments (Category F/ There is further specialization of individual claims — fixed amounts for losses arising from departure from Iraq or Kuwait during August 2, 1990 - March 2, 1991[1] (Category A); fixed amounts for losses resulting from personal injury or death of a relative (Category B); and damages of any type. Individual damage claims are separated into those up to and those exceeding $100,000 (Category C and D, respectively). Iraq is allowed to make legal and factual comments on UNCC policy, but it is not permitted to dispute individual claims, a restriction Iraq has repeatedly protested. The U.N. compensation process does not preclude parallel claims made through the domestic legal systems of U.N. member governments, but claimants must inform the UNCC of any amounts received and these amounts will be deducted from any awards. Members of the armed forces of countries that fought Iraq in the Gulf war may not file claims through the U.N. process, unless they were taken prisoner and mistreated by Iraq. In addition, the costs of allied military operations against Iraq cannot be claimed under the U.N. compensation process.

Claims Filed and Paid

The deadlines for the filing of new claims have expired, and the UNCC has received about 2.6 million claims, from all categories, totaling about $230 billion Kuwaiti claims constitute about 75% of the total. The UNCC has thus far issued 1.3 million awards worth about $10 billion, giving priority in processing and payment to individual claims.

Until December 1996, when Iraq began exporting significant quantities of oil again under the "oil-for-food" Resolution 986, only $13.4 million had actually been paid to claimants. About 4,000 Category B (injury or death of a relative) claimants were paid up to that time. Funds for these payments were derived from frozen Iraqi oil assets transferred to a U.N. escrow account under Resolution 778 (October 1992). Since the start of the oil-for-food program, $3.2 billion has been transferred to the UNCC (as of March 31, 1999). Of that amount, $2.7 billion has gone to pay claims, $125 million has covered UNCC administrative expenses, and the remainder is available for payment and expenses.

The UNCC has acknowledged that the compensation process has been slow and might take many years to finally resolve. UNCC officials have set a goal of processing all claims by 2003. In late 1996, corporate claimants (about $82 billion in total claims) began to receive awards. In December 1996, Kuwait Petroleum Corporation was awarded $610 million to settle a $950 million claim for extinguishing 800 oil well fires set by retreating Iraqi troops in 1991. In April 1999, Israeli firms and individuals were awarded a total of $31 million for damages caused by Iraqi Scud-variant missile attacks (39 fired) on Israel during the Gulf war. In June 1999, KPC received another $2.2 billion in awards, and another state-owned Kuwaiti oil company received an award of $115 million. Governmental claims constitute about $120 billion of the total claims filed, and the UNCC says it will soon begin awarding claims in this category.

U.S. companies appear to have a significant stake in the U.N. compensation process. Over 150 U.S. firms have made claims through the UNCC process with an asserted value of

[1] Many of the mostly South Asian and Arab expatriate workers forced to leave Iraq and Kuwait after the invasion

over $1.5 billion.[2] (Total U.S. claims, about 3,200 in all categories, have an asserted value of about $1.7 billion.) Among U.S. corporate claims, the Bechtel Corp. of San Francisco has filed a claim for losses incurred when the Gulf crisis despoiled the Bekhme Dam project in northeastern Iraq that it was managing. In late June 1999, several U.S. firms received awards, including Saudi Arabian Texaco ($506 million) and oil-service firm Halliburton ($18 million). The U.S. Government seeks $8.8 million in compensation for the eight U.S. departments that contributed scientific or technical help to the Gulf environmental cleanup.[3]

Funding for Compensation

The large number of unresolved claims and the limited funds available for compensation have raised questions about the future of the UNCC process. As noted above, compensation and the UNCC's operating budget are funded by Iraqi oil revenues. At current oil export capabilities of about $10 billion per year,[4] Iraq can generate only about $3 billion annually for compensation. Even if only a fraction of claims filed result in awards, or if sanctions on Iraq were completely lifted, it might take several decades for Iraq to generate sufficient revenues to pay the awards.

The compensation mathematics have led some observers to speculate that the UNCC process will terminate short of completion. If Iraq's leadership changes, before the compensation process is completed and, at some point, Iraq rejoins the international community, Iraq's reintegration will almost certainly spur calls in the international community to terminate the process and ask claimants to abrogate their claims. On the other hand, some countries, such as Germany, continued to make compensation payments even though they had rejoined the international community. Some observers believe the United States should offer an end to the reparations process as an incentive to Iraqis who are willing to overthrow Saddam Husayn and comply with all applicable U.N. Gulf war-related resolutions. Opposition by some Security Council members to continued sanctions on Iraq apparently has led Britain and the Netherlands to include in their draft Security Council Resolution (now under discussion) a provision to temporarily suspend compensation deductions, with the proceeds to go toward increased humanitarian relief. Iraq also has succeeded in persuading some international firms to drop claims before the UNCC in exchange for contracts with Iraq under the oil-for-food program.[5]

CLAIMS AGAINST IRAQI FROZEN ASSETS

Some U.S. claims against Iraq arose before the Iraqi invasion of Kuwait, and are ineligible for consideration under the UNCC process. To try to resolve these claims, the Bush and Clinton Administrations have proposed a plan to seize and distribute to U.S. claimants

and occupation would be covered under this category.

[2] Much of the information in this paragraph is derived from King, Neil. Firms World-Wide Seek Billions to Cover Their Gulf War Losses. *Wall Street Journal,* August 18, 1997.

[3] Nebehay, Stephanie. Billions in Environmental Claims Filed Against Iraq. Reuters, February 4, 1997.

[4] Resolution 1153 (February 20, 1998) allows an increase in Iraqi oil sales to $5.25 billion every six months, and thus an increase in compensation funds generated

[5] Nebehay, Stephanie. Kuwait Accuses Iraq of Extortion At Gulf War Fund. Reuters, June 22, 1999.

the approximately $2.2 billion[6] in Iraqi assets blocked in U.S. financial institutions and their foreign branches. In cases such as this, U.S. claims usually are settled in the context of a reconciliation with the country at issue. Bush and Clinton Administration officials have determined that, in the case of Iraq, the prospects for reconciliation are so limited that the United States should resolve the claims disputes unilaterally.

The Iraqi assets in question were blocked pursuant to President Bush's Executive orders 12722 and 12724 of August 2 and August 9, 1990, respectively. Since the Gulf war, some licenses have been issued to use some of the frozen assets to pay U.S. companies who exported goods to Iraq, prior to the Iraqi invasion, under confirmed letters of credit. These funds were judged by the Office of Foreign Assets Control (OFAC, Department of Treasury) to be the property of the U.S. exporter, and not Iraqi funds. About $3 billion more remain frozen in foreign banks around the world, and remain blocked by their host countries under Resolution 661 (August 6, 1990). Some governments, including that of Saudi Arabia, have released some frozen Iraqi assets, possibly in an effort to improve relations with Iraq.[7]

The U.S. claims on blocked Iraqi assets exceeds the amount of those assets. The claims, which include those from the U.S. government, corporations, and individuals, are estimated to total up to $5 billion. Major U.S. government claims include about $2 billion from the Commodity Credit Corporation and $50 million from the Export-Import Bank for defaulted Iraqi loan guarantees (mostly for the purchase of agricultural exports). Unsettled U.S. claims from the May 17, 1987 Iraqi attack on the U.S.S. Stark include $2.3 million in compensation to the 62 crewmen injured[8], and about $120 million (exact amount undetermined) for damages to the ship itself. U.S. corporate claimants include those, such as ATT, Citicorp, Eastman Kodak, Exxon, Continental Airlines, and others that had contractual obligations Iraq did not fulfill.[9] Other U.S. firms, including tobacco companies and agricultural exporters, want to recoup their losses from exports shipped to Iraq under advised (unsecured) letters of credit that were not able to be paid before U.S.- Iraq business transactions ended. In addition, 3,300 U.S. individuals have registered claims, almost exclusively Gulf war veterans with claims for Guff War Syndrome health damage. The U.S. Foreign Claims Settlement Commission is maintaining a registry of U.S. claimants in anticipation that an Iraq claims process will be enacted by Congress.

Congressional Debate

The limited assets available relative to total claims has created a debate in Congress over claimant priorities. Congress has thus far been unable to resolve that debate and Bush and Clinton Administration claims proposals have not been enacted. In October 1992, the Bush Administration submitted to Congress a draft bill, entitled "The Iraq Claims Act of 1992,"

---

[6] This figure includes about $211 million in frozen assets already transferred to a U.N. escrow account under Resolution 778. Those monies are being refunded to U.S. financial institutions from the proceeds of Iraqi oil sales under the oil-for-food program.

[7] Saudi Arabia Frees $1 million of Iraq's Frozen Assets. Reuters, August 5, 1999.

[8] The United States and Iraq were close to settling this claim at the time of the Iraqi invasion of Kuwait The two sides had agreed to settle on an amount of $ 1.5 million, but Iraq's transfer of the monies was not completed when the invasion occurred. The U.S. government now stands by the original claim of $2.3 million. On April 14, 1989, Iraq paid $27.35 million in compensation to families of the 37 crewmen killed in the attack on the Stark.

[9] Price, David. Who's At the Head Of the Line. *Investor's Business Daily,* February 28, 1997.

that would have seized Iraqi assets and established a claims adjudication process under the Foreign Claims Settlement Commission. The draft bill suggested that priority be given to non-commercial claims from members of the armed forces, including crewmen of the U.S.S. Stark, and other claims arising from Iraq's invasion of Kuwait.

The House and Senate introduced versions (H.R. 3221, S.1401) of the Iraq Claims legislation in mid-1993. Despite substantial debate over which categories of claimants to assign priority to, the House passed the legislation, in much the same form as the Administration draft bill, on April 28, 1994. However, S.1401 did not reach the Senate floor because of opposition from some Senators who wanted to give priority to corporate claimants exporting to Iraq under advised letters of credit. A version of the legislation that gave priority to all categories of corporate claimants was contained in the conference report on the FY1996 foreign aid authorization bill (H.R. 1561). That bill was vetoed because of other issues.

In the first session of the 105th Congress, Iraq claims legislation was incorporated into the Senate version of H.R. 1757, the foreign relations authorization act for FY1998-99. The provision drew opposition from veterans' groups because it excluded Gulf war veterans from the claimant pool. On October 1, 1997, the House passed a motion to instruct its conferees on the bill to strike the Senate provision because of that exclusion. Supporters of the provision maintained that Gulf war veterans had other recourse, such as veterans affairs programs, to be treated for injuries related to the Gulf war, and that there is no tradition of U.S. servicemen and their families suing a U.S. adversary for war losses. The legislation containing this provision was not enacted. In the 106th Congress, Rep. Lloyd Doggett introduced HR. 618, the "Gulf War Veterans' Claims Protection Act of 1999." The bill, which was incorporated into the House version of H.R. 2415, the FY2000 State Department authorization bill, gives priority to claims by members or veterans of the U.S. armed forces. H.R 2415 was passed by the House on July 21, 1999; no similar provision is in the Senate version of the bill.

Other Proposals

The 1997 crisis over weapons inspections in Iraq has generated new proposals for using Iraqi assets frozen by U.S. banks. Iraqi opponents of Saddam Husayn, with support from some Members of Congress, have proposed releasing the frozen assets for their use in a renewed push to overthrow Saddam Husayn. Others suggest using the assets to provide additional humanitarian aid to the Iraqi people, as an additional means of addressing the suffering of the Iraqi people. If written into legislation, these proposals are likely to draw opposition from U.S. claimants on the assets.

Chapter 4

IRAQ: COMPLIANCE, SANCTIONS, AND U.S. POLICY

Kenneth Katzman

MOST RECENT DEVELOPMENTS

President Bush's January 29, 2002 State of the Union message called Iraq part of an "axis of evil" along with North Korea and Iran, prompting speculation of imminent U.S. military action against Iraq. On March 7, Iraq resumed talks with the United Nations over the readmission of U.N. weapons inspectors; a second round of talks began May 1. On March 28, at the Arab League summit in Beirut, Iraq and Kuwait took steps to reconcile.

BACKGROUND AND ANALYSIS

In forty reviews (at 60-day intervals) of Iraqi compliance from the end of the Gulf war in 1991 until August 20, 1998, the U.N. Security Council maintained comprehensive international sanctions on Iraq's imports and exports. The primary ceasefire resolution is Security Council Resolution 687 (April 3, 1991), requiring Iraq to end its weapons of mass destruction programs, recognize Kuwait, account for missing Kuwaitis, return-Kuwaiti property, and end support for international terrorism. Iraq is required by Resolution 688 (April 5, 1991) to end repression of its people.

WEAPONS OF MASS DESTRUCTION (WMD)

A U.N. Special Commission (UNSCOM), chaired during July 1, 1997 - June 30, 1999 by Australian disarmament official Richard Butler (succeeding Rolf Ekeus), and the International Atomic Energy Agency (IAEA) attempted to verify that Iraq had ended all its prohibited WMD programs and to establish a long-term monitoring program to ensure that Iraq remains free of WMD (Resolution 715, October 11, 1991). The monitoring program, accepted by Iraq in November 1993, consisted of visitations and technical surveillance of about 300 sites. Under Resolution 1051 (March 27, 1996), UNSCOM inspected (at point of entry and at end-use destination) of Iraqi imports of any dual use items.

Confrontations over access to suspected WMD sites began almost as soon as UNSCOM began operations in April 1991, prompting adoption of Resolution 707 (August 15, 1991). That resolution required unfettered access to all sites and disclosure by Iraq of all its WMD suppliers. During March 1996 - October 1997, Iraq impeded inspectors from entering Iraqi security service and military facilities, and it interfered with some UNSCOM flights. These actions prompted Resolution 1060 (June 12, 1996) and other Council statements (such as on June 13, 1997) demanding Iraqi cooperation. Resolution 1115 (June 21, 1997) threatened travel restrictions against Iraqi officials committing the infractions. Resolution 1134 (October 23, 1997) again threatened a travel ban and suspended sanctions reviews until April 1998. (France, Russia, China, Egypt, and Kenya abstained.)

1997-1998 Crises

Six days after that vote, Iraq barred American UNSCOM personnel from conducting inspections and, on November 13, 1997, expelled the Americans. Resolution 1137 (adopted unanimously November 12, 1997), imposed travel restrictions on Iraqi officials. (On November 13, 1997, the House adopted H.Res. 322, backing unilateral U.S. military action as a last resort. The Senate did not act on a similar resolution, S.Con.Res. 71, because some Senators wanted it to call for the United States to overthrow Saddam Husayn.) In November 1997 and February 1998, Russia and U.N. Secretary-General Kofi Annan, respectively, brokered temporary compromises that enabled UNSCOM to resume inspections. The February 23, 1998 U.N.-Iraq agreement provided for access to eight "presidential sites" by UNSCOM inspectors and diplomatic observers. Security Council Resolution 1154 (March 2, 1998) accepted that agreement, threatening "the severest consequences" if Iraq reneged. Iraq allowed presidential site inspections (1,058 buildings) during March 26-April 3, 1998, and the United States agreed to lift the travel ban on Iraqi officials and to resume sanctions reviews.

Iraq subsequently refused to implement an UNSCOM plan for completing its work and, in August 1998, barred UNSCOM from inspecting new facilities. The Senate and House passed a resolution, SJ.Res. 54 (P.L. 105-235, signed August 14, 1998), declaring Iraq in "material breach" of the ceasefire. On September 9, 1998, the Security Council unanimously adopted Resolution 1194, suspending sanctions reviews. On October 30, 1998, the Security Council offered an easing of sanctions if Iraq fulfilled WMD and other outstanding requirements, but Iraq demanded an immediate end to sanctions and it ceased cooperation with UNSCOM (but not the IAEA). The U.N. Security Council unanimously adopted Resolution 1205 (November 5, 1998), deeming the Iraqi action a "flagrant violation" of the February 1998 U.N.-Iraq agreement. On November 14, 1998, with the United States about to launch airstrikes, Iraq pledged cooperation, narrowly averting U.S. air strikes but prompting President Clinton to openly declare a U.S. policy of regime change.

Operation Desert Fox and Aftermath

After a month of testing Iraq's cooperation, UNSCOM said on December 15, 1998 that Iraq refused to yield known WMD-related documents and that it was obstructing inspections; the IAEA did not issue similar complaints. All inspectors withdrew and a 70-hour U.S. and British bombing campaign followed (Operation Desert Fox, December 16-19, 1998), directed against Iraqi WMD-capable facilities and military and security targets. After almost one year of negotiations, the Security Council adopted Resolution 1284 (December 17, 1999) by a vote of 11 - 0 (Russia, France, China, and Malaysia abstained), providing for the suspension of most sanctions if Iraq fully cooperates with a new WMD inspection body (UNMOVIC, U.N. Monitoring, Verification and Inspection Commission). Under 1284, Iraq's revenues would be subject to undefined financial controls, exports of dual use items to Iraq would still require U.N. approval, and arms exports would remain banned.

In January 2000, the Security Council selected as head of UNMOVIC former IAEA director Hans Blix, who formulated an organizational plan adopted on April 13, 2000. He reported in August 2000 that UNMOVIC was ready to begin preliminary activities in Iraq.

"Axis of Evil" and U .S. Policy

Amid a growing debate over whether to expand the post-September 11 "war on terrorism" to Iraq and amid fears that Iraq could provide WMD expertise to terrorist groups, on November 26, 2001, and again in his January 29, 2002 State of the Union message, President Bush appeared to threaten unspecified action if Iraq did not readmit U.N. weapons inspectors. In the latter speech he described Iraq as part of an "axis of evil" along with Iran and North Korea. One month prior to the State of the Union speech, there were renewed calls from several members of Congress for the overthrow of Saddam and House passage of HJ.Res. 75 on December 20, 2001, by a vote of 392-12. The joint resolution says that Iraq's refusal to readmit U.N. inspectors is a material breach of its international obligations and a mounting threat to.peace and security, but does not explicitly authorize U.S. military action.

Amid the U.S. threats, on March 7, 2002 Iraq held a meeting with U.N. Secretary-General Annan and UNMOVIC director Blix on the restart of inspections, a meeting Annan called useful. (Similar talks were held during February 26-27, 2001, but made little progress.) Another round of talks, after a delay requested by Iraq, was held May 1-3, and included Blix and IAEA director Mohammad Baradei. Comments by Secretary of Defense Rumsfeld on February 24, 2002 suggested that the United States would accept new inspections only if such inspections were unconditional and comprehensive, a standard that some Administration officials believe Iraq will never meet. Several Western and most Arab governments are opposed to a U.S. military campaign against Iraq, a message reinforced by Arab leaders to Vice President Cheney on his trip to the Middle East in March. Arab leaders voiced opposition to an attack on Iraq at the March 27-28 Arab League summit in Beirut, during which Iraq and Kuwait took some steps to reconcile.

The January 30, 2002 CIA proliferation assessment for Congress, covering January to June 2001, repeats U.S. suspicions of Iraqi rebuilding of and research on WMD but presents little hard evidence of such activity. Britain considered releasing in April 2002 a dossier of Iraqi WMD rebuilding but decided not to, apparently because it concluded that its evidence was not sufficiently convincing. There are also allegations of illicit Iraqi imports of conventional military equipment. A *Jane's Defence Weekly* report of July 25, 2001, says Iraq has been illicitly obtaining spare parts for fighter jets and helicopters from Belarus, Ukraine, and the former Yugoslavia.

The following sums up the status of disarmament efforts in Iraq and outstanding issues.

Nuclear Program

During 1991-1994, despite Iraq's initial declaration that it had no nuclear weapons facilities or unsafeguarded material, UNSCOM/IAEA uncovered and dismantled a previously-undeclared network of about 40 nuclear research facilities, including three clandestine uranium enrichment programs (electromagnetic, centrifuge, and chemical isotope separation) as well as laboratory-scale plutonium separation program. Inspectors found and dismantled (in 1992) Iraq's clandestine nuclear weapons development program, and they found evidence of development of a radiological weapon, which scatters nuclear material without an explosion. No radiological weapon was ever completed, but there is debate over whether Iraq ever tested such a device. UNSCOM removed from Iraq all discovered nuclear, reactor fuel, fresh and irradiated. Following the defection of Husayn Kamil (Saddam's son-in-law and former WMD production czar) in August 1995, Iraq revealed it had launched a crash program in August 1990 to produce a nuclear weapon within one year, and that it had planned to divert fuel from its reactors for a nuclear weapon.

The IAEA, before it ceased work in Iraq, said that Iraq's nuclear program had been ended and that it had a relatively complete picture of Iraq's nuclear suppliers. A May 15, 1998 Security Council statement reflected a U.S. -Russian agreement to close the nuclear file if Iraq cleared up outstanding issues (nuclear design drawings, documents, and the fate of some nuclear equipment), but an IAEA report of July 1998, indicated that some questions still remained. The United States did not agree to close the file. In January 2002, as it has in each of the past 3 years, IAEA inspectors verified that several tons of uranium remained sealed, acting under Iraq's commitments under the 1968 Nuclear Nonproliferation Treaty. However, in May 2000, the IAEA destroyed an Iraqi nuclear centrifuge that Iraq had stored in Jordan in 1991. The IAEA says that the absence of an inspections program creates uncertainty about Iraqi nuclear activities. The United States believes that Iraq retains the expertise (about 7,000 scientists and engineers) and intention to rebuild its nuclear program.

Chemical Weapons

UNSCOM destroyed all chemical weapons materiel uncovered — 38,500 munitions, 690 tons of agents, 3,000 tons of precursor chemicals, and 426 pieces of production equipment items — and the destruction operation formally ended on June 14, 1994. However, the fate of about 31,600 chemical munitions, 550 mustard gas bombs, and 4,000 tons of chemical precursors, remains unknown. Iraq refused to yield an Air Force document, found in July 1998 by UNSCOM, that could explain their fate, although Iraq allowed UNSCOM to take notes from it. In February-1998 UNSCOM discovered that shells taken from Iraq in 1996 contained 97% pure mustard gas, indicating it was freshly produced.

The primary remaining chemical weapons questions center on VX nerve agent, which Iraq did not include in its initial postwar declarations and of which no stockpile was ever located. By 1995 UNSCOM had uncovered enough circumstantial evidence to force Iraq to admit to producing about 4 tons of VX, but UNSCOM believed that Iraq had imported enough precursor — about 600 tons — to produce 200 tons of the agent. In late June 1998, UNSCOM revealed that some unearthed missile warheads, tested in a U.S. Army lab, contained traces of VX, contradicting Iraq's assertions that it had not succeeded in stabilizing the agent. Separate French and Swiss tests did not find conclusive evidence of VX. About 170 chemical sites were under long-term monitoring. Iraq has not signed the Chemical Weapons Convention that took effect April 29, 1997. Recent U.S. government reports to Congress, including the CIA report to Congress on January 30, 2002, have said Iraq has rebuilt some facilities that could be easily converted to chemical weapons production.

Biological Weapons

Iraq did not declare any biological materials, weapons, research, or facilities in its initial declaration to UNSCOM in April 1991, and no biological stockpile was ever uncovered. UNSCOM focused initially on the major research and development site at Salman Pak (gutted and partially buried by Iraq shortly before the first inspection began) and later on the Al Hakam facility south of Baghdad (dismantled by UNSCOM June 20, 1996). In August 1991, Iraq admitted that it had a biological weapons research program. In July 1995, Iraq modified its admission by acknowledging it had an offensive biological weapons program and that it had produced 19,000 liters of botulinum, 8,400 liters of anthrax, and 2,000 liters of aflatoxin and clostridium. In August 1995, Iraq confessed to having produced 191 biological bombs, of which 25 were missile warheads, loaded with anthrax, botulinum, and aflatoxin for use in the Gulf war, but Iraq claims to have destroyed the bombs after the Gulf conflict. UNSCOM monitored 86 biological sites during 1994 -1998.

UNSCOM's position was that Iraq's biological declarations were not credible or verifiable. According to UNSCOM, Iraq imported a total of 34 tons of growth media for producing biological agents during the 1980s, of which 4 tons remain unaccounted for. UNSCOM still lacked information on Iraq's development of drop tanks and aerosol generators for biological dissemination, as well as the fate of the biological munitions. In early April 2001, Iraq wrote to Secretary-General Annan that it plans to refurbish the Doura laboratory, destroyed by UNSCOM in 1996 on the grounds it could be used for biological weapons. Iraq says it needs the plant to produce vaccines against foot and mouth disease.

The October 2001 anthrax-related terrorism in the United States has generated suspicions of Iraqi involvement because Iraq developed anthrax as part of its biological program. No evidence linking the anthrax to Iraq has been announced, and White House spokespersons said in late December 2001 that the anthrax used in the attacks appeared to be from a domestic source, such as a U.S. military laboratory,

Ballistic Missiles

U.N. Security Council Resolution 687 requires the destruction of all Iraqi ballistic missiles with a range greater than 150 kilometers. UNSCOM accounted for 817 of 819 Soviet-supplied Scud missiles, 130 of which survived the Gulf war, as well as all 14 declared mobile launchers and 60 fixed launch pads. U.S. and British analysts, contrary to UNSCOM's assessments, believe Iraq might be concealing 10 to 12 Russian-supplied Scud-type missiles. UNSCOM's last regular report (October 1998) said it had been able to account for at least 43 of the 45 chemical and biological (CBW) warheads Iraq said it unilaterally destroyed in 1991. (The warheads were unearthed in mid-1998.) An additional 30 chemical warheads were previously destroyed under UNSCOM supervision. UNSCOM also accounted for all but 50 conventional Scud warheads, and said it had made progress toward establishing a material balance for Scud engine components. Unresolved issues include accounting for missile program documentation, 300 tons of special missile propellant, and indigenous missile production (30 indigenously-made warheads and 7 missiles).

In December 1995, after Jordan reported seizing 115 Russian-made missile guidance components allegedly bound for Iraq, UNSCOM said Iraq had procured some missile components since 1991, a violation of sanctions. (That month, UNSCOM retrieved prohibited missile guidance gyroscopes, suitable for a 2,000 mile range missile, from Iraq's Tigris River, apparently procured from Russia's defense-industrial establishment.) UNSCOM also had evidence that Iraq, after the Gulf war, conducted secret flight tests and conducted research on missiles of prohibited ranges. Iraq is making progress in developing permitted-range missiles - the Ababil and Samoud programs - according to the January 2002 CIA report to Congress and, prior to Desert Fox, UNSCOM had been monitoring about 63 missile sites and 159 items of equipment, as well as 2,000 permitted missiles. U.S. military officials said after Desert Fox that the bombing had set back Iraq's missile program by two years, damaging production facilities at Taji, Ibn al-Haythim, Al Kindi, and Al Karama.

Human Rights/War Crimes Issues

U.S. and U.N. human rights reports since the Gulf war have repeatedly described Iraq as a gross violator of human rights. In 1994, the Clinton Administration said it might, at some point, present a case against Iraq to the International Court of Justice under the 1948 Genocide Convention. U.N. Rapporteur for Iraq Max Van der Steel's February 1994 report said that Convention might be violated by Iraq's abuses against the Shiite "Marsh Arabs" in southern Iraq, including drainage of the marshes where they live. In February 2002, Iraq allowed the U.N. human rights rapporteur for Iraq, Andreas Mavromatis of Cyprus, to visit Iraq, the first such visit since 1992. Mavromatis expects to make a more extended visit later in 2002.

War Crimes Trial

U.N. Security Council Resolution 674 (October 29, 1990) calls on all states or organizations to provide information on Iraqi atrocities to the United Nations. The Foreign

Relations Authorization Act for FY1992, (P.L. 102-138, October 28, 1991, section 301) stated the sense of Congress that the President should propose to the U.N. Security Council a war crimes tribunal for Saddam Husayn. In later years, similar legislation was passed by one or both chambers, including H.Con.Res. 137, (passed the House November 13, 1997); S.Con.Res. 78, (passed the Senate March 13, 1998); and a provision of the Iraq Liberation Act (P.L. 105-338, signed October 31, 1998).

In the aftermath of the Persian Gulf war, the U.S. Army conducted research into possible war crimes; the report was released on March 19, 1993, after Clinton took office. Since April 1997, the Administration has supported INDICT, a private organization that publicizes alleged Iraqi war crimes and seeks the arrest of 12 alleged Iraqi war criminals. Although apparently lacking international support, in August 2000 then U.S. Ambassador-At-Large for War Crimes David Scheffer said that the United States wanted to see an Iraq war crimes tribunal established within six months, focusing on "nine major criminal episodes." These include the use of chemical weapons against Kurdish civilians at Halabja (March 16, 1988, killing 5,000 Kurds) and the forced relocation of Kurds in the "Anfal" campaign (February 1988, in which an estimated 50,000 to 182,000 Kurds died); the use of chemical weapons use against Iran; post-war crimes against humanity (the Kurds and the Marsh Arabs); war crimes against Kuwait (oil fires, for example) and coalition forces; and other allegations. In FY2001 and again in FY2002, the State Department contributed $4 million to a U.N. "Iraq War Crimes Commission," to be spent if a U.N. tribunal for Iraq war crimes is formed.

RESETTLEMENT OF IRAQI REFUGEES

Desert Storm and postwar rebellions against Saddam created a flood of Iraqi refugees, including 39,000 Iraqis in a camp in Saudi Arabia (Rafha). Of that pool, about 14,000 were ex-soldiers (and their family members) that participated in postwar rebellions or had surrendered to coalition forces. The Bush Administration (1989-1993) agreed to participate in a multinational resettlement program recommended by UNHCR. The total admitted to the United States under the program were about 29,000 Iraqis, of which about 3,800 were ex-soldiers and their families. About 5,000 Iraqis remain in Saudi Arabia as refugees, and the United States is not accepting any more. The FY1994 defense authorization (P.L. 103-160) stated the sense of the Senate that there be no admissions of Iraqi ex-soldiers unless they are certified to have assisted coalition forces after defecting and have not committed any war crimes; the Clinton Administration said these criteria were met. In the wake of the September 1996 northern Iraq crisis, 5,900 Kurds who worked for U.S. relief operations or U.S.-affiliated NGO's in northern Iraq, as well as 650 opposition activists, were resettled in the United States under the Attorney General's parole authority.

SUPPORT FOR INTERNATIONAL TERRORISM/SEPTEMBER 11

Resolution 687 required Iraq to end support for international terrorism, and Iraq made a declaration to that effect to the.U.N. Security Council. Bush Administration officials said in early May 2002 that, after an exhaustive FBI and CIA investigation, no direct link has been found between Iraq and any of the September 11 hijackers. Iraq remains on the U.S. list of state sponsors of terrorism, and according to the State Department's reports on international terrorism, continues to harbor the Abu Nidal Organization and the Palestine Liberation Front of Abu Abbas. Iraq also is paying the families of Palestinian suicide bombers $25,000. An article in the March 25, 2002 edition of *The New Yorker* alleged that Al Qaeda members were relocating to northern Iraq and have contact with Iraqi intelligence, although U.S. officials did not lend credence to these assertions.

IRAQ-KUWAIT ISSUES

Resolution 1284 requires reports on the issues discussed below. However, in contrast to Resolution 687, Resolution 1284 does not make the easing of any sanctions contingent upon Iraqi compliance on these Kuwait-related issues.

Border Delineation and Security/Kuwaiti Sovereignty

Resolution 687 required Iraq to annul its annexation of Kuwait, directed the U.N. Secretary-General to demarcate the Iraq-Kuwait border, and established a demilitarized zone 10 kilometers into Iraq and 5 kilometers into Kuwait. Resolution 773 (August 26, 1992) endorsed border decisions taken by the Iraq-Kuwait Boundary Demarcation Commission (established May 2, 1991) that, in November 1992, finished demarcating the Iraq-Kuwait border as described in an October 1963 agreement between Iraq and Kuwait. The border took effect January 15, 1993. The new line deprived Iraq of part of Umm Qasr port and a strip of the Rumaylah oil field, which straddles the border. On March 18, 1993, the Commission determined the sea border, allowing both countries access to the Gulf. Resolution 833 (May 27, 1993) demanded that Iraq and Kuwait accept the final border demarcation. On November 10, 1994, Iraq formally recognized Kuwait in a motion signed by Saddam Husayn, but Iraqi officials routinely make statements that Kuwait interprets as threatening. At the Arab summit in Beirut (March 27-29, 2002), Iraq reaffirmed its commitment to Kuwait and pledged to cooperate to determine the fate of missing Kuwaitis (see below), earning Iraq an Arab statement of opposition to a U.S. attack on Iraq and a step toward reconciliation with Kuwait.

The 32-nation U.N. Iraq-Kuwait Observer Mission (UNIKOM), established by Resolutions 687 and 689, April 9, 1991), continues to monitor border violations. The United States contributes 11 personnel to the 197 observers in UNIKOM, which is considered a U.N. peacekeeping operation. Under Resolution 806 (February 5, 1993), passed after Iraqi incursions into the demilitarized zone in January 1993 (and other incidents), a 908-member Bengali troop contingent supplements the observer group. Kuwait furnishes two-thirds of UNIKOM's $51 million annual budget. The United States contributes about $4.5 million peryeartoUNIKOM.

Return of Kuwaiti Missing Persons and Property

Security Council Resolutions 686 and 687 require Iraq to account for Kuwaiti and other nationals detained in Iraq during the Persian Gulf crisis. Of an initial 628 Kuwaiti cases, 608 are unresolved (ICRC figure as of May 2000), as are the cases of an additional 17 Saudi nationals. Iraq has admitted to having arrested and detained 126 Kuwaitis, but did not provide enough information to resolve their fate. Only three cases have been resolved since 1995. Since January 1995, Iraq and Kuwait were meeting every month on the Iraq-Kuwait border, along with U.S., British, French, and Saudi representatives, but Iraq has boycotted the meetings since Operation Desert Fox. In February 2000, retired Russian diplomat Yuli Vorontsov was appointed to a new post (created by Resolution 1284) of U.N. coordinator on the issue of missing Kuwaiti persons and unreturned property. Iraq has not yet allowed him to visit Iraq, and in April, June, and August 2000, as well as in March, April, and June 2001, the Security Council has issued statements of concern about the lack of progress. The U.N. Secretary General's August 15, 2001 report on the issue said Iraq continued to be uncooperative. In-April 2002, Iraq offered to receive a U.S. team to discuss the case of missing American serviceman from the Gulf war, Navy pilot Michael Speicher, and Defense Department officials reportedly are considering the offer.

U.N. Security Council Resolutions 686 and 687 require Iraq to return all property seized from Kuwait. In the first few years after the cease-fire, Iraq returned some Kuwaiti civilian and military equipment, including U.S.-made Improved Hawk air defense missiles, and a June 2000 Secretary-General report and a June 19, 2000 Security Council statement did note that Iraq had returned "a substantial amount of property." However, since 1994, U.S. officials have accused Iraq of returning to Kuwait some captured Iranian equipment that was never part of Kuwait's arsenal and of using Kuwaiti missiles and armored personnel carriers during Iraq's October 1994 troop move toward the Kuwait border. The United Nations and Kuwait say Iraq has not returned extensive Kuwaiti state archives and museum pieces, as well as military equipment including eight Mirage F-l aircraft, 245 Russian-made fighting vehicles, 90 Ml 13 armored personnel carriers, one Hawk battery, 3,750 Tow anti-tank missiles, and 675 Russian-made surface-to-air missile batteries. Iraq claims the materiel was left behind or destroyed when Iraq evacuated Kuwait. In the March 7, 2002 talks with U.N. Secretary-General Annan, Iraq pledged to return some historical property to Kuwait.

Reparations Payments

The U.N. Security Council has set up a mechanism for compensating the victims of Iraq's invasion of Kuwait (individuals, governments, and corporations), using 25% (reduced from 30% in December 2000) of the proceeds from Iraqi oil sales. As of March 13, 2002, of a total asserted value of $320 billion claims submitted, the Compensation Commission (UNCC) has thus far approved claims worth about $37.7 billion. Following an April 2002 payout of about $1 billion, which included $800 million in payments to Kuwait, the UNCC has paid out about $14.8 billion. The Commission has paid some corporate and governmental claims, and, as of October 2001, U.S. claimants had received $198 million from the program. In September 2000, the UNCC governing council approved an award to Kuwait of $15.9 billion for oil revenues lost because of the Iraqi occupation and the aftermath of the war (burning oil wells), although current payment schedules will provide only a small fraction of that award (about $50 million) until 2003. In June 2001, the UNCC approved $243 million in payments to all of Iraq's immediate neighbors (except Turkey) for studies of Gulf war environmental damage. Of this amount, $5 million was approved for Iraq's legal expenses to counter the expected environmental reparations claims.

Several legislative proposals ("Iraq Claims Act") to distribute Iraq's frozen assets (about $2.2 billion) in the United States (separate from the U.N. compensation process) were not enacted, because of differences over categories of claimants that should receive priority. In the 107th Congress, H.R. 1632 proposes to distribute Iraq's frozen assets primarily to U.S. victims of the Iraqi invasion of Kuwait. Some might argue that this group of claimants is covered under the U.N. process discussed above and that the frozen assets in the United States should be used for those with claims resulting from events prior to the Iraqi invasion.

U.S. Policy, Sanctions, and the Oil-for-Food Program

As international concerns for the plight of the Iraqi people have grown, the United States has had increasing difficulty maintaining support for international sanctions. The oil-for-food program, established by Resolution 986 (April 15, 1995) and in operation since December 1996, has been progressively modified to improve Iraq's living standards, and the United States has eased its own sanctions to align them with the program. Of the Security Council permanent members, the United States has set the highest standards for full Iraqi compliance. The United States rules out direct dialogue with Iraq on the grounds that Iraq's level of compliance does not justify U.S.-Iraq talks.

"Smart Sanctions" Initiative

During a February 2001 trip to the Middle East, Secretary of State Powell presented a U.S. plan to facilitate exports of civilian equipment to Iraq in exchange for measures to ensure that no militarily useful goods reach Iraq. The Administration portrayed its initiative as an effort to rebuild containment by narrowing differences within the Security Council and limiting sanctions erosion. France, Russia, and China appear to believe that the U.S objective is to keep sanctions on Iraq as part of an overall U.S. effort to destabilize Saddam Husayn.

With phase nine of the oil-for-food program due to expire on June 3, 2001, the Security Council debated integrating the U.S. plan into an authorization for phase ten. Failing to reach agreement, the Council adopted Security Council Resolution 1352 on June 1, 2001, extending phase nine by one month with no changes. Russian opposition prevented Security Council adoption of the U.S. plan by the July 3, 2001 deadline, leading to a Council decision to authorize a 5-month phase ten of the program, with no alterations (U.N. Security Council Resolution 1360), Iraq resumed exporting oil, which it had suspended on June 1, 2001, in protest of the U.S. proposals. Not wanting to jeopardize Russian or moderate Arab cooperation with the war against the Taliban and bin Laden, on November 29, 2001, the United States and Russia, along with the other Security Council members, agreed (Resolution 1382) to authorize a phase eleven with no changes.

There was consensus to work, by the time of the next rollover (May 30, 2002), to agree on a list of goods that would still require review for export to Iraq; a draft listed was attached to Resolution 1382. The United States and Russia agreed on that list on March 28, 2002, and are now negotiating implementation measures, raising hopes for the modified sanctions plan to be adopted at the May 30, 2002 oil-for-food rollover. The United States and Russia also agreed to work to obtain the return of weapons inspectors to Iraq, perhaps in exchange for a broad easing of sanctions under Resolution 1284. According to a *Washington Post* story of January 16, 2002, in December 2001 the United States released holds on $200 million worth of proposed Russian exports to Iraq in order to enlist Russian support for the new sanctions regime.

Amidst these negotiations, on April 8, 2002 Iraq announced a one-month embargo of its oil exports to protest Israel's military incursion into the West Bank, thereby reducing the amount available for civilian imports by at least $1.3 billion, according to the United Nations. In early March 2002, in an effort to stress the risks of easing sanctions, the United States showed satellite photos to the other Security Council members indicating Iraq had converted some trucks imported under the oil for food program for military purposes.

Another issue is that of international flights to Iraq. Since August 2000, France, Russia, and several of Iraq's neighbors have challenged the U.S. interpretation that U.N. Resolution 670 (September 25, 1990) bans passenger flights to and from Iraq; and there has been a revival of significant air traffic into and from Iraq. (The resolution bans flights carrying "cargo," except humanitarian cargo, subject to Sanctions Committee approval.) In early November 2000, Iraq restarted passenger flights within Iraq and its officials have begun flying directly to other countries. The United States has not objected to the internal flights.

France, Russia, and China might also seek to permit new investment in Iraq's energy sector. Such investment is provided for by Resolution 1284 only after Iraq fully complies on outstanding WMD issues. Chinese, Russian, and French firms already have agreed to specific energy investment projects in Iraq, under the condition that the investment ban is lifted. As a possible sign of some easing on this issue, in February 2001 the Sanctions Committee approved plans by two Russian companies (Zarubezhneft and Tatneft) to drill about 100 wells in existing fields in Iraq. The Sanctions Committee also approved a contract between Baghdad and Ankara, signed in December 2001, for a Turkish energy firm to drill 20 wells near Kirkuk.

Previous negotiations on Iraq sanctions sought to prevent Iraq from skirting oil-for-food guidelines in the course of exporting oil. There are continued reports that oil trading companies are paying Iraq surcharges of 20 to 70 cents per barrel of oil, and, in April 2001, the U.S. government warned U.S. firms against buying Iraqi oil from traders that are paying the surcharge. In early 2002, the United States and Britain persuaded the Sanctions Committee to institute a new oil pricing mechanism that would keep Iraq's price closer to the world price and cut down the margin for surcharging. The U.N. official in charge of the oil-for-food program said the new mechanism was affecting the oil contracting process to the point that Iraq's oil exports had fallen about 25%, from about 2.1 million barrels per day (mbd) to about 1.5 mbd.

Formally, comprehensive U.S. trade sanctions against Iraq have been in place since Iraq's 1990 invasion (Executive Order 12722 of August 2, 1990, Executive Order 12724 of August 6, 1990, and the Iraq Sanctions Act of 1990, Section 586 of P.L. 101-513). Since then, U.S. trade regulations have been amended to align them with the oil-for-food program.

U.S. imports of Iraqi oil have soared since 1999 and reached a high of about 970,000 barrels per day in May 2001 — nearly half of Iraq's oil exports. That figure has since fallen to about 600,000 barrels per day in early 2002. In the 107^{lh} Congress, S. 1170, introduced July 12, 2001, would bar U.S. imports of Iraqi oil. The measure was adopted by the Senate on April 18, 2002, as an amendment to an energy bill (H.R. 4). A measure introduced in the 107th Congress (H.R. 742), seeks to ease civilian sanctions while preserving military sanctions and would have eased the licensing procedures for U.S. sales of goods to Iraq under oil-for-food.

Prior to the oil-for-food program, funds for civilian goods and the implementation of U.N. resolutions on Iraq were drawn from frozen Iraqi assets transferred"— or direct contributions—to a U.N. escrow account pursuant to Resolution 778 (October 1992). Total U.S. transfers to the escrow account, which matched contributions from other countries, reached $200 million, the maximum required under Resolution 778. These transfers were being repaid to the United States from proceeds of the oil-for-food program. Resolutions 1284 and 1302 (June 8, 2000) suspended reimbursements until the end of 2000; about $173 million was due back to the United States. Repayments resumed in 2001.

Iraq's Illicit Trade with Its Neighbors

As regional fears of Iraq have eased and sympathy for the Iraqi people has grown, the United States has had difficulty persuading regional governments to enforce the sanctions regime. Common estimates are that Iraq earns up to $2.5 billion in illicit oil export revenues, including receipts from the surcharges discussed above. Improving sanctions enforcement by Iraq's neighbors is key to the U.S. targeted sanctions proposals, although this part of the U.S. plan has run into significant resistance in the region.

Jordan

Since 1992, despite Jordan's economic linkages with Iraq and its advocacy of easing sanctions, the United States has considered Jordan's compliance with the U.N. sanctions regime on Iraq satisfactory. In October 2000, Jordan dismissed Lloyd's International from its role as inspector of goods bound for Iraq and arriving in Jordan at the port of Aqaba, a role enshrined in an agreement between Jordan and the United States in 1993. Recognizing Jordan's economic need, the Sanctions Committee "takes note of Jordan's purchases of discounted Iraqi oil and oil products, which is exchanged for Jordanian goods (approved under the oil-for-food program) and write-downs in Iraqi debt to Jordan. This relationship was renewed in November 2001 at a level of about $500 million for the year, which translates into about 100,000 barrels per day of Iraqi oil exports to Jordan.

Every year since FY1994, foreign aid appropriations laws (P.L. 103-87, P.L. 103-306, P.L. 104-107, P.L. 104-208, P.L. 105-118, P.L. 105-277, P.L. .106-113, and PJL 106-429), have denied U.S. aid to any country that does not comply with the sanctions against Iraq, though these laws do not mention Jordan specifically. The Administration has routinely waived sanctions in order to provide aid to Jordan, which is a key U.S. ally in the Middle East peace process; Congress has not objected to that waiver. Secretary of State Powell has pressed Jordan not to proceed with a planned "free trade agreement" with Iraq that, some fear, could increase the flow of dual use goods to Iraq. It should be noted that virtually all trade with Iraq is, in practice, duty free. In December 2001, Jordan approved a project to build an oil pipeline from Iraq to Jordan, to be operational by 2005.

Turkey

Turkey estimates that it has lost $35 billion as a result of the sanctions. The Turkish government now regulates and taxes the illicit importation of about $400 million per year in

Iraqi energy products by Turkish truck drivers returning from Iraq. That truck traffic resumed in January 2002 at a low level after a 4-month shut down by Iraq - an Iraqi effort to punish the Kurds who earn customs revenue from the trade. U.S. sanctions against Turkey for this trade have been waived each year. In April 2000, Iraq and Turkey neared agreement to increase bilateral trade to about $2.5 billion per year, roughly pre-war levels. Turkey returned an Ambassador to Iraq in January 2001.

Iran/Persian Gulf States

In enforcing the embargo, two U.S. ships lead a Multinational Interdiction Force (MIF) that conducts maritime searches in the Persian Gulf to prevent the smuggling of oil and other high-value exports. The United States has asserted that Iran's Revolutionary Guard has been helping Iraq smuggle out the oil exports in exchange for "protection fees," although Iran did stop some illicit shipments in mid-2000, earning some U.S. praise. From its high of about $600 million in 2000, smuggling through this route has fallen substantially since early 2001, indicating that Iraq is increasing its use of a pipeline to Syria (see below). It should be noted that Iraq receives only half the export value after paying off the Revolutionary Guard and smugglers. In October 2001, the United Nations produced evidence of continued illicit oil exports through the Gulf.

Iranian-Iraqi relations have improved since 1995. The two exchanged 6,000 prisoners from the Iran-Iraq war in April 1998 and smaller batches of prisoners and remains since. In early October 2000, the two agreed to abide by the 1975 Algiers Accords that delineated their border, and Iran's Foreign Minister visited later in the month, a sign of accelerating rapprochement. Iraq's Foreign Minister visited Iran in January 2002, and Iran released over 600 Iraqi prisoners still held. Regarding Iraq's relations with the Gulf monarchy states, in April 2000, the UAE and Bahrain reopened embassies in Baghdad, leaving Kuwait and Saudi Arabia as the only two Gulf monarchies without diplomatic relations with Iraq. As noted above, Kuwait and Iraq, in conjunction with Saudi Arabia, took steps to reconcile at the Arab League summit in Jordan (March 27-28, 2002).

Syria/Lebanon/Egypt

Syria and Iraq began a wanning trend in relations by reopening their border in 1997; this trend has continued since the July 2000 accession of Bashar Assad to the presidency of Syria. Since late 1998, the two countries have benefited from the reopening of the Iraq-Syria oil pipeline, closed since 1982, and Iraq has been sending about 150,000 - 180,000 barrels per day of oil through the line, under a "swap" arrangement in which Syria uses the oil domestically and exports an equivalent extra amount of its own oil. Because of discounts offered to Syria, Iraq earns about $800 million per year from this illicit exportation. Resolution 1284 (paragraph 16) lays the groundwork for the opening of this route, but Syria and Iraq, are resisting controls on this trade. Syria has not implemented its pledge to Secretary of State Powell, made during his February 2001 visit to Damascus, that Syria would place the pipeline under oil-for-food guidelines, and press reports say the Bush Administration has not pressed Syria to uphold this commitment in order to earn Syrian cooperation in the war on terrorism. In May 2001, Iraq and Syria reopened diplomatic missions in each others' capitals.

Lebanon, which is under the heavy influence of Syria, restored diplomatic relations with Iraq October 23, 1998, after a 4-year break. As a sign of warming Iraqi-Egyptian relations, Iraqi-Egyptian trade under the oil for food program and other trade has now reached $1.7

billion annually. On January 18, 2001, the two countries signed a "free trade agreement," although under the condition that it goes into effect when sanctions are lifted. In November 2000, Iraq and Egypt upgraded their interest sections to embassies.

Protecting/Supporting Iraq's Opposition

The post-September 11 debate on Iraq encompasses the question of whether the United States will increase support for the Iraqi opposition.

As of February 2002, the Iraqi opposition has received $24 million in ESF since 1998, with $19 million still to be obligated out of $43 million appropriated. The FY2002 foreign aid bill (H.R. 2506, conference report H.Rept. 107-345) contains a provision authorizing the expenditure of Economic Support Funds (ESI[7]) in FY2002 to change the Iraqi regime, although no dollar amount is specified. The conference report also contains language expressing congressional concern about the results of a State Department audit of the INC's use of U.S.-provided funds and suggesting that the U.S. consider funding other opposition groups in addition to the INC. A U.S.-funded conference of opposition groups, which was to be held in May 2002, is in doubt over divisions within the Administration on how to structure it. In addition, the INC ceased its Liberty TV broadcasts in late April because some of its funding is still being negotiated with the State Department.

Military Action and Long-Term Containment

The current U.S. military posture in the Persian Gulf is focused on containing and deterring Iraq, and some experts believe that a U.S. decision to overthrow Saddam would require the use of U.S. forces. Currently, the United States and Britain enforce two "no fly zones" to provide a measure of protection for Iraq's Kurdish minority and other objects of regime repression and to contain Iraq militarily. To enforce the no-fly zones, the two allies invoke U.N. Resolution 678 (November 29, 1990, authorizing use of force to expel Iraq from Kuwait), 687 (the main ceasefire resolution), 688 (human rights), and the Safwan Accords (the March 3, 1991 cease-fire agreements between Iraq and the coalition forces that banned Iraqi interference with allied air operations). Resolutions 678 and 687 were written under Chapter VII of the U.N. Charter, dealing with peace and security, and are interpreted as allowing military action to enforce these resolutions. Resolution 688 (human rights) was not written under Chapter VII, nor does that or any other resolution establish no fly zones.

To justify Operation Desert Fox, the Administration cited additional justification from Resolution 1154 (see above), which warned of "the severest consequences" for non-compliance. Section 1095 of P.L. 102-190, the Defense Authorization Act for FY1992, signed December 5, 1991, expressed Congress' support for "all necessary means" to achieve the goals of U.N. Security Council Resolution 687. In instances of strikes on Iraq for no fly zone or other infractions, the Administration also has cited congressional action (primarily P.L. 102-1 of January 12, 1991, authorizing military action to expel Iraq from Kuwait).

Kurds/Operation Northern Watch (ONW)

The northern no fly zone was set up in April 1991, to protect the Kurds in northern Iraq. The zone extends north of the 36^{lb} parallel. After the September 1996 Iraqi incursion into northern Iraq, humanitarian aspects of ONW were ended and France ended its ONW participation. On June 25, 2001, Turkey renewed for six months basing rights at Incirlik Air Base for the 24 American aircraft and about 1,300 U.S. forces (plus allied forces). However, Turkey fears that ONW protects the anti-Turkish Kurdistan Workers' Party (PKK), which takes refuge in parts of northern Iraq, and Turkey has made repeated attacks against the PKK there since May 1997.

The two leading Iraqi Kurdish parties, the KDP led by Mas'ud Barzani and the Patriotic Union of Kurdistan (PUK) led by Jalal Talabani, agreed in May 1992 to share power after parliamentary and executive elections. In May 1994, tensions between them flared into clashes, and the KDP turned to Baghdad for backing. In August 1996, Iraqi forces helped the KDP capture Irbil, seat of the Kurdish regional government. With U.S. mediation, the Kurdish parties agreed on October 23, 1996,--to -a cease-fire and the establishment of a 400-man peace monitoring force composed mainly -of Turkomens (75% of the force). The United States funded the force with FY1997 funds of $3 million for peacekeeping (Section 451 of the Foreign Assistance Act), plus about $4 million in DoD drawdowns for vehicles and communications gear (Section 552 of the FAA). Also set up was a peace supervisory group consisting of the United States, Britain, Turkey, the PUK, the KDP, and Iraqi Turkomens. A tenuous cease-fire has held since November 1997 and the KDP and PUK leaders signed an agreement in Washington in September 1998 to work toward resolving the main outstanding issues (sharing of revenues and control over the Kurdish regional government). None of these issues has been fully resolved, but reconciliation efforts have shown substantial progress thus far in 2001. Both parties are represented in the opposition umbrella Iraqi National Congress, but both also maintain ties to Baghdad.

Shiite Muslims/Operation Southern Watch

Shiites constitute a majority in Iraq but historically have been repressed. The U.S.-led coalition declared a no-fly zone over southern Iraq (south of the 32nd parallel) to protect the Shiites on August 26, 1992 (Operation Southern Watch), although the overflights are primarily part of the U.S. containment strategy. The United States and the United Kingdom (but not France) expanded the zone up to the 33rd parallel on September4, 1996; France ended its participation entirely after Desert Fox. In response to Iraq's movement of troops toward Kuwait in October 1994, Security Council Resolution 949 (October 15, 1994) demanded Iraq not deploy forces to threaten its neighbors. The United States and Britain interpret this as authorizing military action if Iraq enhances (in numbers or quality of armament) its forces below the 32nd parallel.

During March 2000-March 2001, Iraqi air defenses fired at or near fixed radar or allied aircraft enforcing the zones on 500 occasions, in many cases provoking U.S. strikes on the activated missile batteries. On February 16, 2001, the United States and Britain struck elements of that network north of the southern no fly zone, in response to Iraq's increasing ability to target U.S. aircraft. U.S. aircraft did not go beyond the zone, but the strike was criticized internationally. Suggesting less U.S. vigilance in its no-fly zone enforcement, coalition aircraft struck Iraqi air defense targets only about 25 times in 2001, despite being fired on by Iraq over 50 times, compared to 47 different strikes in 2000. The U.S. strike activity has continued to be relatively low since September 11, despite the post-September 11 debate over stepped-up U.S. action against Iraq. In late April, the Defense Department said

Iraq had moved anti-aircraft systems into the no fly zones, although U.S. military officials said the activity was not particularly unusual.

Costs of Containment

Saudi Arabia, Kuwait, and the United Arab Emirates contributed a total of $37 billion to the $61.1 billion in incremental costs of Desert Storm, all of which has been paid. From the end of the Gulf war until the end of FY2000, the Defense Department has incurred about $8 billion in costs to contain Iraq and provide humanitarian aid to the Kurds. Of that, about $1.14 billion was spent in FY2000, and just under $100 million was spent for Operation Desert Fox. About $1.1 billion was spent in FY2001, and an FY2001 defense appropriation (H.R. 4576, P.L. 106-259, signed August 9, 2000) provided $3.938 billion in emergency spending for operations over Iraq and in Bosnia and Kosovo.) The Department of Defense, under the Weapons of Mass Destruction Control Act of 1992 (22 U.S.C. 5859a), assisted UNSCOM by providing U-2 surveillance flights (suspended since the December 15, 1998 UNSCOM pullout), intelligence, personnel, equipment, and logistical support, at a cost of about $15 million per year.

Chapter 5

IRAQ: EROSION OF INTERNATIONAL ISOLATION?

Kenneth Katzman and Alfred Prados

INTRODUCTION

Since the Gulf war ended in 1991, the U.S. effort to keep Iraq isolated — and therefore weak militarily — has depended on broad international cooperation, especially in the U.N. Security Council. The policy has succeeded in keeping Iraq strategically weak, but at great cost to the economic well being of the Iraqi people. The humanitarian suffering has reduced the will of many countries to maintain comprehensive sanctions, even though Iraq has refused to allow U.N. weapons inspections since a U.S./British bombing campaign against Iraqi facilities capable of producing weapons of mass destruction (WMD) in December 1998 (Operation Desert Fox). The Security Council has since remained deadlocked on the degree to which incentives should be offered to Iraq to persuade it to resume cooperation with the inspections. Many humanitarian groups and several governments now maintain that weapons inspections and sanctions relief should no longer be linked, while others see sanctions as leverage to force Iraq to disarm.

REGIONAL RELATIONS

Iraq has had some success in reducing its isolation in the Middle East. Relations with several of its neighbors have improved in recent years. Some countries in the region are tolerating Iraqi efforts to circumvent international economic sanctions or calling for their suspension.

Turkey/Northern Iraq

Baghdad has benefited indirectly from continuing rivalries between Kurdish factions in northern Iraq, where the United States and Britain have enforced a no-fly zone. In August

1996, the Iraqi Government exploited disputes between the two leading Iraqi Kurdish factions by intervening briefly at the invitation of the Kurdish Democratic Party (KDP) against the rival Patriotic Union of Kurdistan (PUK). Although Iraqi forces quickly withdrew, they reportedly used their brief incursion to eliminate several U.S.-sponsored opposition networks and the United States closed a military liaison office it had operated in northern Iraq. Allied overflights continue and the United States was able to broker a reconciliation agreement between the KDP and PUK in September 1998; so far, however, the two groups have not held elections to reestablish a joint political leadership as envisioned in the agreement.

Turkish leaders have long been concerned that a power vacuum in northern Iraq provides the Turkish opposition Kurdistan Workers' Party (PKK) with safe haven and a staging area for operations in southeastern Turkey. For the time being, the Turkish leadership seems willing to continue hosting U.S. and British overflights over northern Iraq, while launching periodic cross border raids into northern Iraq against PKK cadres. Some Turkish leaders, however, are concerned that U.S. policies of protecting the Kurdish enclave in Iraq could lead to an independent Kurdish state, which would serve as a model for separatist Turkish Kurds. Turkey also claims that a decade of economic sanctions against Iraq have cost the Turkish economy $30 to $35 billion, although U.S. officials point out that Turkish trade with Iraq under the so-called "oil-for-food" program compensates to some degree for these losses.[1] Turkey reportedly permits its truck drivers to import approximately 2.5 million tons of oil products in spare fuel tanks from Iraq, technically in violation of the international sanctions regime.[2] Iraq donated $10 million worth of oil to Turkey as a good will gesture after the August 1999 earthquake.

Jordan and Iraq

Jordan has distanced itself from Iraq since the early 1990s, but the two countries maintain diplomatic and commercial contacts. During the most recent allied military confrontations with Iraq, beginning in 1998, Jordan called on Iraq to comply with U.N. resolutions but ruled out the use of Jordanian air space to launch attacks against Iraqi targets. On October 7, 1999, on the eve of a visit to the United States, King Abdullah of Jordan told reporters that he would be carrying a message from Iraqi President Saddam Hussein to President Clinton but did not plan to speak on behalf of Iraq. The United Nations continues to acquiesce in Jordanian imports of oil from Iraq (approximately 95,000 barrels per day) since Jordan has no other source of oil at affordable prices. Jordan obtains the oil at a discount, and pays for it through shipments of humanitarian goods to Iraq permitted under the "oil-for-food" program and other pertinent U.N. resolutions. In July 1998, Jordan and Iraq agreed to build a 450-mile pipeline to replace expensive shipments by tanker truck. The project would go into effect when and if U.N. sanctions against Iraq are eased. Funding for the project, estimated at $900 million in March 1999, may be difficult for either country to obtain.

---

[1] Jonathan Wright, U.S. Dampens Turkey's Financial Hopes, Reuters, September 27, 1999.
[2] Steve Bryant, Turkish Quotas Keep Lid On Illicit Disel Trade, Reuters, July 1, 1999.

Iraqi-Syrian Rapprochement

Syrian-Iraqi relations have improved significantly, after decades of geopolitical rivalry. Since mid-1997, the two countries have reopened borders, had discussions on border demarcation, and exchanged trade delegations.

Although they have not restored full diplomatic relations, Syrian officials announced in April 1999 that the two countries will exchange interests sections. Lebanon, which generally adopts Syrian positions on regional affairs, restored diplomatic relations with Iraq on October 1998 after a four-year break. Syria has called on Iraq to observe relevant UN. resolutions, but opposes the use of force against Iraq.

Iraq has also begun purchasing goods from Syria with revenues from oil Iraq is allowed to sell under the U.N.-approved oil-for-food plan.[3] In mid-1998, Syria and Iraq signed an agreement to reopen a 400-kilometer oil pipeline through Syria, closed since 1982. In February 1999, Iraqi officials said repairs on the Iraqi segment of the pipeline were completed. It is not clear whether or not repairs are completed on the Syrian side, and a U.S. State Department official has expressed the view that shipment of Iraqi oil through Syria would require approval by the U.N. Security Council.

Iraq and the Gulf States

The six Gulf Cooperation Council (GCC) states, especially Kuwait and Saudi Arabia, remain fearful of potential threats from Iraq. Several GCC states, however, see strategic and humanitarian benefits to ending Iraq's isolation and supporting its role as a potential counterweight to Iranian military power. Qatar and Oman normalized relations with Iraq shortly after the Gulf war, and both Qatar and the United Arab Emirates (UAE) have called for easing economic burdens on the Iraqi people. In September 1998, several Saudi firms signed contracts to provide supplies to Iraq under the oil-for-food program, and in August 1999, Saudi Arabia released $1 million in Iraqi assets frozen in Saudi banks. In late 1998, a new ferry service began operation between Iraq and the UAE, and Bahrain received permission from the U.N. Sanctions Committee in September 1999 to move people and cargo to Iraq by sea.

Iraq and the Arab League

The 22-member Arab League has taken a more conciliatory stance toward Iraq during 1999. Saddam Hussein initially alienated some League members early in the year by calling for the overthrow of several Arab regimes for acquiescing in U.S.-British strikes on Iraq in December 1998. A communiqué after an Arab League foreign ministers meeting in January 1999 called on Iraq not to pursue provocative policies toward its neighbors; however, the same communiqué expressed "uneasiness and concern" over the use of military force against Iraq and expressed solidarity with the Iraqi people. In September, Iraq's foreign minister

---

[3] In addition to shipments under the U.N.-approved oil-for-food plan, a journalist has alleged that Syrian authorities are permitting illegal shipments of Iraqi oil through Syria. Douglas Jehl, "Syria Sneaks Iraq's Oil Out As Old Foes Become Friends," *The New York Times*, April 26, 1999, p. A6.

chaired an Arab League meeting for the first time since the Iraqi invasion of Kuwait in 1990; the Iraqi minister welcomed the "positive atmosphere" of the meeting but said Iraq would not apologize for its occupation of Kuwait. Arab League Secretary-General Ismat Abd al-Magid of Egypt acknowledged that differences still exist among Arab states toward Iraq, but said the attendees were unanimous in seeking to ease hardships on the Iraqi people and added that none of the League members were opposed to lifting economic sanctions against Iraq.

Iran

Like Iraq, Iran sees itself as the target of U.S. containment efforts, and Iran has been key to Iraq's efforts to break out of its regional isolation. Since 1995, the two countries have been meeting at progressively higher levels, and Iran reportedly has been helping Iraq smuggle varying amounts of oil and other high value exports out of the Gulf in exchange for "protection fees." This illicit exportation has amounted to between $10 million and $20 million per month.[4] However, a number of issues will likely prevent the two neighbors from forging a close alliance. Iran has given no indication it will return to Iraq the 115 combat aircraft flown there at the start of the 1991 Gulf war. In addition, both Iran and Iraq harbor opposition groups fighting to topple the other. Iraq hosts the army of the leftwing People's Mojahedin Organization of Iran (PMOI), and Iran provides some material support to the Supreme Council for the Islamic Revolution in Iraq (SCIRI), a Shiite Islamic fundamentalist political and guerrilla group.

India

India appeared ready to openly defy international sanctions in July 1999 when it announced a $25 million loan to Iraq to purchase 1,000 Indian-made buses. Indian officials noted that they were aware the loan would violate international sanctions.[5] However, U.S. objections led India to announce subsequently that the loan would only be granted if it were approved by the U.N. Sanctions Committee. That same month, India also began negotiating with Iraq to develop the southern Tuba oil field, with the deal to go into effect if and when sanctions on foreign investment are lifted.

U.N. Security Council Developments

The apparent erosion of Iraq's regional isolation has been accompanied by waning Security Council support for maintaining sanctions. Most observers see the United States and Britain increasingly alone in seeking to ensure that Iraq fulfills all its disarmament obligations specified by U.N. Security Council Resolution 687 (April 3, 1991).

The splits within the Council are no more evident than in the debate over a new British/Dutch draft Security Council resolution that would attempt to restore the weapons

[4] Crawley, James. U.S. Sailors On the Lookout for Contraband From Iraq. *San Diego Union-Tribune,* November 18, 1998.

[5] India Says It Will Abide By U.N. Sanctions on Iraq. *Associated Press,* July 30, 1999.

inspection process halted on the eve of Operation Desert Fox (December 16-19, 1998). The draft provides that, following a period of full Iraqi cooperation with new inspections, sanctions on Iraqi exports would be "suspended," and the current U.N. escrow account that holds the revenues of Iraqi oil exports would be phased out in favor of unspecified "financial controls." According to press reports, the United States might agree to a provision suspending sanctions on Iraq's imports as well as exports, as long as an intrusive inspection system is resumed. On September 23, 1999, the five permanent members of the Security Council acknowledged that they had not reached agreement on the new resolution, but would keep working toward an agreement.

Several additional actions by Council members, as well as related developments, suggest that Iraq's international isolation, and Council support for continued sanctions, are weakening:

- Beginning with its non-participation in Operation Desert Fox, France has ended its participation in enforcing the no fly zone over southern Iraq. Earlier, in January 1997, France pulled out of the northern no fly zone enforcement operation following September 1996 U.S. cruise missile strikes on Iraq. The strikes were a response to Iraq's brief incursion into the north (see above). This leaves only the United States and Britain enforcing the two zones.
- With the beginning of the oil-for-food program in December 1996 (U.N. Resolution 986), Iraq returned to the world oil market. Although its oil industry suffered from six years of disuse and lack of repair, the increasing flow of spare parts, coupled with higher oil prices, has enabled Iraq to resume its place as one of the world's five largest oil producers (about 2.7 million barrels per day, with exports about 2.1 million per day).
- In line with Iraq's return to the oil market, international energy firms have signed agreements with it to develop Iraqi energy resources. In March 1997, a Russian consortium (Lukoil, Zarubezhneft, and Mashinoimport) and Iraq signed a $3.5 billion deal to develop Iraq's Al Qurna oilfield. Russian officials stressed that only preliminary feasibility studies would begin before international sanctions on Iraq are lifted. However, Iraq has warned Russia that development work must begin or it will award the contract to other firms. Russian officials visited Iraq in late September 1999 but they did not reach agreement for the Russian team to begin work. In June 4, 1997, Iraq and China signed a $1.2 billion contract for the Chinese National Petroleum Corporation to develop Iraq's Al Ahdab oilfield. In addition, a French-Belgian firm Total Fina, and a French firm Elf Aquitaine have negotiated preliminary agreements to develop other oil fields in Iraq, including the Nahr Umar field. Some believe the commercial interests explain Russian, French, and Chinese willingness to ease sanctions on Iraq.[6]
- The worldwide commercial interest in Iraq has prompted the United States, after some hesitation, to support a provision of the British/Dutch draft resolution that would allow for foreign investment in Iraq's energy industry. The U.S. position might also represent a recognition that, despite the adversarial relationship with Iraq, there is increasing commerce between the two countries. U.S. firms purchase about one-third of Iraq's oil exports under the oil-for-food program. In addition, several U.S.

[6] Efstathiou, Jim. U.K.-Dutch Plan On Iraq Could Trigger Major Oil Deals. *Dow Jones Newswire,* May 20, 1999.

energy firms have had discussions with Iraq about future investments in Iraq's petroleum industry. Those firms include Amoco (now a British firm), Arco, Chevron, Exxon, Mobil, Occidental, Texaco, and Conoco.[7]

- In late September 1999, a delegation from the European consortium Airbus visited Baghdad to discuss supplying aircraft to Iraqi Airways once sanctions are lifted. However, the British/Dutch draft under consideration does not, as of now, provide for an end to the U.N. ban on Iraqi commercial flights.
- The Pope is reportedly planning to visit a religious site in Iraq in early December 1999, and the visit would likely include a meeting with Saddam Husayn.

U.S. Policy Response

The Clinton Administration has tried to counter the impression among many that Iraq is on its way to rejoining the international community. On October 6, 1999, the Administration refused a reported Iraqi overture to begin an official dialogue with the United States. As articulated by State Department spokesman Jamie Rubin, the U.S. position is that the United States is not "interested in" a dialogue, but rather in Iraq's full compliance with all applicable UN. resolutions. On the other hand, it has been suggested that the large quantity of U.S. imports of Iraqi oil — coupled with U.S. willingness to support the easing of sanctions contained in the British/Dutch draft resolution — dilutes the U.S. message that it wants the continued isolation of Iraq.

The Administration has tried to prevent high profile visits to Iraq that might help generate sympathy for Iraqi pleas to end international sanctions. The Administration has said it has attempted to dissuade the Pope from his planned visit to Iraq or, at the very least, from meeting with Saddam Husayn. In August 1999, the Administration strenuously objected to a trip to Iraq by five congressional staff members, and provided none of the customary logistical support. However, no legal means existed to prevent the visit, and it went forward.

The Administration and Congress have sought to break down Saddam Husayn's international legitimacy by publicizing not only Iraq's failure to comply with U.N. resolutions but also its past actions that might constitute war crimes. The Iraq Liberation Act (P.L. 105-338, October 31, 1998) authorizes a draw down of up to $97 million worth of equipment for the Iraqi opposition and recommends that the President push for a war crimes trial for Saddam Husayn and his associates. Administration officials said in September 1999 that the United States is supporting the establishment of a commission on Iraq that would begin finding facts about alleged Iraqi war crimes. Although U.N. Security Council Resolution 674 (October 29, 1990) calls on member states to provide to the United Nations information on Iraqi atrocities, several Security Council members believe that the war crimes issue should not be pursued because it will remove Iraq's incentive to comply with U.N. requirements on WMD and other issues.

The Administration and Congress are supporting organizations that are highlighting alleged Iraqi war crimes. Of the $13 million in additional funds appropriated for the opposition since FY1998, $3 million has been earmarked for INDICT, a group attempting to

[7] Report on Iraq by the Energy Information Administration, an arm of the U.S. Department of Energy. November 1998.

gather and publicize information on Iraqi war crimes. The conference report on the FY2000 foreign aid appropriations bill (H.R. 2606) provides another $2 million for groups performing similar activities, although the bill was vetoed on October 18 over other issues. As of early September 1999, $500,000 has gone to INDICT.[8] The organization has, on several occasions in 1999, persuaded European officials to try to detain visiting alleged Iraqi war criminals. On these occasions, the Iraqis have either departed quickly or canceled planned trips.

[8] Lynch, Colum. U.S. Aids Hunters of Iraqi War Criminals. *Washington Post,* September 4, 1999.

Chapter 6

IRAQ: HUMANITARIAN NEEDS, IMPACT OF SANCTIONS, AND THE "OIL FOR FOOD" PROGRAM

Lois McHugh

ABSTRACT

Much of the Iraqi civilian population is suffering from shortages of food, medical care, and an infrastructure damaged by the 1991 Gulf war. This report discusses these shortages, and what the "oil for food" program, established by the U.N. Security Council, is doing to alleviate them. It discusses the conflicting views about the extent and cause of the civilian suffering and the reliability of the available data.

SUMMARY

Many private and international humanitarian agencies argue that under the U.N. sanctions, Iraqi civilians, and especially children, suffer and die from lack of adequate food and medical supplies despite the "oil for food" program and other international assistance. They argue that the sanctions are inhumane and should be lifted immediately. On the opposing side, defenders of international policy argue that it is not the sanctions causing suffering but deliberate Iraqi policies diverting resources and even manipulating the humanitarian "crisis". Some also accuse Iraqi officials of exaggerating the level of suffering. They point out that Iraq can end the sanctions at any time by meeting the conditions of its 1991 surrender.

The U.N. Security Council established the "oil for food" program in December 1996 to alleviate the impact of sanctions on the civilian population. Since December 1996, the program has been extended and amended to allow more oil to be sold in the face of evidence that civilian suffering continues, but Iraq alleges that the U.S. and British governments deliberately hold up the arrival of humanitarian goods. The United States and Britain argue that the Iraqi government creates the delays itself.

On June 4, 1998, the latest extension of the "oil for food" program began and will allow Iraq to sell oil worth up to $4.5 billion to import humanitarian goods and pay for their distribution during this six month period, bringing the volume of permitted oil exports nearly to pre-Gulf war levels.

This report discusses the conflicting views on the extent and causes of human suffering in Iraq and the reliability of data. It describes and assesses the "oil for food" program, its operation, impact and perceived shortcomings.

BACKGROUND

U.N. sanctions were first applied to Iraq after its invasion of Kuwait in 1990. The 1991 report of a U.N. Under-Secretary-General describing near-apocalyptic destruction in Iraq at the end of the war led the Security Council to establish the current sanctions regime. Security Council resolution 686, adopted on March 2, 1991, prohibited all trade with Iraq including the sale of oil. No limits were placed on Iraq's ability to import food, medicine or other humanitarian goods after the war, however Iraq's foreign assets were frozen. Under a special "oil for food" program, established by Security Council resolution 986 in April 1995, the sale of oil currently allowed may be used only to purchase goods authorized by the U.N. Security Council.

The "oil for food" program is not the only source of food available to Iraq. The Iraqi government controls domestic food production and distribution. This system, prior to the war, provided up to one third of domestic food. The "oil for food" program is also not the only way Iraq currently sells oil. Some oil (about 100,000 barrels per day at below market rate prices) is exported to Jordan under a longstanding program tacitly authorized by the United Nations. Press reports indicate that about $100 million in oil per year is smuggled into Turkey and sold on the black market. Other oil is also exported through Iran and from seaports in the south such as Basra for black market sale. It is not clear how much this benefits the Iraqi government.

The "oil for food" program is not the only source of humanitarian aid to Iraq. Both bilateral and multilateral aid continues to flow into the country as it has since the end of the war. Because U.N. and other humanitarian agencies provide aid to Iraq both through the "oil for food" program and with other funding, it is difficult to determine how much humanitarian assistance is provided outside of the "oil for food" program. It is also impossible to determine the total amount of multilateral and bilateral aid provided by all donors. But UNICEF alone has spent $200 million since the end of the war on programs of health, nutrition, water, sanitation, education and child protection in Iraq. The UNICEF budget for Iraq for 1997, independent of "oil for food" funded assistance, was $16 million, including $7.7 million donated by the United States. UNICEF expects to spend $20 million during 1998 and 1999.[1] Similarly, the UN Development Program budget included $12.8 million for Iraq in 1997. Other international agencies, countries and private voluntary organizations (PVOs) also provide assistance. The European Community's foreign aid program has provided $230 million since the end of the Gulf war[2].

[1] UNICEF. Iraq monthly country situation report. December 1997. p. 1

[2] European Community Humanitarian Office. Speech of the Commissioner. Iraq Humanitarian Meeting. London. April 20, 1998.

Prior to the 1990 Gulf war, Iraq had one of the highest per capita food availabilities in the region due to its relative prosperity, according to the Food and Agriculture Organization (FAO). Food availability has declined sharply since 1990, and, because other countries in the region have not seen similar declines, FAO believes that natural causes are not the reason for the decline. Since the end of the war with Iraq, numerous surveys and studies have been made of the health and nutrition status of the civilian population. Most studies show a continuing decline in health and nutrition of Iraqi civilians, especially children and the elderly. But it is difficult to determine how much of the suffering is due to the sanctions imposed on Iraq and how much is due to other factors. Imposition of U.N. sanctions followed a nearly decade long war between Iraq and Iran, during which spending on the social welfare system declined. The bombing during the Gulf war damaged or destroyed much of the public infrastructure such as water and sewage plants and many public buildings. And since the end of the war, Iraq's government has repeatedly attacked with military force its minority populations in both the north and the south parts of the country leading to destruction of homes and a growing population of displaced persons. There is a government-imposed internal embargo on the northern Kurdish areas which limits trade, financial transactions, and other commerce within Iraq.

Much of the information available on the conditions within Iraq is also questionable. In a closed society such as Iraq, information is provided either with the concurrence of the Iraqi government or in anecdotal form from people fleeing the country. The Iraqi government publicizes estimates that the death toll from the sanctions is 1.5 million, including 500,000 children. Many private and intergovernmental organizations cite these figures as their own. Other groups question the accuracy of the statistics, but have no independent sources of information. All estimates of the number of deaths due to lack of food or medical care vary widely based on the source. In an April 20, 1998 speech calling for a new look at the Iraq sanctions, European Commissioner for Humanitarian Affairs Emma Bonino noted that despite the shortage of reliable information, all the information gleaned from U.N. and private sources led her to the conclusion that the Iraqi social fabric is badly eroded.[3]

Because Iraq has not satisfied U.N. Security Council conditions for a full lifting of the trade embargo, the "oil for food" program was adopted by the Security Council as a way of protecting the Iraqi poor while maintaining pressure on the Iraqi government to abide by the terms of the peace agreement.[4] Iraq did not accept the conditions of the "oil for food" program until December 1996 and the first shipments of goods did not arrive until Spring 1997. Thus the "oil for food" program has been in operation for a little more than a year. At the present time, a full lifting of the oil embargo is tied to certification by U.N. inspectors (UNSCOM) that Iraq has destroyed all chemical and biological weapons and the equipment and raw materials to manufacture them in the future. The problems with the "oil for food" program are political as well as medical and nutritional and have changed over the last year.

[3] European Community. Speech of the Commissioner.

[4] For information on the actions of the U.N. Security Council in the post-Gulf war period, see Iraqi Compliance with Cease-Fire Agreements, by Kenneth Katzman, CRS Issue Brief 92117. Updated regularly.

HUMAN SUFFERING IN IRAQ AND ITS CAUSES

Observers of the Iraqi situation have identified disturbing health and nutrition problems affecting the civilian population. These have been tied to the consequences of war, sanctions, shortcomings of assistance, and the deliberate policies of the Iraqi regime. While the U.N. "oil for food" program was established to alleviate these problems, there is controversy over whether any U.N. run program is able to address them. These problems are:

Malnutrition

Opponents of the U.N. sanctions and critics of the "oil for food" program cite U.N. health evaluations over the 1991-1997 period to argue that the civilian population is suffering under current conditions, with children and other vulnerable groups especially hard hit. These show an increase in infant and child mortality and malnutrition. The most recent UN FAO/World Food Program (WFP) "Food Supply and Nutrition Assessment was released on October 3, 1997[5]. It covered the food supply and nutrition situation for civilians in Iraq based on a June 9- July 8, 1997 visit, when the "oil for food" program had been in operation for two months. The mission based its evaluation on discussions with Iraqi Government Ministries and Departments, UN System Organizations, bilateral agencies and NGOs and on field visits throughout the country. The mission concluded that although there had been some improvements in the food supply situation under the revised "oil for food" program, malnutrition remained a serious problem throughout the country.

A UNICEF survey made in October /November 1997 indicated that nearly 1 million Iraqi children under five years old are suffering from chronic malnutrition in the center and south of Iraq. The Iraqi government maintains that the infant mortality rate has risen sharply since the imposition of sanctions, with government estimates ranging from 5,600 to 6,500 deaths per month in 1998 compared to 389 to 450 deaths per month before sanctions were imposed. Iraq's health ministry figures indicate that 57,000 children under five die each year. UNICEF statistics (which are generally provided by governments) as published in the *State of the World's Children,* show an under five mortality rate of 122 in 1996, compared with 89 in 1989, as shown in an earlier *State of the World's Children.* Beginning in 1991, U.N. assessment missions have observed cases of marasmus and kwashiorkor, the most alarming forms of protein energy malnutrition, indicating that the nutritional health of the population has fallen to dangerous levels. Incidences of stunting, underweight, and wasting among children under five in Baghdad increased from 12%, 7%, and 3%, respectively, in 1991 to 28%, 29%, and 12% in 1995, according to a World Health

Organization survey.[6] (The figures for Baghdad in the July 1997 FAO/WFP survey for stunting, underweight, and wasting of 15%, 11%, and 3.3%, respectively, indicate that even early in the "oil for food" program, the country has made substantial progress, at least in Baghdad, though not to pre-Gulf war levels.)

---

[5] Special Report. FAOAVFP Food Supply and Nutrition Assessment Mission to Iraq. October 3, 1997. Iraqsanc.feo.txt.

[6] World Health Organization. Health Conditions of the Population in Iraq since the Gulf Crisis. March 1996. p. 7 WHO/EHA/96.1.

Others, including the U.S. government, argue that much of the malnutrition seen in Iraq is caused by Iraqi government activities, and is imposed selectively. Iraqi dissident groups point out that the U.N. ration basket was supposed to be an addition to what the Iraqi government provided, and was never intended to provide all the food that the Iraqi population needed. These groups state that the Iraqi government has completely stopped distributing government subsidized food to some groups, leaving the U.N. food basket the only food available for many people. Families of dissidents and army deserters, as well as ethnic and religious minorities have lost their ration cards. The U.N. Special Rapporteur on Human Rights in Iraq noted in his March 1998 report to the Economic and Social Council that "the effect of the embargo is harsher on members of ethnic and religious minorities, and that there exists discrimination in the allocation by the authorities of the limited resources available between rural and urban areas, and against the southern region with respect to the Marsh people."[7] (It should be noted that the U.N. Human Rights Rapporteur has not been allowed into Iraq for several years and this information is acquired second hand.) The U.S. State Department, in a February 28, 1998 Fact Sheet on the Oil for Food program states that Iraq has reduced its own purchases of humanitarian goods and diverted its own stocks to the military, or placed them in warehouses for future use. The United States asserts that Iraq continues to spend its available funds on arms and benefits for the government elite and its supporters. Finally, the United States points out, the assessment team was in Iraq during the 2 months when the Iraqi government refused to sell oil, thereby exacerbating food shortages. In a resolution adopted by the Security Council to mitigate the effect of this Iraqi shutdown of oil sales, the Security Council noted in the text that the Iraqi government bore full responsibility for hardships caused by its decision not to sell oil during the period.

Others have questioned Iraqi statistics on whether there has been an unusually large number of civilian deaths, particularly among children under five. According to the newsletter of the Washington Institute, Iraq's official 1997 census showed a population increase of 3.5 million since 1990 which is consistent with a normal level of births and deaths for the country and a normal rate of infant mortality.[8] The FAO/WFP survey stated that the official Iraqi census showed a population increase between 1987 and 1997 of 6.62 million.

Health

Another cause of the unnatural rise in deaths noted by UNICEF and the WHO, especially among children, is said to be disease due to lack of common medicines, medical equipment shortages and poor sanitation. Critics of the sanctions argue that they are especially damaging in the health area, leading to unnecessary suffering and deaths. U.N. Director of the "oil for food" program in Iraq Dennis Halliday, stated during an interview on March 13, 1998 that "it is tragically the case that the lack of drugs, equipment, supplies, is, indeed, having a devastating impact on young children in particular but also adults."[9] The Secretary-General's March 1998 report[10] noted that despite the feet that a large variety of supplies have been delivered, quantities received to date remain inadequate...often covering only 20 percent of

[7] Report on the situation of human rights in Iraq. p. 20.
[8] Clawson, Patrick. 'Oil for food' or the end of sanctions. Policywatch. 303. February 26, 1998. p. 2.
[9] Transcript of the NewsHour with Jim Lahrer. March 13, 1998.
[10] Report oflhe Secretary-General Pursuant to Paragraph 4 of Resolution 1143 (1997). S/1998/194. March 4, 1998.

requirements. The report suggested that some of the problems were caused by inadequate internal transport at all levels which led to an average time of 5 to 6 weeks to distribute supplies from warehouses to the rest of the country, and that cold chain transport (of medicines which need to be kept refrigerated) is even worse. Other problems were caused by uncoordinated arrival of supplies, such as injectable drugs but no syringes. Some problems he blamed on U.N. personnel. Since the problems exist in both the Northern (U.N. administered) and Central and Southern areas (Iraqi government administered) area, it seems fair to fault U.N. administrators, at least in part. Other problems were caused by the lack of prioritization of needs by Iraqi government personnel, which led to oversupplies of some drugs and very low or no quantities of others, as well as poor communication between health care facilities and the Ministry of Health or even within health facilities. Before the war, Iraq imported an estimated $500 million in drugs and medical supplies annually, or 75 percent of total needs. The other 25 percent were manufactured locally. According to accounts in the press, $200 million worth of medicine was delivered under the "oil for food" program during 1997.[11]

Following the changes made by the Security Council and the U.N. Secretary-General, Eric Fait, U.N. spokesman in Iraq, stated that a May 1998 report by WHO showed that the time lag for delivery of medical supplies has been cut to under four months. He noted that during May, 50 percent of patients received their full prescribed treatment, up from 39 percent six months before. Fifteen percent received none of their prescribed drugs, down from 25 percent.[12]

In other health areas, Iraq continues to maintain a high level of health care with the assistance of the international community. The UNICEF Iraq Monthly Country Situation Report for December 1997 states that the level of childhood disease vaccination coverage has been maintained at greater that 90 percent and that 50 percent of women of child bearing age in high risk areas were vaccinated for tetanus. These statistics are virtually the same as the figures UNICEF provided for 1988-89. The UNICEF publication *State of the World's Children for 1998* states that no vaccination funding was provided by the Iraqi government.

Sanitation

Health experts and Iraqi doctors say malnutrition and increased early childhood deaths are no longer the result of lack of food, as they were before the "oil for food" program. Rather they are caused by lack of safe drinking water and inadequate sanitation. This leads to intestinal diseases that can dehydrate and eventually kill children, especially in rural areas where people are poor and have little knowledge of preventing these problems.[13] UNICEF's December report on Iraq expresses concern that only half of the people in rural areas have access to a water supply from a network, public tap or well, compared to 96 percent of people living in towns and cities. Only 34 percent have a sanitary type of latrine, compared to 97 percent of the urban population. But a comparison with UNICEF's *State of the World's Children for 1991* (which covered the years 1985-88, before the Gulf war) shows similar statistics, with nearly all urban dwellers and 54 percent of rural residents having access to clean water. There were no statistics on sanitary latrines. Water and sanitation are clearly

[11] Reuters. June 7, 1998

[12] Reuters. June 4, 1998.

[13] Struck, Doug. 'Iraqi ingenuity aids survival". Washington Post. May 3, 1998. A22.

problems which predate the sanctions. The U.N. Secretary-General's most recent report estimates the cost of rehabilitating the water and sanitation system at $500 million.

Education

A growing concern is the state of education in Iraq. According to the Iraqi Minister of Education, $170 million is needed for immediate rehabilitation of 7,550 schools at the primary and secondary levels and for essential supplies for students. According to the March 1998 report of the Secretary-General, only 12 percent of the educational supplies of the first year's program have been delivered, which made it impossible for him to assess the program. UNICEF's report on Iraq states that in 1995, only 58 percent of Iraq's 4 million school age children finished primary school, compared to 71 percent completing primary school in 1985-87. This discrepancy may be due in part to internal political disputes which have halted teacher pay by the government in the northern Kurdish areas and the large increase in the number of displaced persons due to Iraqi and Kurdish military activity.

THE OIL FOR FOOD PROGRAM

How the Program Works[14]

Security Council resolution 986 permits Iraq to sell limited quantities of oil over six-month periods. The money generated is deposited into a bank of Iraqi choosing and is used to provide humanitarian goods to Iraqi civilians under close U.N. supervision. The funds are also used to compensate victims of the invasion and occupation of Kuwait and to pay for UNSCOM investigations and other U.N. costs in Iraq. (Thirty percent is provided for compensation and about 5 percent for other U.N. costs, though these percentages can be changed.) After the U.N. Security Council adopts a resolution authorizing the sale of oil for a six month period, the government of Iraq must provide the U.N. Secretary-General with a plan outlining how the Iraqi government plans to spend the oil revenue, which also must be approved by the U.N. Security Council. This must include an agreed upon proportion of aid for the Kurdish areas of the country. The Government of Iraq distributes humanitarian supplies in the south and center of the country and the U.N. Interagency Humanitarian Program distributes supplies in the north due to the internal embargo against the Kurdish areas in the north, But the "oil for food" program provides funds for the entire country. U.N. observers are stationed throughout Iraq to ensure equity and to prevent diversion of food and other humanitarian aid from civilians and to prohibit the misuse of dual use equipment like ambulances or laboratory equipment. The program establishes a ration basket, which, under the latest resolution provides 2500 calories per person per day. Additional assistance is provided directly to vulnerable groups, such as widows with children, the elderly and the handicapped, by U.N. agencies and PVOs throughout the country.

Originally, the "oil for food" program was to be a supplement, available primarily to the poor and vulnerable, in addition to the ration which has been provided by the Iraqi

[14] For more detailed information on the organization of the U.N. sanctions regime, see Iraqi Compliance with Cease-Fire Agreements, by Kenneth Katzman, CRS Issue Brief 92117. Updated regularly.

government for many years. However, it has quickly become the only source of food for many Iraqis.

SHORTCOMINGS/BUREAUCRATIC DELAYS IN THE PROGRAM

The October 1997 FAO/WFP report criticized the slowness of the "oil for food" program. It noted that in the first six months of the "oil for food" program, only 43 percent of the wheat flour and 20 percent of the rice had been received. Some other foods and salt had not arrived at all. The report noted many other examples of delays in both food and medical supplies. U.N. Secretary-General Kofi Annan, in his February 1998 investigation of the delivery system, agreed with many of these complaints. He spoke of "exceptional and unprecedented complexity" in the "oil for food" bureaucracy. He pointed out other delays, noting that only 25% of the phase I and II water and sanitation equipment budgeted has arrived in the south and central parts of Iraq. Though distribution is adequate, delays have occurred in the installation of equipment due to lack of funds and qualified technicians. In the northern governates, 21% of supplies have arrived.[15]

While not disputing bureaucratic slowness, others argued that much of the delay has been caused by the Iraqi government. The March 1998 report of the U.N. Special Rapporteur on Human Rights in Iraq noted that twice the Iraqi government had stopped pumping oil for many weeks, choosing to wait for the Security Council to adopt a new resolution, rather than continuing to pump oil in anticipation of the resolution. "The Special Rapporteur notes that rather than taking every opportunity to facilitate the distribution plan in order to alleviate the suffering of the Iraqi population, the Government of Iraq insists upon arguing about procedural mechanisms."[16] In a similar comment, Britain's International Development Secretary was quoted in the press as saying: "With the volume of resources now available to the government of Iraq there is simply no reason why children should be starving. But they are, and we must help them."[17]

Supporters of the "oil for food" program also argue that the program can and has been improved since it began. Since his February 1998 report, the Secretary-General has worked to improve the response time by recommending that Iraq formulate a distribution plan that will prioritize applications and deliveries. The Security Council Sanctions Committee adopted procedures to process applications within two business days, issue approval letters on the basis of anticipated revenues, and release funds more quickly. Other options are also being adopted to improve the processing time of the program. The monthly WFP emergency report on Iraq, dated April 24, noted that the pipeline has improved greatly, and though some supplies are not sufficient to meet all needs, the supply has become more regular. During April, only rice and infant formula were insufficient, and those were to be supplied from government stocks. The U.N. spokesman in Iraq was quoted in the press as saying that the June ration would be complete, except for legumes (such as peas or beans).[18] WFP's emergency operation for vulnerable groups, including malnourished children, pregnant and

[15] Report of the Secretary-General pursuant to paragraph 4 of resolution 1143(1997). March 4, 1998.

[16] Report on the situation of human rights in Iraq, submitted by the Special Rapporteur, Mr. Max van der Stoel, in accordance with Commission resolution 1997/60. March 10, 1998. E/CN.4/1998/67. p. 21.

[17] Reuters. April 20, 1998.

[18] Reuters. June 4, 1998.

nursing mothers, those in hospitals and other institutions, the internally displaced and refugees, continues to provide aid to 893,000 people with funds provided by donors.

AMENDED "OIL FOR FOOD" EXTENSION

The Security Council adopted SC res. 1153 (February 20, 1998) in response to the problems identified both in the FAO/WFP 1997 study and the U.N. Secretary-General's February 1998 study. The resolution amended the "oil for food" program to more than double the amount of oil that can be sold in order to raise and improve the caloric content of the ration basket and to provide one time infrastructure repair in water, sanitation, electricity, agricultural production, mine clearance, reforestation and education. Thus the purely humanitarian nature of the program has been broadened to include some rebuilding of the country.

The FAO/WFP study of October 1997 reported that the U.N. ration was inadequate in a number of nutrients and provided a low quality of protein. It concluded that sustained improvement in civilian nutrition would require a significant investment in rehabilitating the country's agricultural sector, including better seed, more fertilizer, pesticides, farm machinery, animal feed and vaccines. It also called for repair of irrigation systems, and water and sanitation equipment.

Under the new "oil for food" extension, $3 billion will be available for humanitarian assistance. Of this, $1.113 billion will be for the food sector, to improve the ration basket and address storage and distribution problems. The plan allocates $308 million to the medical services sector with 60% for import of required items for rehabilitation of hospitals and health centers and 40% for medicines. The plan allocates $210 million for rehabilitation of water and sanitation facilities, $411 million for rehabilitating electric power generation units. The $250 million allocated to rehabilitate the agricultural sector will include $80 million to rehabilitate irrigation equipment and $50 million to increase poultry production. The rest will be used for equipment and supplies to enhance domestic food production. The plan allocates $100 million to rehabilitation of schools, $150.5 million to improving the telecommunication system and $300 million for rehabilitation of oil production equipment and facilities. In all of these areas, specific allocations are made for the three Kurdish governates. In addition, $55 million is dedicated to rebuilding Kurdish cities and towns and $11 million for mine clearance activities in Kurdish areas.[19]

IMPACT ON SANCTIONS

Though support for the current sanctions is less unified among Security Council members than it has been in the past, thus far, no Security Council member has indicated a willingness to end the sanctions entirely. The next vote on continuing them will be in September. Nonetheless, Under Secretary for Political Affairs Pickering stated in testimony during May, that after eight years of sanctions, "most states in the world either do not understand or do not

[19] Enhanced Distribution Plan Submitted by the Government of Iraq to the Secretary-General of the United Nations in accordance with the Memorandum of Understanding of 20 May 1996 and Security Council resolution 1153 (1998). U.N. Security Council document S/1998/446. May 29, 1998. p. 3-9.

care that the Iraqi Government is fully responsible for the Iraqi people's suffering-they just want that suffering to end."[20] The Iraqi government has continued to press for an end to the sanctions as the only way to relieve the suffering population, and has received support from many governments and international organizations, both private and governmental. In a July 2, 1998 press release, the Executive Director of the U.N. Iraq Program described the "oil for food" program as a mixed success, excellent in some sectors and not impressive in others. He stressed that the U.N. effort was never meant to meet all the humanitarian needs of the Iraqi people. U.N. Special Envoy to Iraq Prakash Shah was quoted in the press as noting that there is greater awareness among U.N. member states, including Security Council members, of the harm being done to the Iraqi population by the sanctions. He also stated that no country expected the sanctions to go on forever.[21]

Some critics argue that authorizing the sale of $4.5 billion in oil per half year or a total of $9 billion per year in oil sales is actually an end to the sanctions. Average Iraqi oil exports during the 1981-89 period were $9.54 billion per year, adjusting for inflation, or slightly more than will be allowed under the new "oil for food" extension. In addition, the Iraqis are guaranteed the sale of all the oil at a price higher than the current market sale price, which has been moving downward recently. The new extension of the "oil for food" program allows Iraq to import nearly the full range of imports that it would be making without sanctions (the exception being motor vehicles) at about half the pre-war level and to invest in infrastructural improvements.[22]

Supporters of the increased oil sales, on the other hand, say that the tactic will reduce suffering among Iraqis and make it more difficult for the Iraqi government to maintain anti-American/British sentiments and nationalistic fervor.[23] As long as the oil revenue is kept out of the control of the Iraqi government, it hinders Iraq's ability to produce, store, or threaten to use chemical or biological weapons of mass destruction.

Finally, some express concern about a post-sanctions Iraq and how the sanctions should be ended. Kurdish separatist groups are expressing alarm at the potential end of an egalitarian distribution of oil revenue generated supplies and wonder what their future will be in light of the continuing Iraqi internal embargo. Others question how long the Iraqi population will have to wait for their country to be rebuilt and how patient they will be after such a long period of shortages. What safeguards can be put in place to make sure that the Iraqi government will use oil revenue for rebuilding Iraq, given the U.S. and British insistence that the current Iraqi government will try to divert revenues to building up the Iraqi military capability?

[20] Under Secretary of State for Political Affairs Thomas Pickering. Testimony before the Senate Foreign Relations Committee. May 21, 1998. Press release.

[21] Reuters. May 25, 1998.

[22] Clawson, Patrick, p. 1.

[23] Weiss, Thomas G. and Crawford, Neta. A humane way to lessen Iraqi suffering. Boston Globe. December 24, 1997.

Chapter 7

IRAQ: OIL-FOR-FOOD PROGRAM AND INTERNATIONAL SANCTIONS

Kenneth Katzman

SUMMARY

The "oil-for-food" program is the centerpiece of the long-standing U.N. Security Council effort to alleviate human suffering in Iraq while maintaining key elements of the Gulf war-related sanctions regime. In order to ensure that Iraq remains contained and that only humanitarian needs are served by the program, U.N. Security Council resolutions have mandated substantial controls on Iraqi oil exports and humanitarian imports. However, in response to complaints by humanitarian officials and groups working in Iraq that insufficient supplies are reaching the Iraqi people, the Security Council has progressively eased some of the program's restraints.

There is a consensus among observers that the program has eased, but not eliminated, human suffering in Iraq. Many different explanations have been offered for the failure of the program to accomplish all of its objectives. The United States blames Iraq for mismanaging the program and for attempting to import equipment that, at best, will not improve the humanitarian situation and, at worst, could be used in any Iraqi attempt to reconstitute weapons of mass destruction (WMD) programs. On the other hand, the United States has been criticized by the United Nations for exercising excessive scrutiny over equipment purchased by Iraq under the program. The United States has sought to persuade Iraq's neighbors, including Iran, not to help Iraq conduct illicit trade, but the growing regional sympathy for the Iraqi people has resulted in a pronounced relaxation of regional enforcement - or even open defiance - of the Iraq sanctions.

Changes to the program have now become the focus of Bush Administration attempts to shore up strategic containment of Iraq by instituting "smart sanctions." According to official statements, the United States is offering to significantly ease restrictions on exportation of purely civilian goods to Iraq in exchange for greater international and regional cooperation to prevent any arms or weapons-related technology from reaching Iraq. The U.S. plan would also prevent the Iraqi government from receiving the proceeds of illicit oil sales to Iraq's neighbors. The U.S. proposals appear to move away from post-Gulf war linkages between sanctions easing and full Iraqi cooperation with U.N. inspections of Iraq's weapons of mass destruction capabilities.

France, Russia, and China, which are permanent members of the U.N. Security Council, remain skeptical of U.S. proposals, pressing instead for a much broader easing of sanctions on Iraq. Regional governments are hesitant to agree to any changes that would restrict their trade with Iraq, illicit or otherwise. In two rounds of Security Council negotiations, no agreement on a smart sanctions plan was reached, and, on July 3, 2001, the Council unanimously authorized a new, 5-month phase of the oil-for-food program with no alterations (Security Council Resolution 1360).

Background and Structure of the Oil-For-Food Program

The "oil-for-food" program reflects a longstanding U.N. Security Council effort to alleviate human suffering in Iraq while pressing Iraq to comply with all relevant U.N. Security Council resolutions.[1] The program represents a temporary and limited exception to the comprehensive international trade embargo imposed on Iraq as a consequence of its invasion of Kuwait. U.N. Security Council Resolution 687 of April 3, 1991, provided for the international embargo on Iraq's exportation of oil[2] to end once Iraq had fully complied with U.N. efforts to end its weapons of mass destruction (WMD) programs. However, the Security Council judged Iraqi cooperation with the WMD inspection effort to be insufficient to achieve a lifting of that sanction. Without oil export revenues, Iraq was unable to import sufficient quantities of food and medical supplies, and, according to virtually all accepted indicators, living conditions deteriorated sharply during 1991-1995.

The first version of an oil-for-food plan would have allowed Iraq to export $1.6 billion in oil every six months. It was adopted by the Council in 1991 in Resolutions 706 (August 15, 1991) and 712 (an implementing plan adopted September 19, 1991), but Iraq rejected it as too limited in scope and an infringement on Iraq's sovereignty. On April 15, 1995, the Council adopted Resolution 986, which took into account one of Iraq's concerns by allowing the export of $2 billion in oil every six months. Iraq and the United Nations signed a memorandum of understanding on the program on May 20, 1996 (document number S/1996/356) and, after several more months of negotiations on details, the first Iraqi oil exports began on December 10, 1996. After the first year of the program, the Secretary-General determined that the program was not meeting the food and medical needs of the Iraqi people, and Resolution 1153 (February 20, 1998) raised the oil export ceiling to $5.256 billion per 6-month phase. In an effort to provide Iraq an incentive to cooperate with a new program of U.N. weapons of mass destruction (WMD) inspections, the U.N. Security Council, in Resolution 1284 (December 17, 1999), abolished the export limit. This resolution had a number of additional provisions and implications for the oil-for-food program, as discussed below.

---

[1] For a further discussion of Security Council resolutions and requirements on Iraq, see CRS Issue Brief IB92117, *Iraq: Compliance, Sanctions, and U.S. Policy*

[2] That embargo was imposed by U.N. Security Council Resolution 661 of August 6, 1990.

In order to ensure that only humanitarian objectives are served by the program, the oil-for-food program placed substantial controls on Iraqi oil exports and humanitarian imports. Iraq's state-owned oil marketing company (State Oil Marketing Organization, SOMO) negotiates with international oil companies to sell Iraqi oil, but all contracts must be approved by a panel of oil contract overseers reporting to the U.N, Sanctions Committee,[3] which administers the implementation of sanctions on Iraq. Oil is exported through an Iraq-Turkey pipeline and from Iraq's terminals in the Persian Gulf. According to Resolution 986, "the larger share" of oil exports must run through the Turkish route. The proceeds from these sales are deposited directly, by the oil purchasers, into a U.N.-monitored escrow account held at the New York branch of France's Banque Nationale de Paris (BNP). Iraq's oil exports are monitored at the point of exportation by personnel from Saybolt Nederland BV, an energy services firm working under contract to the oil-for-food program.

In each phase of the program, Iraq purchases goods and services directly from supplier firms, in accordance with an agreed distribution plan allocating anticipated revenues among categories of goods to be purchased in that phase. The Sanctions Committee reviews contracts for many goods, particularly those that could have military applications ("dual use items"). The Committee operates by consensus. Any Sanctions Committee member state may place a "hold" on a contract for goods to be imported by Iraq. In deciding whether or not to place a hold on a contract, the U.S. representative on the Sanctions Committee consults with agencies of the U.S. government to determine whether Iraq could use the requested items for military purposes. Under regulations written for the program, the U.S. government allows U.S. firms to buy Iraqi oil and sell goods to Iraq, including oil industry spare parts and equipment. Over the past few years, purchases of Iraqi oil by U.S. firms have ranged between one-third to nearly one-half of Iraq's normal export volume of about 2.1 million barrels per day. (See appendix for an overview of U.S. regulations governing U.S. firms' participation in the program.)

Once a contract is approved, BNP uses the funds deposited in the escrow account to pay letters of credit for the purchased goods. The arriving supplies are monitored at their point of entry into Iraq by about 50 personnel from the Swiss firm Cotecna[4] at four approved border crossings—Umm Qasr on the Persian Gulf; Trebil on the Iraqi-Jordanian border; Walid on the Iraqi-Syrian border; and Zakho on the Iraqi-Turkish border. In Baghdad-controlled Iraq, the Iraqi government distributes imports to the population through a government rationing system, but distribution is monitored by about 158 U.N. workers from the World Food Program, the Food and Agriculture Organization, the World Health Organization, and UNICEF. The U.N. personnel visit ration centers, marketplaces, warehouses, and other installations to ensure that distribution is equitable and accords with the required allocation plans submitted by Iraq for each six month phase. In Kurdish-controlled Iraq, about 65 U.N. workers, accompanied by about 130 U.N. security guards, perform the distribution function.

Under Security Council Resolution 1051 (March 27, 1996), exports to Iraq of dual use items are supposed to be monitored by U.N. weapons inspectors at their point of entry and site of end use in Iraq. This import monitoring mechanism was altered after the previous inspection regime (U.N. Special Commission, UNSCOM) left Iraq in December 1998 just

[3] Sanctions Committee, set up by Resolution 661, consists of representatives of the member states on the U.N. Security Council.

[4] Cotecna replaced Lloyd's Register as point-of-entry monitoring contractor on February 1, 1999.

prior to the U.S./British airstrike campaign against Iraq (Operation Desert Fox, December 16-19). Security Council Resolution 1284 (December 17, 1999) replaced UNSCOM with a new inspection body, the U.N. Monitoring, Verification, and Inspection Commission (UNMOVIC), but Iraq has not allowed UNMOVIC into Iraq. In the absence of inspectors inside Iraq, end use monitoring is performed by some of the 158 U.N. employees who monitor the distribution of civilian goods coming into Iraq. However, these monitors are not trained weapons inspectors, and this has caused the United States and Britain to closely scrutinize, and to place many holds on, exports of dual use items to Iraq.

The oil-for-food program attempts to help Iraq meet its international obligations and ensure equitable distribution of imports to the Iraqi people. The revenues from Iraq's oil sales are distributed as follows:

- 25% is transferred to a U.N. Compensation Commission (UNCC) to pay reparations to victims of Iraq's invasion of Kuwait. The deduction percentage fell to 25% from its previous level of 30% at the commencement of phase nine of the oil-for-food program (December 6, 2000).
- 59% is used to purchase humanitarian items for Baghdad-controlled Iraq. This account was increased from its previous level of 53% when the reparations deduction was reduced in December 2000.
- 13% is used to purchase supplies in the three Kurdish-inhabited provinces of northern Iraq.
- 3%, the remaining amount, pays for U.N. costs to administer the oil-for-food program, as well as UNMOVIC's operating costs.

EFFECTIVENESS OF THE PROGRAM

There is a consensus among U.N. officials and outside observers that the oil for food program has eased substantially, but not eliminated, human suffering in Iraq. Some argue that this result is the best that the international community could have hoped for. The Secretary-General has noted in his reports that the program was never intended to meet all the humanitarian needs of the Iraqi people or to "substitute for normal economic activity."

Few observers question that the program has made vast amounts of funds available for the purchase of food, medicine, and essential civilian goods. Table 1, supplied by the United Nations' Office of the Iraq Program, shows that higher oil prices, coupled with program modifications, have enabled Iraq to generate substantial revenues to fund imports. Iraq is now generating significantly more oil revenue than it did before the U.N. embargo was imposed in 1990 (about $12.5 billion in *total* exports was generated in 1988), although, as noted above, substantial deductions are taken to pay the cost of implementing the program and for reparations payments. During 2000 (phases seven and eight), Iraq generated a total of about $17 billion in oil revenues. From inception until May 9, 2001, the program has yielded $24.24 billion,[5] after all deductions, for the purchase of civilian goods for Baghdad-controlled Iraq.

[5] The figure includes interest earned on the escrow account that hold Iraq's oil revenue.

Table 1. Revenue Generated by Oil-For-Food Program (Through June 1, 2001)

Phase Number(each phase is six months)	Volume Sold(millions of barrels)	Value of Export ($billion)	Average Price per Barrel ($)
One Begun December 10, 1996 - $2 billion ceiling)"	120	2.15	17.92
Two	127	2.125	16.73
Three	182	2.085	11.46
Four Ceiling raised to $5.2 billion by Resolution 1153	308	3.027	9.83
Five	360.8	3.947	10.94
Six Ceiling temporarily raised an additional $3 billion	389.6	7.402	19.00
Seven Ceiling lifted permanently by Resoution 1284	343.4	8.285	24.13
Eight (June 9, 2000 -December 5, 2000)	375.5	9.564	25.50
Nine (December 6, 2000 -July 3, 2001)	285.8	6.533	22.92
Totals/Averages	2,492	45.135	18.11

Source: U.N. Office of the Iraq Programme.
[http://www.un .org/Depts/oip/latest/basicfigures.html].

a. Applicable U.N. Security Council resolutions allowed Iraq to generate revenue, over and above the ceilings, to pay the costs of transit fees for exporting oil through Turkey, which explains why some figures might exceed stated ceilings.

Food

Of the oil-for-food revenues generated, $6.7 billion worth of food has arrived in Iraq since the inception of the program. In his May 18, 2001 report on the program, U.N. Secretary-General Kofi Annan notes that, in Baghdad-controlled Iraq, the Iraqi government is now importing and distributing food sufficient to maintain about 90% of the U.N. target caloric intake of 2,472 kilocalories per person per day. The full ration was achieved only during December 2000. The report notes that few families can buy additional food and some sell part of their distributed rations in order to buy other goods on the open market. The Secretary General's report does not identify any food problems for the three Kurdish provinces, which is consistent with press reports that food has become relatively abundant there, sometimes to the detriment of local agricultural production. Annan's report adds that food distribution suffers from the dilapidated state of Iraq's transportation system.

Health and Sanitation

The Secretary General's assessments of health conditions in Iraq are somewhat less optimistic, although $1.2 billion in health supplies have arrived in Iraq since the inception of the oil-for-food program. The Secretary General's May 18, 2001 report indicates improvement in the health sector over the past year, but it notes that "shortages of drugs and hospital equipment are still being reported." The report attributes the shortages both to the slow pace of Iraqi contracting as well as Sanctions Committee holds on hospital equipment. In the related area of water and sanitation, the Secretary General's report says that there has been some recent improvement because of the arrival of vehicles and purification chemicals and equipment to install water piping.

In mid-1999, UNICEF released its first country wide survey of infant and maternal mortality in Iraq since 1991. The survey took a number of precautions to ensure that the survey results would not be altered or modified and UNICEF is confident that the survey information is accurate. It showed that infant mortality in the southern and central sections of Iraq (under the control of the Iraqi government) rose from 47.1 deaths per thousand live births during 1984-1989 to 107.9 deaths per thousand during 1994-1999. The under five-year-old mortality rate rose from 56 to 130.6 per thousand live births in the same time period. In the northern part of Iraq, (currently under the protection of the international community) the mortality rate has declined over the same period: infant mortality dropped from 63.9 per thousand live births in 1984-1989 to 58.7 in 1994-1999 and under five-year-old mortality dropped from 80.2 per thousand live births to 71.8 per thousand. See chapter 2 of the report, which is available online on the UNICEF Web site at [http://www.unicef. org/reseval/iraqr. htm].

Education

The Secretary General's May 18, 2001 report identifies significant shortages of materials and equipment throughout the education sector. According to his earlier report of September 8, 2000, Iraq's literacy rate (53.7% of adults and 70.7% of the youth) "has remained fixed for a number of years." The report adds that school enrollment in Baghdad-controlled Iraq has dropped as families have sent their children to work, while enrollment has risen in the Kurdish-controlled provinces because of improving economic conditions there.

Explanations for Continuing Difficulties in Living Conditions

A number of factors contribute to the difficulties in living conditions that continue to be reported in Iraq. The United States and Britain tend to place most of the blame on Iraq, alleging that it disregards the needs of its people. U.N. administrators of the program criticize Iraq on similar grounds, but they also attribute program deficiencies to U.S. and British policy, which they allege slows or halts the flow of infrastructure equipment that is required to realize the program's benefits.

The issue of contract holds on infrastructure equipment has been one of the most contentious that the United Nations has tried to address. U.N. reports on the program claim that infrastructure equipment, such as trucks, communications gear, forklifts, electricity, and water treatment equipment, are crucial to the timely distribution and proper storage and functioning of foodstuffs and medical products. According to the Secretary General's May 18, 2001 report, the total value of contracts still on hold is $3.71 billion. Of this amount, holds on spare parts for the oil industry constitute about $442 million.

In response to international criticism of the holds, the United States asserts that 90% of all contracts are approved and that the holds have had minimal impact. The United States maintains that all contracts must be scrutinized to ensure that no equipment will be used to rebuild WMD programs, especially because U.N. weapons inspectors are not in Iraq to monitor dual use exports that are shipped there. U.S. officials say they also want to ensure that no contract is being awarded solely to encourage political support for Iraq from parent governments and that all contracts submitted for review must provide required technical specifications. On June 1, 2001, in conjunction with Security Council debate over facilitating the flow of civilian equipment to Iraq, the United States announced it was lifting its holds on $800 million worth of goods, including equipment for sanitation, housing, electricity generation, transportation, and the energy sector. Later in June, the United States lifted holds on about $80 million worth of contracts for Chinese firms to sell telecommunications and energy equipment to Iraq, possibly in an effort to induce China to sign on to the U.S. "smart sanctions" plan (see below).[6]

U.N. reports express the hope that the United States and Britain will release some of their holds, but the reports also criticize Iraq. U.N. reports cite Iraq for often failing to follow U.N. procurement recommendations and for failing to efficiently distribute program imports, particularly medicine and medical equipment. Reports by the Secretary-General in 1999 noted three month delays in Iraq's movement of medicine from the main receiving warehouse to hospitals and clinics.[7] The September 8, 2000 U.N. report criticized Iraq for refusing to allow U.N. experts to conduct a comprehensive assessment of the humanitarian situation, as stipulated in U.N. Security Council Resolution 1302 (June 8, 2000). The Secretary General's May 18, 2001 report criticizes Iraq for failing to submit purchase applications for health, education, and water treatment supplies, as well as energy equipment for phase nine. U.N. reports do not accuse Iraq of purposely diverting imports from the program to the military or regime supporters, although some U.S. reports, such as a February 28, 1998 State Department fact sheet, say Iraq has diverted other food stocks to these elements.

Some of the fault appears to lie with factors outside the control of any particular party. The Secretary General's September 8, 2000 report attributes the decline of the health sector, in part, to the departure from Iraq of foreign and Iraqi health professionals.

Resolution 1284 and Other Initiatives to Improve Program Effectiveness

U.N. Security Council Resolution 1284, adopted December 17, 1999, as well as other recent Security Council and Sanctions Committee decisions, was intended to improve the provision of relief for the Iraqi people and offer Iraq an incentive to readmit U.N. weapons inspectors. (For full text of Resolution 1284, see [http://www.un.org/Docs/SCTses/1999/99scl284.htm].) The following highlights key provisions of it and related decisions:

- As noted previously, Resolution 1284 eliminated the limit on the amount of oil Iraq could export, in order to enable Iraq to generate more revenues for humanitarian purchases. All proceeds from the oil sales must still be deposited in the U.N.-supervised escrow account
- Resolution 1284 began the process, continued in subsequent oil-for-food program rollover resolutions, of easing restrictions on the flow of civilian goods to Iraq. The resolution directed the Sanctions Committee to draw up lists of items, in several categories, that would no longer be subject to Sanctions Committee review, and therefore would not be vulnerable to holds. The accelerated approval procedures for

[6] Lynch, Colum. Trade Deal Won Chinese Support of U.S. Policy on Iraq. *Washington Post,* July 6, 2001.
[7] Aita, Judy. "U.N. Concerned About Medicines Distribution in Iraq." *USIS Washington File,* May 21, 1999.

foodstuffs and educational goods began on March 1, 2000, and continued with pharmaceuticals, medical supplies, medical equipment, and agricultural equipment (March 29, 2000). Subsequent oil-for-food rollover resolutions made eligible for the new procedures water treatment and sanitation supplies (August 11, 2000) goods for the housing sector (February 26, 2001) and electricity supplies (May 24, 2001).

- Resolution 1284 laid the groundwork for foreign investment to explore for and produce oil in Iraq, although the Resolution made this investment contingent on full Iraqi cooperation with the new U.N. weapons inspection body, U.N. Monitoring, Verification, and Inspection Commission (UNMOVIC). In late 2000, the Sanctions Committee approved two Russian firms (Tatneft and Slavneft) to drill new wells in existing fields, but exploration of new fields is not permitted.
- Resolution 1284 created incentives for Iraq to cooperate with UNMOVIC by promising that, if Iraq fully cooperates with the new body, export and import sanctions would be suspended. Iraq would once again be allowed to control its own revenues, although subject to strict but unspecified financial controls, according to the resolution. Arms exports to Iraq would still be banned and exports of dual use items would still be subject to scrutiny by the Sanctions Committee.
- Resolution 1284 also made some oil industry spare parts eligible for a streamlined approval process - contracts for such equipment are scrutinized by the same Sanctions Committee panel of oil overseers that review Iraq's oil sales contracts, without requiring full Sanctions Committee review. U.N. Security Council Resolution 1293 (March 31, 2000) increased to $600 million, from $300 million, the value of oil industry spare parts that Iraq could import per oil-for-food phase. This decision was taken in response to recommendations by the U.N. Secretary-General that improving the humanitarian situation was contingent on the rehabilitation of Iraq's ability to export its oil.

In late September 2000, the United States reached agreement with Russia and France that, beginning in phase nine of the oil for food program (commencing December 5, 2000) the amount of revenue to be deducted for reparations payments would fall to 25% from 30%. This freed substantial additional funds for humanitarian relief.

Transactions with Iraq Outside the Oil-for-Food Program

As discussed in previous sections, the oil-for-food program provides humanitarian relief without giving the Iraqi government revenues or authority to import militarily-useful goods. As a consequence, Iraq has sought to skirt the program's restrictions. It is conducting illicit trade with its neighbors, and it appears to view the oil-for-food program and other international donations as a substitute for, rather than a supplement to, its pre-existing supply purchase program. On February 29, 2000, the Clinton Administration accused the Iraqi government of using its resources to build nine lavish palaces (valued at about $2 billion) and to import non-essential items such as cigarettes and liquor.[8] Some fear that Iraq is also using its own reserves, or illicitly generated revenues, to import militarily useful equipment. U.N. weapons inspectors seized illicitly imported missile guidance systems in 1995. In February 2001, the United States struck an air defense network that was being upgraded with the help of a Chinese firm, according to press accounts.

International Donations

UNICEF, the World Food Program (WFP) the U.N. Development Program (UNDP), the European Community (ECHO), the International Committee of the Red Cross (ICRC), governments, and private relief organizations such as Catholic Relief Services and Save the Children continue to provide additional relief to supplement the oil-for-food program. UNICEF, ECHO, and WFP focus their humanitarian aid on the South and Central part of the country rather than on the economically better off Kurdish north.

It is impossible to determine precisely the total amounts of bilateral and multilateral aid by all donors. However, the U.N. Secretary-General's recent reports and statements have suggested that these aid sources are declining, possibly because donors believe the oil-for-food program is satisfying Iraq's needs. Secretary-General Annan has called for increased international assistance to Iraq, and Resolution 1284 "encourages" countries and international organizations to provide supplementary humanitarian aid and educational materials to Iraq. After Baghdad's incursion into the Kurdish north in late August 1996, the United States virtually ended its assistance program for northern Iraq, which had been about $45 million per year. The incursion caused all American-based humanitarian relief organizations in northern Iraq to leave in fear of Iraqi reprisals against them.

There is no single source for information on humanitarian assistance to Iraq. A recent report of the Organization for Economic Cooperation and Development (OECD), which provides donor information for the years 1994 through 1998, indicates that Iraq received a total of $76.36 million in bilateral assistance in 1998.[9] This does not include any funds provided by U.N. agencies but does include grants by the European Commission (ECHO). A Washington-based official of the European Commission said in June 2001 that the European Union has given over $200 million in aid to Iraq since 1991.

Relief Flights

Since September 2000, Iraq has derived an unknown amount of additional aid from flights, most of which carried some relief aid, intended to challenge the U.S. and British interpretation of U.N. Security Council Resolution 670 (September 25, 1990). The Resolution requires the banning of flights to or from Iraq that are carrying any "cargo to or from Iraq or Kuwait other than food in humanitarian circumstances, subject to authorization by the Council...." or the Sanctions Committee. Prior to September 2000, the U.S. interpretation prevailed that all flights to Iraq require Sanctions Committee authorization prior to takeoff. Since September 2000, several dozen flights carrying officials and humanitarian donations to

[8] Alcohol is classified as a food, so the imports are technically legal under the international sanctions regime in place since Iraq's August 2, 1990 invasion of Kuwait.

[9] Geographical Distribution of Financial Flows to Aid Recipients. Disbursements, Commitments, Country Indicators. 1994-1998. OECD. 2000.

Iraq have taken place, some of which proceeded before receiving formal approval. The United States criticized those governments that allowed flights to proceed without approval, but no U.S. or U.N. measures were taken against those flights or governments. Nor has the United States taken any action against Jordan and Syria, which have begun allowing charter passenger air service to and from Iraq. The United States maintains that Resolution 670 is intended to ensure that any cargo or material destined for Iraq could be inspected to ensure it is not carrying contraband goods. France, Russia, and other governments, although not opposed in principle to inspecting cargo bound for Iraq, argue that passengers are not "cargo" and that the U.S. interpretation that the Resolution restricts all flights to Iraq is not correct.

One donation to Iraq in November 2000 drew strong U.S. criticism and a sanction. A member of the royal family of Qatar presented Saddam Husayn with a Boeing 747 jumbo jet as a "gift." The Qatari, Hamad bin Ali bin Jabr Al Thani, heads the Gulf Falcon air services company, which gave him access to the aircraft. On November 24, 2000, the Clinton Administration announced that exports and reexports of many U.S. goods would need specific Commerce Department approval for sale to Mr. Al Thani or his businesses. U.S. officials said that sanctions were imposed to ensure that U.S. goods would not be improperly diverted to Iraq.

Illicit Trade

Baghdad is using its neighbors, as well as its outlet to the Persian Gulf, as conduits to conduct illicit trade. Iraq is doing so to earn funds that it can fully control, as well as to import prohibited goods, including items such as automobiles and consumer electronics. Iraq's neighbors are increasingly cooperative in these efforts because of sympathy with the Iraqi people, and out of the apparent belief that Saddam is likely to remain in power. The total value of Iraq's illicit exports is about $2 billion to $2.5 billion. After paying smugglers and other middlemen on various export routes, the Iraqi government receives about $1.5 billion, a figure derived by adding the estimates of revenue Iraq receives from each outlet discussed below. The following are the main routes for illicit trade with Iraq:

- Since the Gulf war, Jordan has notified the Security Council that it imports Iraqi oil (up to 100,000 barrels per day) at below-market prices in exchange for civilian goods and write-downs of Iraq's debt to Jordan. Iraq's oil exports to Jordan will be worth about $450 million for 2001. The United States supports the Sanctions Committee decision to "take note of the Jordanian purchases, neither approving them nor deeming them a violation. The Administration has routinely waived unilateral sanctions on Jordan that could be imposed because of this trade.[10] In October 2000, Jordan cancelled an agreement with Lloyd's Registry, in force since 1993, for the firm to inspect Iraq-bound cargo in Jordan's port of Aqaba. This inspection agreement covered goods other than those imported under the oil-for-food program; goods imported under the program are monitored at all points of entry, including the Iraq-Jordanian border.

[10] Every fiscal year since 1994, Congress has included a provision in foreign aid appropriations cutting U.S. aid to countries that violated the Iraq embargo.

- Iraq conducts much of its illicit trade through the Gulf, apparently with cooperation from Iran. The U.S. Navy estimated in March 2000 that Iraq would export about $1 billion in oil products through the Gulf in 2000, but the U.S. Ambassador to the United Arab Emirates said in March 2001 that the volume had fallen substantially, to a "low ebb." Previous lulls took export volumes through this route down to levels that would now be worth about $500 million per year. Of this amount, about one half goes to Iraq, one quarter goes to smugglers and middlemen, and one quarter goes to Iran's Revolutionary Guard for "protection fees" to allow the shipments to hug its coast and avoid capture. Many believe Iraq's illicit Gulf exports have fallen because Iraq is diverting oil to the Syrian route, where there are fewer middlemen to pay. In early November 2000, Iraq openly admitted it is using its Gulf ports for contraband imports by announcing it would import 30,000 Toyota automobiles "from Qatar and the United Arab Emirates."[11] Neither of these Gulf states have land borders with Iraq and both of them have called for the easing of Iraq sanctions.
- In late 2000, according to several press reports, Iraq began sending about 150,000 barrels of oil per day through an Iraq-Syria pipeline, closed since 1982 but now repaired. This route is said to earn Iraq about $700 million per year. This exportation is reputedly under a bilateral agreement with Syria under which Syria refines the Iraqi oil for domestic use, pays Iraq about $15 per barrel, for the oil, and frees up extra Syrian oil for export, allowing Syria to profit. Resolution 1284 states the Security Council's "intention" to allow new oil export routes, such as this line, and the U.S. and British position is to oppose the reopening of this line unless it is brought under the oil-for-food program and its monitoring and control mechanisms.
- Iraq is estimated to conduct about $400 million per year in illicit trade with neighboring Turkey, of which about $120 million goes to Iraq, according to diplomats in the region. Most of the trade is in the form of 450 Turkish trucks per day carrying Iraqi oil products through the Iraqi Kurdish areas into Turkey in spare fuel tanks. The Turkish government taxes and regulates the illicit imports. As in the case of Jordan, the U.S. Administration has routinely waived the imposition of U.S. sanctions on Turkey for permitting this illicit trade.

DEBATE OVER THE FUTURE OF IRAQ SANCTIONS

The oil-for-food program remains the centerpiece of a broader debate over the future of international sanctions on Iraq. This debate intensified in May and June 2001 when the five permanent members of the U.N. Security Council attempted to incorporate into an oil-for-food rollover a U.S. plan to implement "smart sanctions" on Iraq. The smart sanctions plan represents an effort, articulated primarily by Secretary of State Colin Powell at the beginning of the Bush Administration, to rebuild a consensus to contain Iraq. It would do so by maintaining only those sanctions that apply to limiting Iraq's military capabilities.

The smart sanctions plan is intended to defuse criticism by several governments, including permanent members of the U.N. Security Council France, Russia, and China, that

[11] "Iraq to Import 30,000 Toyota Vehicles." *Dow Jones Newswire*, November 1, 2000.

the United States is using international sanctions to promote the overthrow of the Iraqi government or to punish Iraq indefinitely for the invasion of Kuwait. These governments appear to believe that no amount of Iraqi cooperation with the United Nations will be sufficient to satisfy the United States that sanctions should be eased further, and some have moved unilaterally to skirt or erode the sanctions regime. The Bush Administration says that, in part due to opposition from these and other governments, the sanctions regime was collapsing and needed to be rebuilt.

With phase nine of the oil-for-food program set to expire on June 4, 2001, the permanent five members of the Security Council began discussions on the U.S. smart sanctions plan. The U.S. plan centered on a trade-off in which restrictions on the flow of civilian goods to Iraq would be greatly eased and, in return, Iraq's illicit trade with its neighbors would be brought under the oil-for-food program and its monitoring and control mechanisms. Differences between the permanent members over how to implement these measures prevented agreement by the expiration of phase nine. In adopting Security Council Resolution 1352 on June 1, 2001, the Security Council agreed to a one month extension of phase nine, until July 3, 2001. The resolution contained language indicating that the Security Council would work to reach agreement on the smart sanctions plan by that expiration date. In protest at what it saw as a U.S. effort to forestall further erosion of the sanctions regime, Iraq stopped exporting oil upon passage of Resolution 1352, asserting that it would resume oil exports if and when the oil-for-food program were renewed with no changes.

The Security Council did not reach agreement on the smart sanctions plan by July 3, 2001, choosing instead to authorize an unaltered phase ten of the oil-for-food program (Security Council Resolution 1360 of July 3, 2001, adopted unanimously). However, the permanent members are expected to continue to try to reach agreement on the smart sanctions plan by the end of phase ten. The following are the key elements of the smart sanctions plan that the permanent members have debated, and most of these issues were continued in a U.S.-backed British draft resolution[12] circulated in late June:

- **List of Restricted Items**. A major point of dispute has been the criteria for placing items on a list of goods that would continue to need Sanctions Committee review. The United States circulated a draft list of items that it maintains needs to be comprehensive in order to ensure that Iraq cannot acquire militarily-useful technology. Under the U.S. smart sanctions plan, any item not on the new list (with the exception of arms, which would be banned for sale to Iraq) would no longer need Sanctions Committee review. Russia and France maintained that the proposed list, which included such goods as high performance computers, optical sensing technology, drilling equipment, aircraft spare parts, and marine sensing gear[13], was too extensive, and would have the net effect of hindering the rebuilding of Iraq's civilian infrastructure. However, France and China ultimately agreed to a compromise list, according to U.S. officials.
- **Border Controls.** This issue has been a major point of contention as well, as Iraq's neighbors have clearly asserted their opposition to controlling illicit trade with Iraq

[12] CRS was provided with a copy of the late June British draft resolution by journalists who follow the issue.

[13] A May 24, 2001 draft of the list of goods that would still be subject to review is at [http://www.cam.ac.uk/societies/casi/info/annex010524.html].

on the grounds that doing so would harm their economies. The British draft resolution called on the U.N. Secretary-General to consult with Iraq's neighbors to formulate a plan for them to buy up to 150,000 barrels per day of oil from Iraq, with the proceeds to be held in escrow. The draft also called for the United Nations to enhance its border monitoring procedures to ensure that no contraband goods reach Iraq. Many believe that Iraq's gradual reintegration into the Arab and regional fold - coupled with their own economic needs - will prompt the neighboring states to look for and find ways to avoid any new program to control their trade with Iraq.

- **Flights.** The British draft resolution attempts to gain some control over international civilian flights to Iraq by requiring that their cargo be inspected at designated airports outside Iraq. The draft would also permit Jordan to return six Iraqi Airways passenger aircraft grounded in Amman since the Gulf war, and Tunisia to return four planes there.
- **Foreign Investment/Exploration.** The British draft "expresses an intention" to permit foreign companies to provide services in Iraq. Some diplomats interpreted this as implicitly including energy exploration services, although most observers believe that a Security Council resolution would need to make energy investment permission explicit. Russia, France, and China have pressed for investment in Iraq's energy sector, and companies from these countries have reached agreement with Iraq to develop several oil fields if and when the prohibition on foreign exploration is lifted.
- **Surcharges.** The British draft attempts to end the reported practice of paying Iraq a surcharge of about 50 cents per barrel of oil, which goes into the coffers of Iraq's government. The surcharges are reportedly being paid by small oil trading firms, such as those from Russia, Ukraine, Sudan, and other countries. The draft stipulates that a list of companies authorized to do business with Iraq be drawn up, a list which it is widely understood would include only large, well known international oil firms that would not pay Iraq these surcharges.

Appendix: Overview of U.S. Regulations Governing U.S. Participation in the Oil-for-Food Program[14]

The Iraqi Sanctions Regulations implement Executive Orders No. 12722 (August 2, 1990) and 12724 (August 9, 1990). The Iraq Sanctions Act of 1990 (Section 586 of P.L. 101-513, signed November 5, 1990 reinforces those executive orders. The August 9 executive order amended the August 2 executive order to align U.S. sanctions with U.N. Security Council Resolution 661 (August 6, 1990), in keeping with the United Nations Participation Act (22 U.S.C. 287c). The regulations have since been modified to allow for U.S. participation in the oil-for-food program. Key provisions of the U.S. sanctions include the following:

[14] Source: Iraq: What You Need to Know About the U.S. Embargo. An Overview of the Iraqi Sanctions Regulations - Title 31, Part 575 of the U.S. Code of Federal Regulations. U.S. Department of the Treasury, Office of Foreign Assets Control [http://www.treas.gov/ofac/].

U.S. firms may apply to the Office of Foreign Assets Control (OFAC) of the Treasury Department for specific licenses for the following activities under the oil-for-food program:

- "the sale and exportation to Iraq of medicines, health supplies, foodstuffs, and materials and supplies for essential civilian needs." The goods can be sold, subject to a license, to the government of Iraq or to a U.N. entity distributing aid under the program.
- "the purchase and exportation from Iraq of Iraqi-origin petroleum and petroleum products;"
- "the trading, importation, exportation or other dealings in or related to Iraq-origin petroleum and petroleum products outside Iraq; and"
- "the sale and exportation to Iraq of parts and equipment that are essential for the safe operation of the Kirkuk-Yumurtalik (Iraq-Turkey) pipeline system in Iraq."

In addition:

- The regulations "generally" prohibit "the performance of contracts in support of industrial, commercial, public utility, or governmental projects" in Iraq. U.S. persons may not provide financing or consulting services to a foreign country company where those services would benefit such projects in Iraq. U.S. persons may not provide consulting services or goods, in connection with Iraqi projects, to foreign subsidiaries of U.S. corporations, although foreign subsidiaries themselves are not subject to U.S. regulations.
- All transfers of funds by U.S. persons to the government of Iraq or to persons in Iraq, are prohibited, as are "all commitments or transfers of credit, financial transactions, or contracts."
- All transportation-related services, or the use by U.S. persons of vehicles, ships or aircraft registered in Iraq, are prohibited. Travel-related transactions by U.S. persons are also prohibited, with the exception of travel related to journalism, or U.S. government or United Nations business.

Chapter 8

IRAQ: POST WAR CHALLENGES AND U.S. RESPONSES, 1991-1998

Alfred B. Prados

ABSTRACT

This chapter reviews cease-fire terms that followed the Gulf war in early 1991; highlights provisions that Iraq has tended to violate; describes ensuing confrontations between the United States and Iraq since 1991, together with international reactions; and summarizes related points of congressional interest. The chapter is designed as a source of ready reference for congressional offices interested in previous instances of use of force by the United States against Iraq after the Gulf war.

SUMMARY

Iraq has not fully complied with terms of the cease-fire agreements that followed the expulsion of Iraqi forces from Kuwait in early 1991. Several Iraqi violations of cease-fire provisions have resulted in brief military confrontations between Iraq and the United States, supported in some cases by other allied forces. Iraqi violations prompting a U.S. military response have fallen into four general categories: obstruction of UN. weapons inspection teams, involvement in international terrorist acts, failure to abide by air exclusion zones imposed by the allies over parts of Iraq, and troop movements that could threaten Kuwait or internal targets of repression by the Iraqi Government.

In January 1993, the United States conducted several air strikes against Iraqi missile facilities and other military targets. The allied strikes followed a series of Iraqi challenges, including violations of no-fly zones, interference with weapons inspections, and unauthorized removal of materiel from the demilitarized zone with Kuwait. In June of that year, the United States launched missile strikes against an Iraqi intelligence headquarters building in response to evidence that Iraq had organized an attempt to assassinate former President George Bush.

Further confrontations took place in the mid-1990s. In October 1994, Iraq moved elite troops south toward Kuwait in an effort to pursue demands that the U.N. Security Council set a firm time table for removal of a ban on oil exports by Iraq. Iraq subsequently withdrew its forces, after the United States began deploying more forces to the Gulf region. In August 1996, Iraq moved three divisions into the allied-protected Kurdish enclave in northern Iraq, allegedly at the invitation of one of the two rival Iraqi Kurdish factions. The United States responded with air and sea-based missile strikes directed against military targets in southern Iraq. Although Iraqi forces quickly withdrew from the Kurdish enclave, several news reports indicate that the Iraqi incursion disrupted a U.S. covert action aimed at toppling the Iraqi regime.

The United States began a force build-up in the Gulf region in late 1997, in response to Iraq interference in the conduct of U.N. weapons inspections. Military action was averted on two occasions by last minute agreements with Iraq in November 1997 and February 1998. Tensions mounted once again in late 1998 after Iraq reneged on its earlier promises to cooperate with the U.N. weapons inspection regime, leading to further confrontations.

International support for U.S. employment of force against Iraq has eroded, especially in cases when Iraqi actions do not appear to threaten Kuwait or other neighbors directly. Middle East countries, in particular, have become uneasy over U.S. military action against Iraq and are increasingly reluctant to provide facilities for such operations.

Prior to the 1991 Gulf war, Congress authorized military action to force Iraqi compliance with U.N. Security Council resolutions by H.J.Res. 77 (P.L. 102-1). The Bush and Clinton Administrations have consulted with Congress during subsequent military confrontations, although there has been criticism from some Members who felt that consultation was insufficient in specific cases.

INTRODUCTION

In February 1991, a U.S.-led coalition of allied military forces expelled Iraqi forces that had occupied Kuwait since August 1990. Several cease-fire agreements followed the termination of hostilities on February 28, 1991. Periodic Iraqi violations of cease-fire terms and other provocative acts by Iraq precipitated a series of brief confrontations with the United States over the next six years. A more extended series of confrontations began in late 1997.

This report reviews cease-fire terms that followed the Gulf war in early 1991; highlights provisions that Iraq has been prone to violate; describes resulting confrontations between the United States and Iraq between 1991 and 1998, together with international reactions; and summarizes related points of congressional interest. The purpose of this report is to facilitate ready reference to the circumstances surrounding previous uses offeree, or preparations to use force, by the United States against Iraq in the years following the Gulf war of 1991.

CEASE-FIRE TERMS AND VIOLATIONS

The Agreements

Cease-fire arrangements following the war consisted of three agreements that are summarized below. The first two were temporary and the third established a permanent cease-fire. Some additional requirements have been levied on Iraq as well.

Resolution 686

On March 2, 1991, the United Nations Security Council passed Resolution 686, which imposed several conditions on Iraq. Resolution 686 demanded that Iraq cease all hostile actions against allied forces, accept earlier U.N. resolutions, release Kuwaiti citizens and others detained in Iraq, begin returning property seized in Kuwait, and accept liability for damages resulting from its invasion of Kuwait. Also, the resolution demanded that Iraq appoint military commanders to meet with allied military commanders to arrange the military details of a cease-fire.

The Safwan Accords

The Safwan Accords refer to the cease-fire agreements made between allied military commanders and Iraqi officers, under the provisions of Resolution 686, above. On March 3, 1991, the U.S. commander, U.S. Army General H. Norman Schwarzkopf and other allied commanders met with Iraqi officers at the town of Safwan in southern Iraq and agreed on several matters: return of prisoners of war, removal of mine fields, and procedures to prevent any further outbreaks of fighting between Iraqi and allied forces. The Safwan Accords also provided for a temporary cease-fire line, with the understanding that allied forces would remain in southern Iraq until a permanent cease-fire agreement came into effect. Furthermore, the Accords banned flights by Iraqi fixed wing aircraft throughout Iraq to avoid threats to allied forces temporarily remaining in southern Iraq, but permitted flights by Iraqi helicopters (with some restrictions on armed helicopters). The ban on Iraqi aircraft flights was relaxed when allied forces left Iraq in May 1991; however, the United States and western allies believe it continues to apply over areas in which allied combat aircraft still operate in support of U.N. resolutions (i.e. the no-fly zones over northern and southern Iraq, as discussed below).[1]

Resolution 687

On April 3, 1991, the U.N. Security Council passed Resolution 687, which established a formal cease-fire and imposed a number of long-term requirements on Iraq. Resolution 687, sometimes known as the omnibus cease-fire resolution, provided for demarcation of the border between Iraq and Kuwait, a U.N. guarantee of the border, and a U.N. observer force to monitor the border area. The resolution called on Iraq to return Kuwaiti property it had seized and to release Kuwaiti and foreign citizens it had detained, required Iraq to compensate victims of its aggression, and demanded that Iraq agree to refrain from terrorist acts. In

[1] The terms of the Safwan Accords have not been formally published. For discussion of the meeting at Safwan and the main points agreed upon, see H.R.H. Prince Khaled bin Sultan, *Desert Warrior*, New York, Harper zind Collins, 1995, pp. 421-438. General bin Sultan was the Saudi Arabian commander of joint Arab and Islamic forces in the allied coalition.

addition, the resolution required Iraq to agree to the removal or dismantling of its weapons of mass destruction and to end its programs to develop such weapons (i.e., chemical, biological, or nuclear weapons and longer range missiles). The resolution retained restrictions on imports to Iraq, except for food, medicine, and essential civilian supplies; banned shipments of military equipment to Iraq; and continued to ban Iraqi exports until the U.N. Security Council is satisfied that Iraq is free of mass destruction weapons. Of note, Resolution 687 was enacted under Chapter VII of the U.N. charter (peace and security); hence, the provisions of this resolution can be enforced through military action.

Other Terms and Conditions

Since passing Resolution 687, the Security Council has adopted over 25 resolutions and statements to implement or amplify the terms of the basic cease-fire agreement. Of particular significance was Resolution 688 adopted on April 3, 1991. This resolution, which demanded that Iraq cease repression of its population, was aimed especially at terminating Iraqi reprisals against Kurds in the north and Shi'ite Muslims in the south, both of whom had revolted in the aftermath of the Gulf war. Resolution 688, however, was not enacted under Chapter YE of the U.N. charter, and opinions differ within the international community over the criteria for enforcing its terms.

Iraqi Violations

Iraq reluctantly accepted the omnibus cease-fire Resolution 687 on April 6, 1991; the U.N. Security Council has found Iraq not to be in full compliance with the terms of this resolution. On seven occasions between 1991 and 1993, the Security Council found

Iraq in "material breach" of the provisions of Resolution 687. The Council has not agreed on this wording since June 1993, reflecting to some extent an erosion of the former international consensus behind forcing Iraq to comply with cease-fire terms.[2] Subsequent resolutions and statements by the Council, however, have continued to warn Iraq of "serious consequences" of violating the terms of U.N. resolutions.

Iraqi actions prompting a U.S. military response have fallen into four general categories, as summarized below. In addition, Iraq has engaged in other cease-fire violations that have not resulted in a direct confrontation with the United States. These include failure to return missing Kuwaiti property and to account for approximately 600 Kuwaitis and other foreign citizens who are believed to be still under detention in Iraq.

Weapons Inspections

Resolution 687 established an inspection regime to find and eliminate Iraqi weapons of mass destruction, including chemical and biological agents, nuclear facilities, and missiles with ranges exceeding 150 kilometers (93 miles). The resolution also stipulated that Iraq was to provide the U.N. Secretary-General a list of all such weapons in its possession within 15 days. In addition, Resolution 707 requires Iraq to allow U.N. weapons inspectors to use their own 'aircraft, and Resolution 715 provides for long term monitoring of Iraqi facilities that

[2] For a listing of occasions when the Security Council found Iraq in "material breach" of cease-fire terms, see Greg Saiontz, "A Chronology of Diminishing Response: UN Reactions to Iraqi Provocations since the Gulf War," Research Notes, The Washington Institute for Near East Policy, June 3, 1997, pp. 1-5.

could be used to develop mass destruction weapons. Iraqi authorities have interfered frequently with the conduct of inspections, concealed important evidence of programs to develop weapons of mass destruction, and repeatedly provided incomplete and inaccurate declarations of the extent of its past programs to develop mass destruction weapons. U.N. inspectors gradually have discovered weapons plants and programs not initially revealed by the Iraqis in their initial list or in subsequent declarations to the United Nations.

Terrorism

Resolution 687 requires Iraq to assure the Security Council that it will not commit or support terrorist acts. Iraq remains on an annual list of countries identified by the U.S. State Department as supportive of international terrorism. In the spring of 1993, Iraq was implicated in a plot to assassinate former President George Bush while on a visit to Kuwait.

No-Fly Zones

The United States, together with Britain and France, began enforcing air exclusion zones over northern and southern Iraq, respectively, in 1991 and 1992. U.S. officials base the no-fly zones primarily on Resolution 688, which demands that Iraq end repression of its population (notably Kurds in the north and Shi'ite Muslims in the south), and on the Safwan Accords, which forbid Iraq to interfere with allied air operations over Iraq. Some countries question this interpretation, arguing that Resolution 688 was not passed under Chapter VII provisions (peace and security) and does not by itself permit military action to enforce its terms. Iraq maintains that the no-fly zones constitute an illegal infringement on its sovereignty and has occasionally fired on allied planes conducting overflights to enforce these zones. (Map 1 shows the no-fly zones in Iraq.)

Troop Movements

In conjunction with establishing the northern no-fly zone in 1991, the United States and its allies warned Iraq not to move ground forces into a portion of the zone where the allies had established a protected enclave for Iraqi Kurds. On at least one occasion, in the summer of 1996, Iraq briefly moved forces into Kurdish controlled areas, as discussed below. Previously, in October 1994, the apparent deployment of Iraqi armored forces toward Kuwait led to Security Council Resolution 949, which demanded that Iraq complete the withdrawal of these units and refrain from threatening its neighbors in the future. (U.S. and British officials sometimes interpret this resolution as imposing a "no-drive" zone in the south, in addition to the no-fly zone already in place in that area.)

Map 1. Iraq: No-Fly Zones

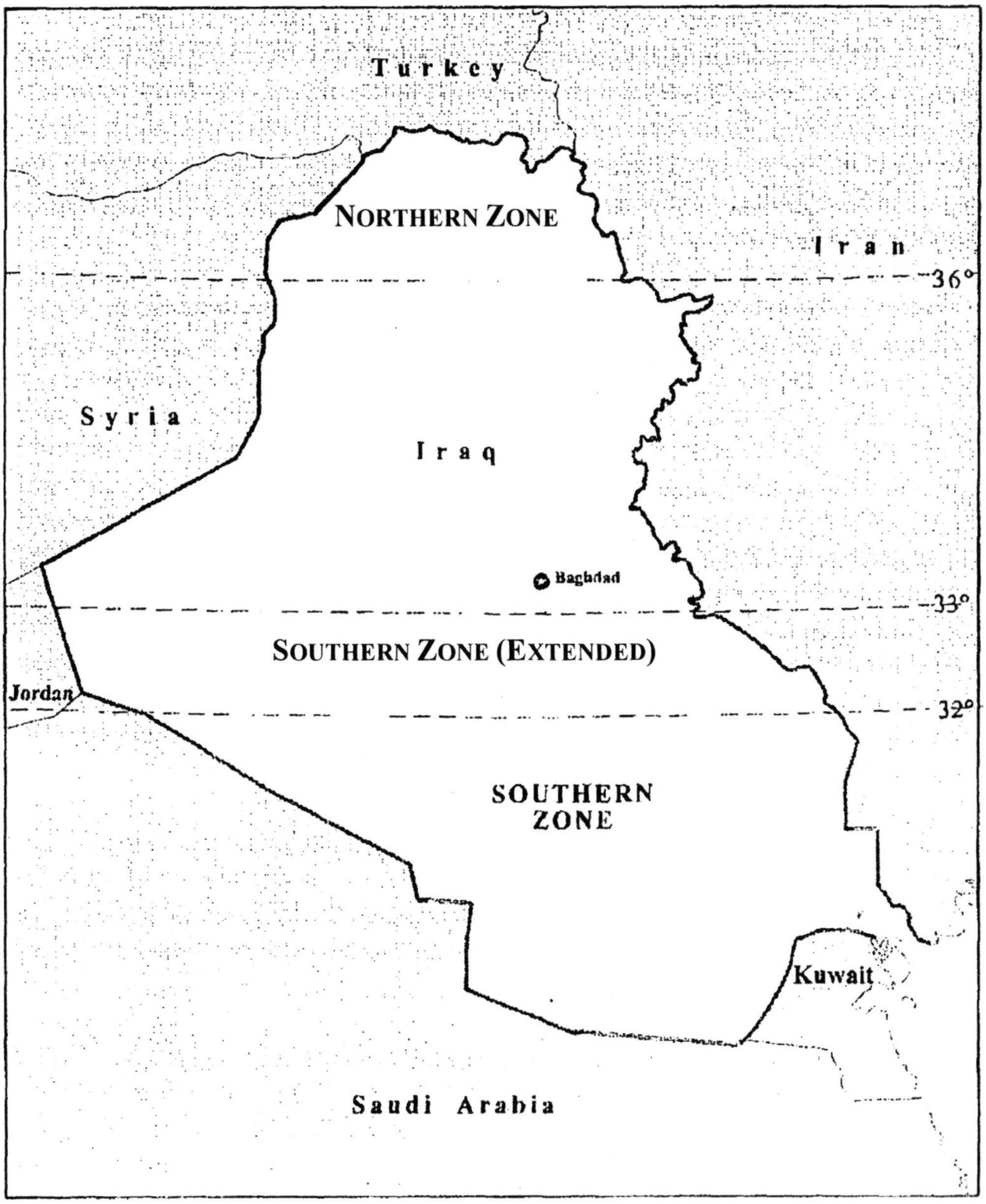

Adapted by CRS from Magellan Geographix. Used with permission.

THE COURSE OF THE CONFRONTATIONS

Early Incidents, 1991-1992[3]

Iraqi defiance of cease-fire terms initially took the form of obstructing thc work of U.N. weapons inspectors seeking to identify and dismantle Iraqi weapons of mass destruction. Iraqi interference affected the conduct of inspections by two groups: the International Atomic Energy Agency (IAEA), charged with inspecting Iraqi nuclear programs, and the U.N. Special Commission (UNSCOM), established pursuant to Resolution 687 and charged with inspecting chemical and biological weapons and medium and long range missiles. Listed below are some of the more notable incidents that occurred during the year following the establishment of the U.N. weapons inspection regime in June 1991.

- Between June and August 1991, Iraqi officials periodically denied IAEA inspectors access to sites they wanted to visit, provided information on several weapons programs that later proved to be false, and at one point fired shots over the heads of weapons inspectors.
- On two occasions in September 1991, Iraqi officials refused to allow U.N. inspectors to depart installations where they had gathered documentation, insisting initially that the inspectors return documents they were carrying.
- In January and February 1992, Iraqi officials refused to allow UNSCOM inspectors to destroy certain missiles and related equipment the inspectors had identified as subject to dismantling under relevant U.N. decisions.
- In July 1992, Iraq officials refused to let UNSCOM inspectors enter the Iraqi Ministry of Agriculture, which the inspectors believed to be housing proscribed material.

The Security Council described the confrontations in June-August 1991, January-February 1992, and July 1992 as "material breaches" by Iraq of cease-fire terms. The Council condemned Iraqi obstruction of U.N. inspectors in September 1991 but did not describe it as a material breach. (The January-February 1992 confrontation resulted in two findings of "material breach," giving a total of four such findings by the Security Council in 1991 and 1992.) None of these incidents led to military action or deployments on the part of the United States or other members of the Security Council. The findings of "material breach," however, may have strengthened the hand of the United States in responding to subsequent violations, as described below.

[3] For further information, see Greg Saiontz, "A Chronology of Diminishing Response: UN Reactions to Iraqi Provocations since the Gulf War," Research Notes, The Washington Institute for Near East Policy, June 3, 1997, pp. 1-3.

January 1993 Confrontation[4]

Tensions mounted during 1992 as several developments led Iraq to mount more aggressive challenges to restrictions imposed after the Gulf war. In April 1992, in a step condemned by the Iraqi Government, Kurdish groups in northern Iraq held elections for a provisional parliament under the umbrella of U.S. and allied air protection. In August, the United States, Britain, and France imposed a second no-fly zone, this time over southern Iraq, in response to increasing Iraqi military campaigns against Shi'ite Muslim guerrillas in the south. Later, on November 23, a U.N. commission established by Resolution 687 completed demarcation of the Kuwaiti-Iraqi border, awarding to Kuwait additional territory including a former Iraqi naval base and several oil wells. Iraq condemned the findings of the commission. In addition, the outcome of presidential elections in the United States may have impelled Iraqi President Saddam Hussein to test the willingness of the outgoing Bush Administration and the incoming Clinton Administration to continue enforcing terms of the cease-fire.

The allied air actions that began on January 13 against Iraq were prompted by an intensifying confrontation between Iraq and the United States, its coalition partners, and the United Nations in three areas: violations of the no-fly zones, obstruction of weapons inspections, and incursions into the demilitarized zone between Iraq and Kuwait.

No-Fly Zone Violations

On December 27, 1992, the United States shot down an Iraqi jet that had violated the allied imposed "no-fly zone" in southern Iraq. Subsequently, Iraq redeployed 8 SA-3 and 12 SA-2 anti-aircraft missile launchers in the no-fly zone in a manner threatening to coalition aircraft patrolling the zone. On January 6, 1993, the United States, Britain, France, and Russia gave Iraq 48 hours to move the missiles to their original locations or face possible military action. Despite Iraqi statements that it would not comply, and after examining intelligence reports on the movement of the missiles, the White House announced January 9 that Iraq had complied with the ultimatum. However, the White House noted that action could be taken without warning if Iraq redeployed the missiles in a threatening manner. On January 11, then Director of Central Intelligence Robert Gates said that Iraq was continuing to shift anti-aircraft missiles in the exclusion zones in both southern and northern Iraq, but that it was too early to determine whether or not the deployments threatened allied aircraft. On January 12, the Commander-in-Chief of U.S. forces in Europe, U.S. Army General John Shalikashvili, said that Iraq had put its anti-aircraft missiles in the northern no-fly zone on operational status. On several subsequent occasions, Iraq again activated its targeting radar in the no-fly zones, precipitating confrontations with coalition aircraft.

Obstruction of Weapons Inspections

On January 7, 1993, Iraq told the United Nations that it would no longer permit U.N. weapons inspectors to use their own aircraft to fly into or land in Iraq. It said the inspectors could use chartered Iraqi aircraft (all Iraqi air travel is banned by U.N. sanctions, however.) Iraq did not specifically ban U.N. U-2 or helicopter surveillance flights, however. On January 10, Iraq banned the flight into Iraq of 70 inspectors who were returning to Iraq after the holidays. Meanwhile, on January 8, the Security Council called Iraqi interference with U.N.

[4] For further information, see Facts on File Yearbook 1993, pp. 29-30; issues of *The Washington Post, The New*

inspections unacceptable, described it as a "material breach" of cease-fire terras, and warned Iraq of serious consequences of its actions.

Iraq-Kuwait Border Incursion

Meanwhile, on November 2, 1992, the United Nations had warned Iraq not to remove weapons from the demilitarized zone between Iraq and Kuwait without permission from the U.N. Iraq-Kuwait Observer Mission (UNIKOM). (UNDCOM was created by Resolution 687 to monitor the Iraq-Kuwait border.) On January 10, 1993, according to a spokesman for UNIKOM, 500 Iraqis (some armed) crossed into the demilitarized zone, seized weapons, including four Silkworm missiles, under guard by UNIKOM, and returned to Iraq. (UNIKOM is a monitoring force, and is neither empowered nor able to resist militarily a large Iraqi incursion across the border.) The equipment had been left behind by Iraq when it retreated from Kuwait in the Persian Gulf war. On January 10, emissaries from the United States, Britain, France, and Russia, visited Iraq's Ambassador to the United Nations to protest the seizure. The Security Council, which met on January 11, once more found Iraq in "material breach" of cease-fire terms on the basis of its accumulated violations. On the same day, several hundred Iraqis again entered the zone and began dismantling weapons warehouses, and resumed this activity on January 12 and early on January 13. Iraq claimed that UNIKOM gave it permission to clear the weaponry from the zone. Moreover, Iraq initially refused to remove six police posts from territory allotted to Kuwait, although on January 18, U.N. officials said Iraq had done so.

Allied Air Strikes

On January 13, 1993, U.S.-led coalition forces conducted air strikes against eight Iraqi antiaircraft missile sites and related control facilities in the no-fly zone of southern Iraq (south of the 32nd parallel). Subsequently, Administration officials called the raid a success in that it seriously degraded Iraq's air defense network, although several targets were not hit. The raid involved 600 U.S. military personnel from the various services and approximately 110 allied aircraft. According to a Defense Department spokesman, the United States and former Desert Storm partners Britain and France participated in the raid; however, there are indications that one or more other countries (possibly from the Persian Gulf region) may have participated as well.[5] Iraqis said the attack killed 19 and wounded 15, many of them civilians. U.S. officials acknowledged that an apartment building in the southern city of Basra was hit, presumably by mistake. Meanwhile, the United States announced the deployment of the 1st battalion, 19th regiment, 1st Cavalry Division from Fort Hood, Texas (about 1,100 soldiers) to Kuwait to join 300 U.S.

Special Forces troops already there and underscore U.S. commitments to Persian Gulf security.

York Times, The Wall Street Journal during January and February 1993.

[5] The Defense official, asked by reporters if Saudi aircraft had participated in the strikes, answered: 'Members of the coalition, to include the French and the British, participated. I'm not going to name other countries." Defense Department Background Briefing, Jan. 13, 1993, carried by Reuters newswire. The press noted that the air strike was "joined by Britain, France, and at least one other undisclosed ally." Barton Gellman and Ann Devroy, "U.S. Delivers Limited Air Strike on Baghdad," *The Washington Post,* Jan. 14, 1993, p. Al.

Iraqi Reactions

The raid apparently prompted some early concessions from Baghdad. Despite a defiant post-raid speech by Saddam Hussein, Iraq's Ambassador to the United Nations told the president of the United Nations Security Council that Iraq would permit flights by UN. inspectors in their own aircraft, and that incursions into the demilitarized zone with Kuwait would cease. However, Iraq vowed that it would continue to resist enforcement of the no-fly zones, and Saddam instructed the military to fire on coalition planes over Iraqi territory.

When Iraq failed to respond to a U.N. request to land a U.N. aircraft carrying weapons inspectors to Iraq, the United States, Britain, and France delivered an ultimatum to Iraq that it provide such clearance by 4:00 PM EST on Jan. 15, 1993. Before the deadline expired, Iraq said the U.N. aircraft could land, but that Iraq could not guarantee its security, since allied operations were taking place in the southern no-fly zone. The U.N. Special Commission (UNSCOM) conducting the inspections rejected that condition and said it would file a new flight request. On January 16, Iraq said it would permit the flights and guarantee their security, but only if the flights enter Iraqi airspace from Jordan, and not from the south. (The U.N. flights generally enter from the south, flying from Bahrain, where UNSCOM maintains a field office.) UNSCOM again rejected this condition, as well as a January 17 Iraqi proposal that the flights could enter from the south if the coalition suspended its patrols of the no-fly zone during the U.N. flights. On January 19 at 1:30 p.m. EST, as the incoming Clinton Administration prepared to take office, Iraq's ruling Revolutionary Command Council offered a "cease-fire... to enable the new Administration to study the no-fly zones."[6]

Further Actions

Sporadic military action continued from January 17 to January 23, 1993, in response to further Iraqi provocations. Iraq activated targeting radar in the northern no-fly zone and refused to grant unconditional clearance to U.N. inspection flights (January 17); challenged allied aircraft in the northern no-fly zone and, according to a report not confirmed by the Pentagon, fired a Scud missile at the city of Dhahran in Saudi Arabia (January 18); challenged the northern no-fly zone and directed anti-aircraft fire at coalition aircraft (January 19); directed a radar beam search at U.S. aircraft in northern no-fly zone (January 21); tracked U.S. aircraft with air defense radar (January 22); and apparently directed anti-aircraft fire at U.S. aircraft in the northern zone (January 22 or 23). In the latter two cases, Iraq denied tracking or firing at U.S. aircraft.

In retaliation, coalition aircraft conducted a strike at an Iraqi S A-6 ground radar in northern Iraq, shot down an Iraqi MiG-23, and launched 45 cruise missiles at the Zafaraniya manufacturing complex outside Baghdad (January 17); the coalition struck air defense installations in both the northern and southern zones and shot at (probably shooting down) an Iraqi warplane (January 18); the coalition fired cluster bombs and air-to-surface missiles at Iraqi anti-aircraft guns in the northern zone and the United States moved four U.S. warships (including the aircraft carrier *Kennedy)* toward the eastern Mediterranean on a contingency basis (January 19); U.S. aircraft fired a missile and dropped cluster bombs on Iraqi ground radar in the northern zone (January 21); a U.S. F-4G "Wild Weasel" fired two missiles at an Iraqi air defense battery in the north (January 22); and a U.S. A-6 Intruder aircraft fired a

[6] R. Jeffrey Smith and Julia Preston, "Baghdad Declares Good Will Cease-Fire," *The Washington Post,* Jan. 20, 1993, p. Al.

laser-guided bomb at an Iraqi anti-aircraft position in the southern zone (January 22 or 23). Regarding the January 17 missile strikes at Zafaraniya plant (which the Bush Administration said had been used to make components for Iraq's nuclear program), one cruise missile went off course and hit the al-Rashid Hotel in Baghdad, killing at least three civilians. Iraq said 21 were killed in attacks on January 18.

Bush Assassination Attempt

The Alleged Plot

Tensions between the United States and Iraq increased during the spring of 1993, as Iraq continued its failure to cooperate fully with U.N. weapons inspections and reportedly concentrated forces near the Kurdish enclave. In the meantime, the Government of Kuwait informed the U.S. Administration that it had discovered evidence that Iraq sponsored an attempt to assassinate former President Bush and destabilize Kuwait during his April 14-16 visit to Kuwait. The Kuwaitis captured a small van loaded with 180 pounds of explosives, and confiscated detonators, timing devices, and other bomb components. Kuwait apprehended and tried 14 suspects, ultimately sentencing six to death (five Iraqis and one Kuwaiti) and seven to prison terms; one defendant was acquitted.[7] One of the Iraqi defendants testified that Iraqi intelligence was behind the plot. Federal Bureau of Investigation (FBI) agents and other U.S. intelligence officers were sent to Kuwait to conduct their own investigation, and reported back to the President on June 24, 1993, that their findings confirmed the view that Iraq was behind the plot. Iraq has denied that it sponsored the attempt.[8]

Some in the Administration and Congress called for retaliation, including air strikes, against Iraq if it were clear that Iraq had sponsored the plot; others pointed out that U.S. policy toward Iraq already was strict and few other options were available. Skeptics questioned the validity of evidence obtained from Kuwaiti investigation of the suspects.

U.S. Missile Strikes

On June 26, 1993 (June 27, Baghdad time), the U.S.S. Peterson, a Spruance-class destroyer in the Red Sea, and the U.S.S. *Chancethrsville,* a Ticonderoga-class cruiser in the Persian Gulf, began launching 23 Tomahawk missiles toward the Iraqi intelligence headquarters in western Baghdad. The Tomahawk is a 20-foot long missile that flies at 550 mph about 50 feet above the ground to avoid radar, carrying a 1,000-pound conventional warhead some 700 miles. Tomahawks were used because they are not manned, and therefore do not place U.S. Armed Forces personnel at risk, and because they have a success rate estimated to be as high as 80%. About one hour after launch, 20 of the Tomahawks hit the 6-winged headquarters building in the center of the intelligence complex.

Later that evening, President Clinton said CIA and FBI reports provided compelling evidence that Iraqi intelligence forces were behind the attempted assassination of former President Bush in April and that the United States was justified in acting against Iraq under the self defense provisions of Article 51 of the United Nations Charter. Defense Secretary Les

---

[7] After a long trial, the sentences were finally imposed in June 1994. "Kuwait Sentences Six to Death for Plotting to Kill Bush," *The New York Times,* June 5, 1994, p. 6.

Aspin and Chairman of the Joint Chiefs of Staff General Colin Powell said the intelligence headquarters was selected as the target because the Iraqi intelligence services had been linked to the attempt on President Bush, because it was a discreet target, and because it was at the low end of a spectrum of possible targets that included the Ministry of Defense, the Presidential Palace, military bases, or others. Early U.S. damage estimates described the attack as a qualified success, although three of the Tomahawks missed their targets and hit nearby residential areas, destroying several houses and killing 8 and wounding 12 civilians. (Iraq claims to have shot down four of the missiles.) The President said the raids crippled Iraq's military intelligence capability, but some observers suggested that this capability was not severely damaged because of redundancies in the system.[9]

In brief follow-up actions, on June 27, the United States moved the aircraft carrier U.S.S. *Theodore Roosevelt* and destroyers *Arleigh Burke* and *Spruance* from the Mediterranean to the Red Sea. (The carrier U.S.S. *Nimitz* left the Persian Gulf on June 17 at the end of its 6-month tour.) Two days later, a U.S. F-4G "Wild Weasel" aircraft fired a HARM missile at an Iraqi radar, in response to Iraqi actions that appeared to threaten U.S. planes patrolling the southern no-fly zone over Iraq.

U.N. Camera Installation

In an unrelated incident in early June 1993, Iraqi officials refused to allow a UNSCOM team to install six cameras at two test sites to maintain continuing surveillance of Iraqi weapons programs. Iraq subsequently agreed to their installation. Meanwhile, however, on June 18, a statement by the President of the U.N. Security Council described Iraq's failure action in impeding installation of the cameras and failure to destroy certain banned chemical materials as "a material and unacceptable breach" of relevant provisions of Resolution 687. This was the last occasion on which the Security Council issued a finding of "material breach" against Iraq.[10]

October 1994 Troop Movements[11]

Iraqi Moves

During the week of October 3, 1994, Iraq issued warnings of unspecified consequences if the ban on exporting Iraqi oil were not lifted in conjunction with the bi-monthly UNSCOM report to the Security Council due on October 10. Iraq also warned that it would stop cooperating with UNSCOM. (The UNSCOM report, formally presented to the Security Council October 11, said that a long-term weapons monitoring program had begun, but, contrary to Iraqi desires, the report did not set a timetable for testing the monitoring system.)

---

[8] According to one report, the Iraqi intelligence service linked to the plot was headed by a son of Saddam Hussein. R. Jeffrey Smith, "Iraqi Officer Recruited Suspects in Plot Against Bush, U.S. Says," *The Washington Post,* July 1, 1993, p. A18.

[9] R. Jeffiey Smith and Ann Devroy, "Clinton Says U.S. Missiles 'Crippled,'" *The Washington Post,* June 29, 1993; Haine Sciolino, "Clinton Overstates Impact of Raids, His Aids Warn," *The New York Times,* June 29, 1993, p. 6.

[10] Greg Saiontz, "A Chronology of Diminishing Response: UN-Reactions to Iraqi Provocations since the Gulf War," Research Notes, The Washington Institute for Near East Policy, June 3, 1997, p. 5.

[11] See Facts on File Yearbook 1994, pp. 745-746; issues of *The Washington Post, The New York Times, The Wall Street Journal* in October 1994.

Meanwhile, in early in October, Iraq began ordering at least two divisions (Hammurabi, al-Nida) of elite Republican Guard troops to join approximately 40,000 regular troops in southern Iraq, around the city of Basra. By October 9, according to statements by U.S. officials, Iraq had about 80,000 troops in or heading toward southern Iraq, assuming all Iraqi units were eventually filled out.[12] The lead elements of the Iraqi deployment reportedly went as close as 12 miles from the border with Kuwait. Kuwait responded by moving most of its 16,000-person force to the border with Kuwait, a much larger display offeree than it demonstrated in August 1990. Nonetheless, Kuwait's force remained too small and poorly armed and trained to deter Iraq, should Iraq want to invade again, even though Iraq had lost more than half its weaponry in the 1991 Persian Gulf.

U.S. Response

On October 7, Secretary of Defense William Perry called the Iraqi troop movements a cause for concern, and other U.S. defense officials said the troop movements, which included the transport of ammunition and support equipment, were not consistent with routine troop rotations. President Clinton said on October 7 and again on October 8 that "it would be a grave error for Iraq to repeat the mistakes of the past [the August 1990 invasion of Kuwait] or to misjudge either American will or American power." He said the United States would honor a commitment to defend Kuwait and to enforce U.N. resolutions on Iraq. Press reports cited several U.S. defense officials as saying that they not believe Iraq intended to invade Kuwait again, but that Iraq's record of belligerence made it wise to be prepared. At the height of the crisis, there were reports that the Administration was considering striking the Iraqi force even if it did not invade Kuwait, in a possible effort to erode Iraq's military capability even further.

In a rapid response operation entitled "Vigilant Warrior," the United States began reinforcing approximately 13,000 U.S. Army, Navy, Air Force, and Marine troops already in the Gulf, together with equipment prepositioned in Kuwait. Had the crisis not abated, the new forces would have included: two additional Patriot missile batteries; 350 additional combat aircraft, including B-52 bombers, F-117 Stealth fighters, F-15's, F-16's, A-10 attack aircraft, AWAC's surveillance aircraft, and U-2 reconnaissance aircraft; the 18,000-member 1st Marine Expeditionary Force; and 16,000 Army troops from the 24th Mechanized Infantry Division. An additional 156,000 troops were placed on alert. The United States also moved the carrier U.S.S. George Washington from the Adriatic Sea into the Red Sea, within striking range of Iraq. Among U.S. allies, Britain sent two ships, six Tornado aircraft, and a battalion of troops to the Gulf. France, which had supported the idea of setting a firm timetable for allowing Iraq to resume oil sales, sent a frigate to the Gulf. As the crisis began to wind down in mid-October, however, the United States scaled back the deployment of both ground and air forces to the region.

International reaction tended to condemn the Iraqi troop movements and support U.S. and allied deployments to the Gulf. (See International Reactions, below.) On October 8, the U.N. Security Council expressed grave concern about the Iraqi troop movements and Iraqi threats to stop cooperating with UNSCOM. One option reportedly under consideration by the Clinton Administration was to seek U.N. approval for a military exclusion zone or a "no-tank zone" in

[12] U.S. officials noted that the Iraqi forces menacing Kuwait were equipped with weapons captured from Kuwait, including over 200 Soviet-manufactured armored personnel carriers and a battalion of U.S.-made M109 self-propelled howitzers. Michael R. Gordon, "As Iraqis Scimp, Their President Lives Lavishly," *The New York Times*, Nov. 14, 1994, p. A3.

southern Iraq, south of the 32nd parallel, to supplement the no-fly zone in that area. On October 15, the United States succeeded in gaining unanimous Security Council approval of Resolution 949, demanding that Iraq remove forces recently deployed to the south and avoid further deployments that would threaten its neighbors. The resolution invoked Chapter YE (peace and security) of the U.N. Charter but did not specify means of enforcement. U.S. Ambassador to the U.N. Albright said the resolution gave the United States authority to strike Iraq if it moved Republican Guards near Kuwait again, but other Security Council members did not endorse that view.[13]

The Crisis Recedes

There are strong indications that the U.S. response, together with support from the Security Council and other allies, caused Iraq to rethink its strategy. Between October 7 and 9, Iraqi officials made several conciliatory statements, and in a speech to the U.N. General Assembly, Iraqi Deputy Prime Minister Tariq Aziz hinted that Iraq might even recognize Kuwait. On October 10, Iraq's Ambassador to the United Nations said Iraq was redeploying troops from the border area because of "Security Council concerns," although he said Iraq reserved the right to move troops anywhere on its territory. Between October 11 and October 16, U.S. officials noted increasing evidence that Iraqi units were withdrawing, and then Secretary of State Warren Christopher confirmed this trend on October 16. On November 10, 1994, after the crisis had receded, Iraq formally recognized Kuwait in a motion passed by the Iraqi National Assembly and signed by President Saddam Hussein.

Motivation behind the Iraqi troop movements of early October remains obscure. Most analysts believe that Iraqi President Saddam Husayn was attempting to attract international attention to his argument that Iraq has complied sufficiently with certain provisions of Resolution 687 to justify lifting of the oil sale boycott. Some believed Saddam Hussein thought the United States might seek compromise rather than military confrontation in view of current preoccupations with Haiti, North Korea, and Bosnia. Still others theorized that internal economic pressures impelled Saddam to demonstrate to the Iraqi people that he was taking decisive action to obtain lifting of economic sanctions. According to a minority view, reportedly shared by some U.S. military officials, Iraq did not plan to threaten Kuwait, and Iraqi troop movements were prompted by fear of heightened allied air operations previously under way.[14]

Iraqi Defections to Jordan

No major U.S.-Iraqi confrontations occurred for almost two years after Operation Vigilant Warrior; however, in 1995, a potential Iraqi threat to Jordan prompted a brief augmentation of U.S. forces in the Gulf region. On August 8, 1995, two sons-in-law and key aids of Iraqi President Saddam Hussein defected to Jordan and were given political asylum. One of the defectors, General Hussein Kamil Hassan, was the principal architect of Iraq's programs to develop mass destruction weapons. Following his defection to Jordan, Hussein

[13] In nearly identical diplomatic notes on October 20, 1994, the United States and Britain warned Iraq against moving reinforcements south of a line running roughly 150 miles north of the border with Kuwait. Julia Preston and Thomas W. Lippman, "Allies Warn Iraq Against Troop Shifts," *The Washington Post,* Oct. 21, 1994, p. Al.

Kamil reportedly provided information to U.S. and Saudi Arabian representatives on the status of Iraqi weapons programs. At the same time, Jordanian officials emphasized that the decision to grant asylum to Hussein Kamil was taken on humanitarian rather than political grounds. Frustrated in his attempts to gain support from other Iraqi opposition groups or foreign governments, Hussein Kamil and his brother unwisely returned to Iraq in 1996 where they were promptly murdered, probably on orders of the Saddam Hussein Regime.

There were initial concerns in August 1995 on the part of U.S. and Jordanian officials that Iraq might retaliate against Jordan for granting asylum to the defectors.[15] The United States took several precautionary steps in August 1995 to protect Jordan under an operation called "Vigilant Sentinel."[16] An aircraft carrier (the U.S.S. *Theodore Roosevelt*) was moved to the eastern Mediterranean within aircraft range of Iraq, while another (the U.S.S. *Abraham Lincoln*) was held in the Persian Gulf for an additional month pending arrival of a replacement, to avoid a one-month gap hi carrier coverage. During August, 2,000 to 3,000 U.S. Marines and 4,000 Jordanian troops held a previously scheduled two-week exercise; a joint U.S.-Kuwaiti military exercise was advanced by two months; and an unspecified number of additional U.S. military personnel were alerted for possible deployment to the Persian Gulf. Finally, shiploads of U.S. military equipment normally stationed in the Indian Ocean and western Pacific were shifted closer to the Gulf region.[17] In the event, Iraq acted with restraint and no further U.S. deployments proved necessary at that time.

The Incursion of August 1996[18]

Events and Responses

Meanwhile, internal strife which erupted between the two principal Iraqi Kurdish factions in 1994 provided Iraq and neighboring countries with opportunities to exploit the growing disarray in the allied-protected Kurdish enclave in northern Iraq. (Map 2 shows Kurdish inhabited areas in Iraq and in neighboring countries.) One of the two leading Kurdish factions, the Patriotic Union of Kurdistan (PUK), had seized the Kurdish provisional capital of Irbil after feuding broke out between the two factions in May 1994. In the summer of 1996, Saddam Hussein sought to exploit internecine strife among the Kurds by intervening on the side of a rival faction, the Kurdistan Democratic Party (KDP).

On August 31, 1996, an Iraqi force estimated at three armored divisions (30,000-40,000 personnel) invaded Irbil, which lies approximately 7 miles within the allied-imposed no-fly zone. Iraq moved at the invitation of KDP leader Massud Barzani. Over the next few days, and without much additional Iraqi help, the KDP captured major Kurdish cities from the

---

14 David A. Fulghum, "Iraq Invasion Threat Reassessed by Military," *Aviation Week and Space Technology,* Nov. 14, 1994, pp. 18-20.

15 Then U.S. Secretary of Defense William Perry told reporters that 'There have been some unusual deployments of Iraqi military forces" but added that there was "nothing that leads us to believe that any invasion is underway or planned." Bradley Graham, "U.S. Speeds Troops to Kuwait, Plays Down Chance of Iraqi Attack," *The Washington Post,* Aug. 23, 1995, p. A24.

16 President Clinton praised Jordan's decision to grant the defectors political asylum and said "the United States considers Jordan our ally and entitled to our protection if their security is threatened as a result of this incident." Alison Mitchell, "U.S. to Protect Jordan from Iraq, Clinton Says," *New York Times,* Aug. 11, 1995, p. A10.

17 Bradley Graham, "U.S. Bolsters Gulf Force to Counter Iraq," *The Washington Post,* Aug. 18, 1995, pp. Al, A27.

18 See Facts on File Yearbook 1996, pp. 637-638; issues of *The Washington Post, The New York Times, and The Wall Street Journal* in September 1997.

PUK, which was supported by Iran. Numerous PUK members and other Kurds fearful of the apparent extension of Iraqi Government influence in northern Iraq sought refuge in Iran. PUK militia subsequently regrouped and launched a counterattack on October 13, recapturing significant portions of territory they had previously lost, and the situation remained fluid. Iran denied allegations by both KDP and Turkish officials that the PUK counterattack received Iranian military support.

The United States expressed grave concern, put forces in the Persian Gulf region on alert, and warned Iraq to withdraw. On September 3, at 12:15 a.m. Eastern Daylight Time (7:15 a.m., Iraq time), U.S. forces launched 27 cruise missiles at military targets in the southern part of Iraq, 14 from the U.S. S. Laboon guided missile destroyer and the U.S.S. Shilo cruiser in the Persian Gulf, and 13 from two B-52 bombers that flew from Guam. President Clinton also announced that he was widening the no-fly zone over southern Iraq (extending it northward from the 32nd to the 33rd parallel) and would not allow a limited oil sale by Iraq under a recent U.N. resolution to take place until Iraq abandons its aggressive policies. On September 4, U.S. forces fired an additional 17 missiles from three surface ships and one submarine, in what a Pentagon spokesman described as a mopping-up operation, designed to destroy Iraqi air defenses that might threaten allied enforcement of an expanded no-fly zone. Subsequently, a U.S. F-16 fighter aircraft fired two anti-radiation missiles at an Iraqi radar. Later on the same day, President Clinton announced that the U.S. mission had been largely accomplished.

In mid-September, in response to further Iraqi provocations (see below), the United States dispatched eight F-l 17A stealth fighters to Kuwait, four B-52 bombers to the British base at Diego Garcia in the Indian Ocean, two Patriot missile batteries to Saudi Arabia, and a second aircraft carrier along with additional aircraft and air defense units to the region. (The second aircraft carrier returned home in October.) On September 13, a reinforced squadron of U.S. F-l 6 fighter aircraft was deployed to Bahrain. On September 17, President Clinton ordered approximately 3,000 U.S. Army troops from the 1st Cavalry Division at Ft. Hood, Texas to deploy to Kuwait, joining an additional U.S. 1,200 troops already there. By late September, U.S. troop strength in the region, including personnel embarked on ships, approached 30,000. On November 29, then U.S. Secretary of Defense William Perry said the 4,200 troops in Kuwait would depart before Christmas, but added that 1,800 Marines would remain offshore for rapid deployment and that the F-l 17A stealth fighters would remain in Kuwait as a warning to Iraq and Iran.

Iraq quickly repaired some damaged air defense missile sites despite U.S. warnings not to do so, and during September 11-13, unsuccessfully fired six SA-6 surface-to-air missiles at U.S. fighter aircraft patrolling northern and southern Iraq. The Administration threatened further responses, and demanded that Iraq stop targeting U.S. aircraft enforcing the no-fly zones and remove mobile surface-to-air missiles from the zones. Iraq, which had earlier threatened to fire at allied planes overflying these zones, announced on September 13 that it would "suspend our military reactions" to allied enforcement of the no-fly zones, while still refusing to acknowledge their validity. Iraqi forces largely evacuated the Kurdish enclave, but some Iraqi intelligence agents reportedly remained in these areas.[19]

---

[19] Tim Weiner, "Iraq Pulling Out, But Leaving Spies Behind, U.S. Says," *The New York Times,* Sept. 6, 1994, p. Al.

Map 2. Kurdish Inhabited Areas

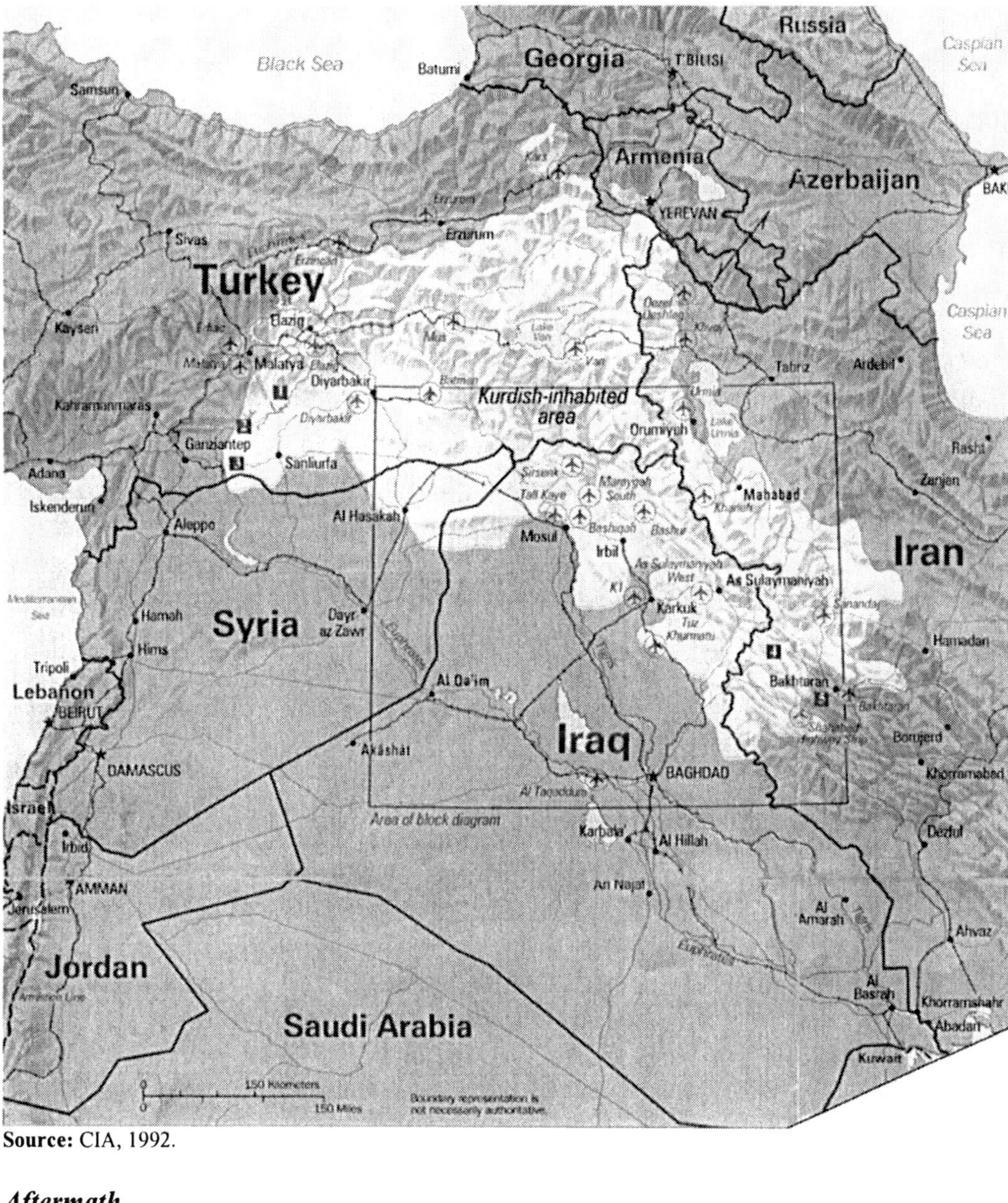

Source: CIA, 1992.

Aftermath

Unrest in northern Iraq has continued, with recurrent fighting between the rival Kurdish KDP and PUK factions. The scene has been further complicated by several Turkish cross-border operations directed against a dissident Turkish Kurd faction, the Kurdistan Workers' Party (PKK), who have launched raids against Turkey from safe havens in northern Iraq. Some observers believe Turkey is maintaining a small force in northern Iraq on a more or less permanent basis to forestall further infiltration by the dissident KDP guerrillas.[20] Meanwhile,

[20] Kelly Couturier, "Rival Factions Complicate Turkey's Pursuit of Kurds," *The Washington Post,* Oct 25, 1997, p. A13; Umit Enginsoy, "Infighting Hampers Turkey's Kurdish Security Plan," *Defense News,* Nov. 3-9, 1997, p. 24. Several Arab states have criticized Turkey's cross-border operations in northern Iraq.

on January 1, 1997, the former allied protective umbrella over northern Iraq, Operation Provide Comfort, was modified and renamed Operation Northern Watch. France, which had joined the United States and Britain in Provide Comfort, does not participate in Northern Watch.

A by-product of the Iraqi incursion and Iraq's temporary cooperation with the KDP was the disruption of U.S. intelligence operations aimed at toppling the regime of Saddam Hussein. U.S. agents reportedly fled just before Iraqi troops briefly moved north, and Iraqi intelligence officers captured and executed approximately Iraqi 100 opposition figures.[21] The United States ultimately evacuated over 6,000 persons who had worked on U.S. supported humanitarian programs in northern Iraq and a smaller number (about 600) of opposition figures to Guam where they were screened for political asylum in the United States. Iraq did not repeat its August incursion 1996 into the Kurdish enclave; however, the following year saw an increase in other Iraqi challenges that led to more serious confrontations with the United States and its allies.

Further Confrontations: 1997 and Beyond

The Mounting Crisis over Inspections

Between mid-1993 and 1996, members of UNSCOM were able to carry out their inspections of Iraqi weapons programs with relatively little interference by the Government of Iraq. Increasing attempts by Iraq in 1997 to impede U.N. weapons inspections prompted demands by the U.N. Security Council that Iraq cease its interference or face further sanctions. Iraqi officials complained that U.S. pressure on the Security Council and UNSCOM was prolonging economic sanctions against Iraq. On October 29, 1997, Iraq barred participation by U.S. personnel in UNSCOM inspections, demanded the departure of all U.S. UNSCOM personnel within 7 days, and called for termination of U.S.-piloted flights by U-2 reconnaissance aircraft. Iraq followed on November 13 by expelling U.S. inspectors, and chief UNSCOM inspector Richard Butler withdrew most of the other inspectors the following day. A crisis was averted after a diplomatic initiative by Russia, which undertook to work for the speedy lifting of sanctions against Iraq and seek "balanced representation" on U.N. inspection teams. U.S. officials denied that they had agreed to any conditions in exchange for Iraqi compliance with U.N. demands.

Iraqi officials continued to complain about the alleged predominance of U.S. and British personnel on inspection teams, and insisted on their right to bar inspectors from an unspecified number of "presidential sites" on grounds of national sovereignty. On January 12, 1998, Iraq declared three specific locations to be "sensitive sites" and off limits to U.N. inspectors seeking to visit them, although the Iraqis permitted access to them later in the day. On January 16, a U.S.-led team, which was investigating Iraqi methods of concealing mass destruction weapons programs, left Iraq%fter being barred for three days from conducting an inspection. Iraqi officials asserted that the team was unbalanced inasmuch as it consisted largely of Americans and British and that team leader Scott Ritter, a former U.S. Marine

[21] The Iraqi regime reportedly had already discovered another opposition network in June 1996 and executed 100 Iraqi dissidents belonging to that group as well. R. Jeffrey Smith and David B. Ottoway, "Anti-Saddam Operation Cost CIA3100 Million," *The Washington Post,* Sept. 15, 19%, pp. 1, 29; Evan Thomas, Christopher Dickey and Gregory L. Vistica, "Bay of Pigs Redux," *Newsweek,* March 23, 1998, pp. 36-37.

officer and veteran of numerous similar inspections, was engaged in spying on Iraq. U.N. and U.S. officials denied the accusations concerning Ritter and emphasized that Iraq cannot dictate the composition of U.N. inspection teams. The following day, President Saddam Hussein announced that Iraq would expel all U.N. weapons inspectors if sanctions against Iraq were not removed within six months. Also on January 17, the Iraqi Foreign Ministry criticized U.S. rejection of an offer by Russia to replace the U.S. U-2 reconnaissance aircraft with Russian planes. (The U-2 flights have continued despite an Iraqi threat to fire on them.) By early February, U.S.-led retaliatory action against Iraq seemed imminent.

The February 23, 1998 Agreement

Intensive diplomatic efforts in early and mid-February centered on attempts to find a formula for inspecting eight "sensitive" sites under conditions that the United Nations and Iraq would accept. The United States insisted that two principles must govern any agreement on the conduct of inspections: full access by UNSCOM to sites throughout Iraq, and respect for the integrity of the U.N. Special Commission process. On February 17, the U.N. Security Council reportedly endorsed a plan that would give U.N. inspectors full access within Iraq, while allowing diplomats from U.N. Security Council member countries to accompany U.N. inspectors on visits to the eight "presidential" compounds. The presence of diplomats would serve as a face-saving gesture for Iraq by signifying international recognition of Iraq sovereignty. On February 23, after three days of negotiations, Secretary-General Annan and Iraqi Foreign Minister Tariq Aziz signed an agreement with the following principal provisions:

- Reconfirmation by Iraq that it accepts relevant U.N. resolutions
- Commitment of U.N. member states to "respect the sovereignty and territorial integrity of Iraq"
- "Immediate, unconditional, and unrestricted access" by UNSCOM and IAEA within Iraq, with respect for Iraqi concerns relating to "national security, sovereignty, and dignity"
- Special procedures to apply to inspections at eight "presidential sites" defined in an annex to the agreement
- Efforts to accelerate the inspection process, and an undertaking by the Secretary-General to bring to U.N. Security Council members the concerns of Iraq over economic sanctions.

Under the special procedures governing inspections at the eight sites, the U.N. Secretary-General established a "Special Group" comprising diplomats appointed by the Secretary-General and experts drawn from UNSCOM and IAEA. Reports by the Special Group were to be submitted by the Executive Chairman of UNSCOM through the Secretary-General to the Security Council. Inspections of the eight sites took place between March 26 and April 3, 1998, and revealed no evidence of prohibited weapons systems, but the senior inspector said "It was clearly apparent that all sites had undergone extensive evacuation."[22] Other

[22] Barbara Crossette, "Inspectors Report Lack of Progress in Verifying Iraqi Disarmament," *The New York Times*, April 17, 1998, p. 1.

inspections proceeded relatively smoothly during the next few months, but many questions about Iraq's weapons programs remained unresolved as of mid-1998.

Meanwhile, on March 3, the U.N. Security Council unanimously passed Resolution 1154, co-sponsored by Britain and Japan, which commended the initiative of the Secretary-General in securing commitments from Iraq, stressed that Iraq must comply with its obligations, and warned that "any violation [of the agreement or other pertinent resolutions] would have severest consequences for Iraq." President Clinton and Secretary of State Madeleine Albright described the agreement as a "step forward" for U.S. policy of containing Iraq, but the President commented that "What really matters is Iraq's compliance, not its stated commitments." Secretary Albright said of the agreement that "The proof is in the testing."

Force Deployments and Drawdown

A U.S. force build-up in the Gulf region began in October 1997 as tensions with Iraq mounted. For several months thereafter, the United States maintained two aircraft carriers in the Gulf, and three during a brief period in February 1998 (the *U.S.S. Nimitz, U.S.S. George Washington,* and *U.S.S. Independence*). In November 1997, during the early stages of the crisis, the United States sent six F-117A stealth fighters to Kuwait; eight B-52 bombers to the Indian Ocean base of Diego Garcia (British territory); and an Air Expeditionary Force consisting of 32 combat aircraft (12 F-15 fighters, 18 F-16 fighters, and 2 B-l bombers) to Bahrain, accompanied by additional personnel to man a Patriot missile battery to protect the aircraft.

On February 4, as the crisis intensified, Secretary Cohen announced additional deployments to the Gulf region. According to subsequent press reports, these included the following: the 24th Marine Expeditionary Unit (approximately 2,000-2,200 personnel) to the Gulf; 6 more F-l 17A stealth fighters to Kuwait; 6 more B-52 bombers to Diego Garcia; 6 more F-16s and one more B-l bomber to Bahrain; and additional U.S. Army troops to join 1,500 already in Kuwait. According to a subsequent order on February 16, the Army troops include approximately 5,000-6,000, comprising mechanized infantry units to complete a brigade, a 24-helicopter aviation unit, and communications personnel. These deployments brought U.S. force levels to a peak level of almost 45,000 personnel (including over 20,000 on ships); approximately 35 combat and support ships, and over 350 aircraft (including approximately 275 fighters and bombers). Force levels of over 35,000 were maintained from March through May. (See Table 2 for comparative U.S. force levels in the Gulf since 1997.)

Meanwhile, Britain moved an aircraft carrier, the *Invincible,* with 19 Harrier jets to the Gulf, as well as 6 more Harriers and 8 Tornado fighters (12 Tornados are already in the region). At least ten other countries offered small contingents. A senior State Department official told reporters on March 4 that some 20 nations were ready to participate in a military coalition against Iraq, but did not name them; on March 17, Secretary of Defense Cohen said a total of 25 nations were ready "to be with the United States should military action become necessary.")

During May, as the crisis continued to recede, Administration officials became increasingly concerned that the large-scale U.S. military presence in the Gulf was affecting U.S. force readiness and creating domestic problems for U.S. allies. On May 26., President Clinton ordered a reduction of U.S. forces, beginning with the return of; one of the two aircraft carriers to the Pacific. Several other units were subsequently withdrawn: the Air Expeditionary Force in Bahrain (approximately 40 combat aircraft) in early June; "Stealth" fighters in Kuwait; a brigade and other ground force units in Kuwait; and some of the 14 B-52 bombers and support aircraft in Diego Garcia. After these and other withdrawals, according to Defense officials, U.S. forces in the Gulf returned to an average of approximately 20,000 personnel, varying perhaps as much as 2,000 above or below that level. Allied countries also reduced or ended their Gulf deployments. U.S. Defense officials noted that the United States was leaving "a very powerful force of cruise missiles" in the Gulf and noted that forces in the region could be quickly reinforced.

Epilogue

A relative lull during the spring and summer of 1998 was followed by increasing tensions in the fall, as Iraq mounted further challenges to U.N. operations. Late in 1998, after testing Iraq's compliance with yet another pledge to cooperate unconditionally with UNSCOM, the United States once more expanded its forces in the Gulf and, in conjunction with British forces, mounted retaliatory strikes against a wide range of Iraqi targets for a four-day period in December. Smaller scale military strikes against Iraq continued thereafter, in response to a steady patter of Iraqi violations of the no-fly zones over northern and southern Iraq.

International Reactions

Reactions during Earlier Crises

International reactions to U.S. reprisals against Iraq have been mixed, and have varied to some extent according to the nature of the crisis that precipitated a U.S. military response.[23] Much of the international community has supported U.S. retaliation against Iraqi actions that appeared to threaten Kuwait, for example during the crisis brought on by Iraqi troops deployments in October 1994. The international community has been less supportive of U.S. military responses to Iraqi actions that are not perceived as major violations of cease-fire terms or threats to another country. Some countries, particularly in the Middle East, question the imposition of no-fly zones over parts of Iraq and tend to sympathize with Iraqi efforts to assert control over its own territory. For example, many Middle East countries—including some U.S. allies—were critical of U.S. missile strikes against Iraq after its brief incursion into the Kurdish enclave in August 1996. A consistent exception to Arab unease with U.S. retaliation against Iraq has been Kuwait, where memories of the Iraqi invasion remain fresh.

In January 1993, the United States responded to a three-fold Iraqi challenge including border violations, interference with weapons inspections, and defiance of no-fly zones; at least two of these actions were violations of a U.N. resolution (Security Council Resolution 687) passed under Chapter VII (peace and security) provisions. Moreover, the operation was multilateral, in that two European allies, Britain and France, participated in the operation, although France voiced reservations. International reactions were favorable among much of the industrialized world and largely muted elsewhere. Besides Britain and France, countries expressing support included Denmark, the Netherlands, Spain and Japan. Russia first backed

[23] For more information on international reactions, see Reuters news wire articles and other press reports during the various confrontation periods described above, for example, John M. Goshko, "U.N. Divided on Role in Iraq Conflict," *The Washington Post,* Sept. 5, 1996, p. A19; Charles Trueheart, "U.S. Raids on Iraq Get Little European Support," *The Washington Post,* Sept. 6, 1996, p. A30.

the allied raids but later suggested that they might be "out of proportion" to the provocation. Arab governments generally remained silent or balanced their criticism of Iraqi provocation with statements of regret that the United States and western allies did not make similar efforts to enforce U.N. resolutions regarding Bosnia and Israel. Although the Arab Gulf states did not openly endorse the U.S. retaliatory measures, one or more of them may have provided assistance to the allied strikes, as explained above.

The June 1993 strikes in response to Iraq's alleged attempt to assassinate former President Bush represented a unilateral action by the United States under Article 51 of the U.N. Charter, which authorizes actions taken in self defense. Thus, it differed from the January strikes, which represented a combined allied operation to enforce U.N. Resolution 687, and international support for the June operation was somewhat less evident. Western allies and Russia expressed general approval, with strongest support coming from Britain, Germany, and Belgium. Within the Middle East, there was little support for the U.S. air strikes, even among members of the former allied coalition, and widespread criticism that the United States had applied a dual standard in attacking Iraq while permitting atrocities against Muslims in Bosnia. With the exception of Kuwait, which praised the U.S. action, Gulf states were officially silent. Criticism or reservations regarding the U.S. attack were expressed by other Muslim, non-aligned, and Communist (or former Communist) countries. China voiced concern and hoped that all sides would avoid actions that might worsen the situation. The Vatican, though not taking sides, deplored the loss of civilian life. A large number of countries, however, remained silent on the subject.

By contrast, in October 1994, much of the international community condemned the Iraqi troop movements toward Kuwait and supported the U.S. and allied deployments to the Gulf. Two factors contributed toward this increased level of international support: first, Iraqi actions were perceived as constituting a threat to Kuwait; and, second, allied reactions were limited to troop deployments rather than direct military action. Russia, France, and Turkey, which had favored some easing of the trade embargo against Iraq, hardened their positions at least temporarily as a result of Iraqi actions. Egypt and the Gulf states all supported the U.S. deployments. Jordan's King Hussein, who was sympathetic to Saddam in the 1990-91 crisis, echoed U.S. warnings to Saddam not to repeat past mistakes. Several Jordanian newspapers, however, appeared to sympathize with Iraq by calling for the easing of sanctions. The Palestine Liberation Organization expressed little support for Saddam during the crisis but its statements were weaker than the United States wanted!

A different picture emerged during the next confrontation in August 1996. The movement of Iraqi ground forces into the Kurdish enclave in northern Iraq, though it violated understandings in place since 1991, was not technically a violation of the allied-imposed no-fly zones. A perception that Iraq was not violating any formal cease-fire arrangements was probably a contributing factor to a lack of widespread support among U.S. allies for the subsequent reprisals undertaken by the U.S. Government.[24] Britain, Canada, Germany, and Japan supported the U.S. strikes; NATO formally endorsed them, but some NATO members expressed reservations. France refused to participate in patrolling the expanded portion of the southern no-fly zone and, shortly afterwards, withdrew from patrolling the northern zone.

[24] A year later, Saudi Minister of Defense Prince Sultan bin Abd al-Aziz told reporters that "... frankly, the aggressor and the aggressed were both Iraqi, so we felt it was difficult to intervene." Scott Peterson, "Saudi Prince's View: We're the Most Permanent US Ally," *Christian Science Monitor*, Sept. 2, 1997, p. 1.

Russia called the situation "extremely dangerous" and China called for restraint from both Washington and Baghdad. The U.N. Security Council deadlocked on a British draft resolution condemning Iraq's actions. In the Middle East, Jordan and Turkey refused to permit U.S. air strikes from their territory and Saudi Arabia did not offer the use of its bases for that purpose.[25] Only Kuwait and Bahrain appeared to endorse the U.S. action by agreeing to host temporary deployments of additional U.S. combat aircraft.

Recent Reactions

European and Arab allies agreed that Iraq must honor U.N. Security Council resolutions when Iraq began to challenge U.N. inspections in late 1997; however, most were opposed to using military force or favored it only as a last resort. As the crisis worsened in early 1998, Secretary of State Albright visited regional allies and reported that "the U.S., Egypt, Jordan, Kuwait, Saudi Arabia, Bahrain, and the Palestinian Authority are of one mind on this crisis caused by Iraq's defiance of the Security Council."[26] She added that "none of the Arab leaders, specifically, urged me to tell the president not to use force."[27] None except Kuwait, however, voiced enthusiasm over using force against Iraq, and there were widespread expressions of relief in the Arab World over the February 23 agreement which averted retaliatory strikes against Iraq for the time being.

Regional allies were particularly reluctant to serve as staging areas for attacks on Iraq. During the February crisis, only Kuwait agreed to allow U.S. air strikes against Iraq from their territory, although there were conflicting reports over Bahrain's stance.[28] Oman agreed to station U.S. support aircraft (five KC-10 tankers) on its territory. Saudi Arabia's Defense Minister said his country did not favor strikes against Iraq, and on February 9, Secretary Cohen said he would not seek permission to launch U.S. fighters or bombers from Saudi territory.[29] Cohen suggested that Saudi authorities might allow U.S. non-combat aircraft (tankers, transports, radar jammers) to operate from Saudi Arabia and might agree to the movement of U.S. fighter aircraft stationed in Saudi Arabia to other Gulf states for use in combat operations. Another Defense official thought Saudi Arabia would have permitted use of Saudi air space by U.S. combat aircraft based in other Gulf states.[30] Turkish officials said they would study any U.S. request to use bases in Turkey for air operations against Iraq, but said they had not received such a request.

In the event, U.S. military reprisals were averted until the end of the year. By late 1998, international support for use offeree against Iraq had grown somewhat stronger as Iraq was

---

[25] Saudi Minister of Defense Prince Sultan told reporters that the use of Saudi basis "was not requested from us. If it was requested we would have rejected it." "Saudi against hosting U.S. raids on Iraq," Reuters newswire, Sept. 11, 1996, 02:53 PET.

[26] Mark Huband, "Arabs lukewarm on Albright' s call to back air strikes," *Financial Times*, February 4, 1998, p. 8.

[27] John Lancaster and Barton Gellman, "Mideast Leaders Don't Deny U.S. Support on Iraq," *The Washington Post*, February 4, 1998, p. A21.

[28] According to some press reports, Bahrain signaled a willingness to let the United States mount attacks from its territory. Steven Lee Myers, "U.S. Will Not Ask to Use Saudi Bases for a Raid on Iraq," *The New York Times*, February 9, 1998, p. Al. On February 17, however, Bahrain's Minister of Information said his country " has not allowed the use of its territories for any military action against Iraq." Reuters News Wire, February 17, 1998, 12:26 PET.

[29] Ibid.

[30] Id. Also, Bradley Graham, "U.S. to Avoid Strikes From Saudi Bases," *The Washington Post*, February 9, 1998, p. Al.

repeatedly seen to be obstructing U.N. operations and Saddam Hussein called for the overthrow of various Arab regimes. Most regional allies, however, remained unwilling to serve as staging areas for U.S. air or missile strikes against Iraq.

Trends

A review of international reactions to U.S.-Iraqi confrontations since 1991 shows erosion of support for retaliation against Iraq. Indicative of this trend is the reluctance of the U.N. Security Council since 1993 to find Iraq in "material breach" of Resolution 687, despite its frequent attempts to obstruct the work of U.N. weapons inspectors and its failure to observe certain other provisions of the resolution. Some Council members, like Russia, have essentially ruled out a finding of "material breach" by insisting on a narrow interpretation of the term that would exclude most of Iraq's recent challenges.[31] Altered international conditions, including growing Arab disillusionment with broader U.S. Middle East policies, U.S.-Russian tensions, Arab perceptions that Iraq is no longer a major threat, and concerns among Arabs and others over the effect of sanctions on the Iraqi population have made it increasingly difficult to replicate the broad-based coalition the United States was able to assemble in response to the Iraqi invasion of Kuwait in 1990.

Declining support within the Arab world for military action against Iraq has been particularly apparent. Although Arab countries formed an important component of the allied coalition that defeated Iraq in 1991,[32] subsequent U.S. confrontations with Iraq have not seen comparable levels of Arab support, for several reasons. First, none of Iraq's subsequent provocations involved the invasion and occupation of another Arab state. Second, Arab public opinion has increasingly blamed the United States for the sufferings of the Iraqi people under U.N.-imposed economic sanctions. Third, as Arab-Israeli peace negotiations have faltered, Arabs have complained that the United States is applying a dual standard, by using force to make Iraq comply with cease-fire provisions but not exerting pressure on Israel to comply with terms of various peace agreements. Finally, some Arab governments that would privately welcome the departure of Saddam Hussein are unwilling to support limited U.S. measures that provoke the Iraqi dictator but do not remove him from power, leaving him in a position to extract future revenge on his neighbors.[33]

---

[31] Russia's U.N. Ambassador has said, "A material breach of the cease-fire resolution would mean that Iraq invaded Kuwait again." Christopher S. Wren, "U.N. Resolutions Allow Attacks on the Likes of Iraq," *The New York Times*, Feb. 5, 1998, p. A6.

[32] Nine Arab countries committed forces to the allied coalition. On August 10, 1990, the Arab League voted for a resolution condemning the Iraqi invasion, supporting U.N. Security Council resolutions on Iraq, and endorsing the dispatch offerees to the Gulf. The vote was 12 in favor, 3 opposed, 2 abstaining, 3 expressing reservations, plus one absentee. Foreign Broadcast Information Service—Near East, August 13, 1990, pp. 1-2.

[33] There are indications that some Gulf leaders, while fearful of "pinprick attacks" that would leave them exposed to subsequent Iraqi reprisals, would privately support U.S. military actions on a scale sufficient to undermine or overthrow Saddam Hussein's regime. Douglas Jehl, "On the Record, Arab Leaders Oppose U.S. Attacks on Iraq," *The New York Times*, Jan. 29, 1998, p. A6.

ROLE OF CONGRESS

Congress authorized the President to use the U.S. Armed Forces to implement pertinent U.N. resolutions in Public Law 102-1 (HJ.Res. 77), passed by Congress on January. 12, 1991, and signed into law by President Bush on January 14, 1991, two days before Operation Desert Storm began. Congress reaffirmed its approval of the use offeree against Iraq in the Defense Authorization Act for FY1992 (Section 1095, P.L, 102-190, December 5, 1991). According to news reports, the Administration continues to cite P.L. 102-1 as a legislative basis for using force against Iraq.[34]

The Administration consulted with Congress during subsequent confrontations with Iraq. Prior to taking military action against Iraq on January 13, 1993, President Bush informed congressional leaders of his intention to launch air strikes against Iraqi missile sites. In the first hours after the strikes, several Members of Congress voiced their approval of the use offeree. According to reports, President Clinton conferred with selected Members of Congress prior to the June 26, 1993 attack on the Iraqi Intelligence headquarters. Most Members of Congress supported the President's action, although some believed the President should have pursued diplomatic avenues before resorting to military action, and some questioned the wisdom of launching the Tomahawks at night when civilians were more likely to be at home.[35] Congress was out of session at the height of the October 1994 Iraqi troop movements crisis but the Administration kept Congress and the public informed through speeches, briefings, and news conferences. The same was true of the response to Iraq's incursion into the Kurdish enclave, which occurred at the end of the 1996 summer recess.

The question of congressional authorization for use of force has arisen again hi the context of Iraq's challenges to U.N. inspection teams in late 1997 and 1998. On November 13, 1997, the House of Representatives passed House Resolution 322, which expressed the sense of the House that the United States should assure compliance with U.N. resolutions and supported military action if diplomatic efforts were unsuccessful. On January 28, Senator Trent Lott introduced a resolution (S.Con.Res. 71) with bipartisan support, urging the President to take all necessary and appropriate actions to respond to the threat posed by Iraq's refusal to end its weapons programs. Some Members wanted the resolution to call for a long term plan to eliminate threats posed by Iraq through such measures as overthrowing the regime of Saddam Hussein. In the end, Members were unable to agree on revisions and the resolution did not pass.

Other Members expressed a different concern, namely, that a resolution along the lines of the proposed S.Con.Res. 71 could provide the Administration with a "blank check" for military escalation. For example, Representative Roscoe Bartlett introduced House Concurrent Resolution 226, which stated the sense of Congress that the United States should not take military action against Iraq unless authorized by a law enacted after adoption of this resolution. Section 3002 of the House version of H.R. 3579, the Emergency Supplemental

---

[34] 102-1 has no expiration date, and some specialists in international law agree with the Administration's position that it provides sufficient authority to use force against Iraq. Philip Shenon, "U.S. To Use '91 Law to Justify Air Strikes on Iraq," *The New York Times,* February 4, 1998.

[35] Rep. Ron Dellums, then Chairman of the House Armed Services Committee (now the House National Security Committee), criticized the Administration for foiling "to consult effectively with Congress on the specific exercise of military force." Mary Jacoby, "Dellums Slams Clinton for Not Consulting Hill on Strike," *Roll Call,* July 1, 1993, pp. 1,17.

Appropriations bill, would have banned offensive action against Iraq unless authorized by a law enacted after the passage of H.R. 3579. This provision was included in a modified non-binding form as Section 17 in the enrolled bill signed by the President (P.L. 105-174, May 5, 1998). According to Section 17, it is the sense of Congress that funds made available by this act should not be used for offensive operations against Iraq unless authorized by a subsequent law.

Congress has also appropriated funds to defray the costs of increased U.S. force deployments to the Gulf since late 1997. The Emergency Supplemental Appropriations Act for FY1998 (P.L. 105-469, March 27, 1998) contained $1.31 billion to cover unanticipated costs of the build-up in the Persian Gulf through September 1998. For additional information on costs of U.S. military deployments and operations in the Gulf region, see IB94049, Iraq-U.S. Confrontation: 1997-1999.

Table 1. Comparative Military Strengths and Inventories: Gulf States

Country	Military Personnel	Tanks	Other Armored Vehicles	Field Artillery		Attack Heli-copters	Combat Aircraft	Naval Units	
				Towed	Self-Propelled			Surface Combat-ants	Sub-marines
Saudi Arabia	162,500	910	3,055	248	200	45	358	8	0
United Arab Emirates	64,500	231	1,148	46	90	49	99	0	0
Oman	43,500	77	92	91	18	0	47	0	0
Kuwait	15,300	249	456	0	41	20	76	0	0
Qatar	11,800	34	248	12	28	18	18	0	0
Bahrain	11,000	106	411	36	13	26	24	1	0
Total: Allies	*308,600*	*1,607*	*5,410*	*433*	*390*	*158*	*622*	*9*	*0*
Iraq	429,000	2,700	2,900	1,800	150	120	316	2	0
Iran	475,000	1,400	1,025	2,170	290	109	315*	3	3

* Includes aircraft flown from Iraq to Iran during 1991 Gulf war.

Source: International Institute for Strategic Studies, *The Military Balance 1998-1999.* Note: Figures shown here do not include materiel beh'eved to be in storage and inoperable.

Table 2. Comparative U.S. Force Levels in Persian Gulf: 1997-1999

Date	Personnel	Aircraft	Ships	Source of Data
mid-1997	20,000	200	20	News reports and transcripts
03/1998	44,700	355*	34	DOD NB* 05/19/98, 08/12/98
06/1998	29,800	195	21	DODNB 06/18/98
08/1998	19,650	165	20[b]	DOD NB 08/1 2/98
11/1998	23,500	173	23	DODNB 11/10/98
12/1998	29,900	348	37	AFPS** 12/28/98
03/1999	24,400	189	30	AFPS 03/05/99

a. Interpolated b. Estimated

* Department of Defense News Briefing

** Armed Forces Press Service

Chapter 9

IRAQ: U.S. EFFORTS TO CHANGE THE REGIME

Kenneth Katzman

SUMMARY

In his January 29, 2002 State of the Union message, President Bush characterized Iraq as part of an "axis of evil," along with Iran and North Korea. The President identified the key threat from Iraq as its development of weapons of mass destruction (WMD), and the potential for Iraq to transfer WMD to the terrorist groups it sponsors. The President's speech left observers with the clear implication that the Administration is planning to take additional steps to achieve the ouster of Iraq's President Saddam Husayn and his Ba'th Party regime. In comments after the speech, senior U.S. officials reiterated that it was already U.S. policy to work toward a change of Iraq's regime.

The President's comments raised the possibility that the Administration might try to go beyond previous efforts to destabilize Iraq by aiding internal opponents of the regime. Those efforts have been pursued, with varying degrees of intensity, since the end of the Gulf war in 1991. According to several experts, past efforts to change the regime floundered because of limited U.S. engagement, disorganization of the Iraqi opposition, and the efficiency and ruthlessness of Iraq's several overlapping intelligence and security forces. Some past U.S. efforts focused on an attempt to promote a military coup from within Iraq's regime, while other U.S. activities consisted primarily of supporting organized opposition groups composed of groups outside Iraq's current power structure.

Some experts believe that the removal of Saddam Husayn would require substantially more U.S. assistance to the opposition than has been dedicated to this purpose previously, or the direct use of U.S. armed force. Some are concerned that Saddam's removal could lead to the fragmentation of Iraq and not necessarily produce a stable regime that is attuned to U.S. values and U.S. interests. There are also concerns that most Western and virtually all Arab governments have publicly stated opposition to a U.S. military effort against Iraq.

An alternative view is that the Iraqi opposition is stronger than widely believed, and that a minor amount of U.S. help could bring it to power. Some believe that almost any successor regime would be preferable to that of Saddam Husayn, and that Saddam's removal would almost certainly bring an end to Iraq's WMD programs. Advocates of forceful steps to change Iraq's regime maintain that Iraq's neighbors would support a U.S. overthrow effort, even if it involves the direct use of U.S. military force, provided the effort succeeds. Congress, in various legislative measures including the 1998 Iraq Liberation Act, has made clear its support for changing Iraq's regime. However, some Members have questioned the costs and risks of strategies currently under discussion.

INTRODUCTION

The United States has been attempting to change Iraq's regime since the 1991 Persian Gulf war, although achieving this goal was not declared policy until 1998. In November 1998, amid a crisis with Iraq over U.N. weapons of mass destruction (WMD) inspections, the Clinton Administration stated that the United States would seek not only to contain Iraq, but to promote a change of regime. Bush Administration officials say this is still the policy of the United States. This paper discusses past and current U.S. efforts to oust Saddam Husayn and the current debate over the implementation of that policy.

PAST ATTEMPTS TO OUST SADDAM

Prior to the launching on January 16, 1991 of Operation Desert Storm, an operation that reversed Iraq's August 1990 invasion of Kuwait, President George H.W. Bush called on the Iraqi people to overthrow Saddam. Within days of the end of the Gulf war (February 28, 1991), opposition Shiite Muslims in southern Iraq and Kurdish factions in northern Iraq, emboldened by the regime's defeat and the hope of U.S. support, launched significant rebellions.[1] The revolt in southern Iraq reached the suburbs of Baghdad, but enough Republican Guard forces had survived the war to defeat the Shiite rebels by mid-March 1991. The Kurds, benefiting from a U.S.-led "no fly zone" established in April 1991, were able to carve out an autonomous zone in northern Iraq, and remain free of Iraqi rule today.

According to press reports, about two months after the failure of the Shiite uprising, President George H.W. Bush forwarded to Congress an intelligence finding stating that the United States would undertake efforts to promote a military coup against Saddam Husayn; a reported $ 15 million to $20 million was allocated for that purpose.[2] The Administration apparently believed -- and this view apparently still is shared by many experts and U.S officials — that a coup by elements within the current regime could produce a favorable new government without fragmenting Iraq. Many observers, however, including neighboring governments, feared that Shiite and Kurdish groups, if they ousted Saddam, would divide Iraq into warring ethnic and tribal groups, opening Iraq to influence from neighboring Iran, Turkey, and Syria.

[1] Shiites constitute about 65% of Iraq's population but historically have been repressed and under-represented in governing bodies by the members of the Sunni Muslim sect. Kurds, who are not Arabs, constitute about 20% of the population of about 20 million.

[2] Tyler, Patrick. "Plan On Iraq Coup Told To Congress." *New York Times*, February 9, 1992.

An Opposition Coalition Emerges

Reports in July 1992 of a serious but unsuccessful coup attempt suggested that the U.S. strategy might ultimately succeed. However, there was disappointment within the George H.W. Bush Administration that the coup had failed and a decision was made to shift the U.S. approach from promotion of a coup to supporting the diverse opposition groups that had led the postwar rebellions. The Kurdish, Shiite, and other opposition elements were coalescing into a broad and diverse movement that appeared to be gaining support internationally. Congress more than doubled the budget for covert support to the opposition groups to about $40 million for FY1993.[3]

The Iraqi National Congress

The Iraqi National Congress (INC) served as the vehicle for U.S. support. The INC was formed when the two main Kurdish militias — the Kurdistan Democratic Party (KDP), headed by Masud Barzani, and the Patriotic Union of Kurdistan (PUK), headed by Jalal Talabani — participated in a June 1992 meeting in Vienna of dozens of opposition groups. In October 1992, the major Shiite groups came into the coalition when the INC met in Kurdish-controlled northern Iraq. Selected to chair the INC's Executive Committee was Ahmad Chalabi, a secular Shiite Muslim and U.S.-trained mathematician who had fled Iraq to Jordan in the late 1950s, before the Ba'th Party took power in Iraq (July 1968). He eventually chaired the Petra Bank there, but later ran afoul of Jordanian authorities on charges of financial malfeasance. Chalabi maintains that the Jordanian government was pressured by Iraq to turn against him.

The INC initially appeared viable because it brought under one banner varying Iraqi ethnicities and diverse political ideologies, including nationalists, ex-military officers, and defectors from Iraq's ruling Ba'th Party. The Kurds provided the INC with a source of armed force and a presence on Iraqi territory. Its constituent groups nominally united around a platform that appeared to match U.S. values and interests, including human rights, democracy, pluralism, the preservation of Iraq's territorial integrity, and compliance with U.N. Security Council resolutions on Iraq.[4] However, many observers doubted its commitment to democracy, because most of its groups have an authoritarian internal structure, and because of inherent tensions among its varied ethnic groups and ideologies.

Some observers believe the Kurds would seek independence or full autonomy from a post-Saddam Iraq. Turkey, which has a sizable Kurdish population in the areas bordering northern Iraq, particularly fears independence for Iraq's Kurds. Turkey believes that outcome would likely touch off an effort to unify into a broader "Kurdistan." Iraq's Kurds have been fighting intermittently for autonomy since their region was incorporated into the newly formed Iraqi state after World War I. In 1961, the KDP, then led by founder Mullah Mustafa Barzani, began an insurgency that has continued until today, although interrupted by periods of autonomy negotiations with Baghdad. The PUK split off from the KDP in the 1960s. Together, the PUK and KDP have about 35,000 fighters. A small Kurdish Islamic faction, the

---

[3] Sciolino, Elaine. "Greater U.S. Effort Backed To Oust Iraqi." *New York Times,* June 2, 1992.

[4] The Iraqi National Congress and the International Community. Document provided by INC representatives, February 1993.

Islamic Movement of Iraqi Kurdistan (IMIK), is headed by Shaykh Ali Abd-al Aziz. Based in Halabja, Iraq, the IMIK has been publicizing the effects of Baghdad's March 1988 chemical attack on that city.

Several outside experts have concerns about the alliance between Iran and another INC component, the Iraqi Shiite Islamic fundamentalist group called the Supreme Council for the Islamic Revolution in Iraq (SCIRI). SCIRI was set up in 1982 to increase Iranian control over Shiite opposition groups in Iraq and the Persian Gulf states. Its leader, Ayatollah Muhammad Baqr al-Hakim, was the late Ayatollah Khomeini's choice to head an Islamic Republic of Iraq. It has as many as 5,000 fighters organized into a "Badr Corps" (named after a major battle in early Islam) that conducts forays from Iran into southern Iraq to attack the Iraqi military and officials there. Although Iran has improved relations with Iraq over the past few years, Iran's Revolutionary Guard - which is politically aligned with Iran's hard line civilian officials - reportedly continues to provide the Badr Corps with weapons and other assistance. However, many Iraqi Shiites view SCIRI as an Iranian creation and SCIRI/Badr Corps operations in southern Iraq have not been known to spark broad popular unrest against the Iraqi regime. SCIRI has periodically distanced itself from the INC and has publicly refused to attend opposition meetings in the United States or accept U.S. assistance.

The Fragmentation of the Opposition

The differences within the INC led to its near collapse in the mid 1990s. In May 1994, the KDP and the PUK began clashing with each other over territory, customs revenues levied at border with Turkey, and control over the Kurdish enclave's government based in Irbil. The PUK lined up support from Iran while the KDP sought and received countervailing backing from its erstwhile nemeses, the Baghdad government. The infighting contributed to the defeat of an INC offensive against Iraqi troops in March 1995; the KDP pulled out of the offensive at the last minute. Although it was repelled, the offensive did initially overrun some of the less well-trained and poorly motivated Iraqi units on the front lines facing the Kurds. Some INC leaders have pointed to the battle as an indication that the INC could succeed militarily in the future if it were given additional resources and training.

The infighting in the INC caused the United States to briefly revisit the "coup strategy" by renewing ties to a separate group, Iraq National Accord (INA).[5] The INA consisted of military and security defectors who were perceived as having ties to disgruntled officials currently serving within their former organizations. The INA's prospects appeared to brighten in August 1995 when Saddam's son-in-law Husayn Kamil al-Majid — architect of Iraq's weapons of mass destruction programs — defected to Jordan, suggesting that Saddam's grip on the military and security services was weakening. Jordan's King Hussein agreed to allow the INA to operate from there. However, the INA became penetrated by Iraq's intelligence services and, in June 1996, Baghdad dealt it a serious setback by arresting or executing over 100 INA sympathizers in the military. Its leader, Dr. Iyad Alawi, claims that the INA continues to operate throughout Iraq, and it apparently has rebuilt itself to some extent since the June 1996 arrests.

[5] An account of this shift in U.S. strategy is essayed in Hoagland, Jim. "How CIA's Secret War On Saddam Collapsed." *Washington Post*, June 26, 1997.

Iraq's counteroffensive against the opposition was completed two months later. In late August 1996, the KDP asked Baghdad to provide armed support for its capture of Irbil from the rival PUK. Iraq took advantage of the request to strike against the INC base in Salahuddin, northern Iraq, as well as against remaining INA operatives throughout northern Iraq. In the course of its incursion in the north, Iraq reportedly executed two hundred oppositionists and arrested as many as 2,000 others. The United States evacuated from northern Iraq and eventually resettled in the United States 650 oppositionists, mostly from the INC.

REBUILDING AN OPPOSITION STRATEGY

For the two years following the opposition's 1996 setbacks, the Clinton Administration had little contact with the opposition. In those two years, the INC, INA, and other opposition groups attempted to rebuild their organizations and their ties to each other, although with mixed success. On February 26, 1998, then Secretary of State Madeleine Albright testified to a Senate Appropriations subcommittee that it would be "wrong to create false or unsustainable expectations" about what U.S. support for the opposition could accomplish. However, Iraq's obstructions of U.N. weapons of mass destruction (WMD) inspections during 1997-98 led to growing congressional calls for overthrowing Saddam Husayn, and contributed to the Clinton Administration's open declaration in November 1998 that it is U.S. policy to change Iraq's regime.

A congressional push for a regime change policy began with a FY1998 supplemental appropriation (P.L. 105-174, signed May 1, 1998) that, among other provisions, earmarked $5 million in Economic Support Funds (ESF) for the opposition and $5 million for a Radio Free Iraq, under the direction of Radio Free Europe/Radio Liberty (RFE/RL). The radio service began broadcasting in October 1998, from Prague. Of the ESF, $3 million was devoted to an overt program to coordinate and promote cohesion among the various opposition factions, and to highlighting Iraqi violations of U.N. resolutions. The remaining $2 million was used to publicize evidence of alleged Iraqi war crimes, retrieved from the Kurdish north, and subsequently placed on 176 CD-ROM diskettes.

Reflecting congressional views that the overt coordination program did little to challenge Iraq's regime, a provision of the FY1999 omnibus appropriation (Section 590 of H.R. 4328, P.L. 105-277, signed October 21, 1998), earmarked $8 million in ESF to the opposition, with the stipulation that at least $3 million in ESF be given directly to the INC and at least another $2 million be used for opposition activities inside Iraq itself. The provision also appeared to indicate that many in Congress believed that the INC was the most effective vehicle to implement the regime change policy. The remaining $3 million went to the opposition-led INDICT (International Campaign to Indict Iraqi War Criminals) organization for publicizing Iraqi war crimes issues. The $2 million for use inside Iraq was spent on humanitarian projects mainly in the Kurdish north, according to the State Department. Another $ 10 million in ESF for the opposition was provided by the FY2000 foreign aid law (passed by reference in P.L. 106-113, signed November 29, 1999). Of that amount, $2 million was earmarked for war crimes issues.

Iraq Liberation Act (ILA)

The clearest indication of congressional support for a more robust U.S. overthrow effort was encapsulated in another bill introduced in 1998 - the Iraq Liberation Act *(ILA,* H.R. 4655, P.L. 105-338, signed into law October 31, 1998). The ILA gave the President authority to provide up to $97 million in defense articles (and $2 million in broadcasting funds) to opposition organizations to be designated by the Administration. The Act's passage was widely interpreted as an expression of congressional support for the concept, advocated by INC chairman Ahmad Chalabi and some U.S. policy experts, to promote an insurgency by using U.S. airpower to protect opposition-controlled enclaves. President Clinton signed the legislation despite reported widespread doubts within the Clinton Administration about the chances of success in promoting an insurgency inside Iraq. In January 1999, career diplomat Frank Ricciardone was named as the State Department's "Coordinator for the Transition in Iraq," - the chief liaison with the opposition. On February 5, 1999, after consultations with Congress, the President issued a determination (P.D. 99-13) that the following organizations would be eligible to receive U.S. military assistance under the Iraq Liberation Act: the INC; the INA; the Islamic Movement of Iraqi Kurdistan (MIK); the KDP; the PUK; the Movement for Constitutional Monarchy (MCM); and SCIRI. The IMIK and the MCM, in particular, are considered small movements that cannot contribute much to an overthrow effort.

In May 1999, in concert with an INC visit to Washington, the Clinton Administration announced it would draw down $5 million worth of training and "non-lethal" defense equipment under the ILA. In late 1999, three opposition members began civil administration training at Hurlburt air base in Florida and, in June 2000, the Clinton Administration announced that another 145 oppositionists would undergo similar training. The Defense Department-run courses provide civil affairs training, including instruction in field medicine, logistics, computers, communications, broadcasting, power generation, and war crimes issues. However, the Clinton Administration asserted that the opposition was not sufficiently organized to merit U.S. provision of lethal military equipment or combat training. These limitations reflected divisions within and outside the Clinton Administration over the effectiveness and viability of the opposition, and over the potential for the United States to become militarily embroiled in civil conflict in Iraq.

CONTINUED DEBATE OVER POLICY

U.S. efforts after 1999 to rebuild and train the opposition did not end the debate within the Clinton Administration over this component of Iraq policy. In hearings and statements, several Members of both parties expressed disappointment with the Clinton Administration's decision not to give the opposition lethal military aid or combat training. Many took those decisions as an indication that the Clinton Administration was skeptical of the overthrow strategy in light of past failures to oust Saddam Husayn. Others believed the Clinton Administration erred in publicly declaring a policy of overthrow, on the grounds that a public declaration raised expectations of U.S. action to achieve that objective. Opponents of the overthrow policy maintained that nothing short of substantial direct U.S. military involvement would guarantee an opposition victory, and that such involvement was risky and not justified by the threat posed by Iraq. Other critics suggested the United States focus instead on rebuilding an international coalition to contain Iraq, in part by achieving reentry into Iraq of the U.N. weapons of mass destruction inspectors that had been absent from Iraq since December 15, 1998.

As a reflection of continued congressional support for the overthrow effort, a provision of the FY2001 foreign aid appropriation (H.R. 4811, P.L. 106-429, signed November 6, 2000) earmarked $25 million in ESF for "programs benefiting the Iraqi people," of which at least: $ 12 million was for the INC to distribute humanitarian aid inside Iraq; $6 million was for INC broadcasting; and $2 million was for war crimes issues. According to the appropriation the remaining $5 million could be used to aid the seven groups eligible to receive assistance under the ILA. Taking note of congressional sentiment for INC distribution of aid inside Iraq, on September 29, 2000 the Clinton Administration reached agreement with the INC to provide the organization with $4 million in FY1999 ESF (one half the total earmark available) to develop an aid distribution plan and to gather information in Iraq on Iraqi war crimes. Three days before it left office, the Clinton Administration issued a required report to Congress that noted that any INC effort to distribute aid in areas of Iraq under Baghdad's control would be fraught with security risks to the INC, to Iraqi recipients of such aid, and to any relief distributors with which the INC contracts.[6] On February 2, 2001, the Bush Administration confirmed that, shortly after President Bush took office, the Treasury Department's Office of Foreign Assets Control (OFAC) granted the INC a license to proceed with the information gathering portion of the humanitarian aid distribution plan.

BUSH ADMINISTRATION POLICY

Bush Administration policy toward Iraq appears to have changed after the September 11 terrorist attacks, even though no hard evidence has come to light linking Iraq to those attacks. The shift toward a more assertive policy became clear in President Bush's State of the Union message on January 29, 2002, when he characterized Iraq as part of an "axis of evil," along with Iran and North Korea.

Pre-September 11 Policy

Throughout most of its first year, the Bush Administration continued most elements of Clinton Administration policy. With no clear consensus within the new Administration on how forcefully to proceed with an overthrow strategy, Secretary of State Powell focused on strengthening containment of Iraq, which the Bush Administration said had eroded substantially in the year prior to its taking office. Secretary Powell visited the Middle East in February 2001 to enlist regional support for a modification of the U.N. sanctions regime to ensure that no weapons-related technology reaches Iraq. His plan offered to alter the U.N.-sponsored "oil-for-food" program by relaxing U.N. restrictions on exports to Iraq of civilian equipment and needed non-military technology.[7] The United States asserted that this step would alleviate the suffering of the Iraqi people. Powell, who has sometimes openly

[6] U.S. Department of State. *Washington File.* Clinton Sends Report on Iraq to Congress. January 17, 2001.

[7] For more information on this program, see CRS Report RL30472, *Iraq: Oil For Food Program,* July 10, 2001, by Kenneth Katzman.

expressed skepticism about the opposition's prospects, barely raised the regime change issue during his trip or in his March 7, 2001 testimony before the House International Relations Committee, at which he was questioned about Iraq.[8]

Even though several senior officials had been strong advocates of an overthrow policy, many of the questions about the wisdom and difficulty of that strategy that had faced previous administrations were debated in the Bush Administration.[9] Aside from restating the U.S. policy of regime change, the Bush Administration said little about the regime change strategy throughout most of its first year. During his confirmation hearings as Deputy Secretary of Defense, a reported strong advocate of overthrow, Paul Wolfowitz, said that if there were a real option to overthrow Saddam Husayn, "I would think it was worthwhile," although he also stated that he did not yet see a "plausible plan" for changing the regime. Like its predecessor, the Bush Administration declined to provide the opposition with lethal aid, combat training, or a commitment of direct U.S. military help. It eliminated the separate State Department position of "Coordinator for the Transition in Iraq," further casting doubt on its enthusiasm for the overthrow strategy. The Bush Administration also refused to back the INC plan to rebuild its presence inside Iraq by distributing humanitarian aid. However, these possibilities were left open pending the outcome of a policy review.

Possibly signaling skepticism about the value of the INC in an overthrow plan, there were some indications that the Bush Administration began to build ties to opposition elements other than the INC, such as ex-military officers or ex-Ba'th Party officials. In March 2001, a senior official seemed to suggest to journalists that covert options were under consideration, saying that, "The INC has a role to play, but there may be other things we want to do."[10] Some viewed the outreach to non-INC figures as a signal that the Bush Administration might be considering returning to the "coup strategy" pursued on several occasions in previous administrations.

Many in Congress, on the other hand, continued to support the INC as a viable and immediately available vehicle for achieving regime change. Partly in deference to congressional sentiment, according to several observers, the Bush Administration continued to expand its ties to the INC. In August 2001, the INC began satellite television broadcasts into Iraq, from London, called Liberty TV. The station was funded by the ESF aid appropriated by Congress, with start-up costs of $1 million and an estimated additional $2.7 million per year in operating costs.[11]

Policy Post-September 11

Bush Administration policy toward Iraq became notably more assertive after September 11. Almost immediately after the U.S.-led war on the Taliban and Al Qaeda in Afghanistan began in early October 2001, speculation began building that the Administration might try to change Iraq's regime through direct use of military force as part of a "phase two" of the war on terrorism. Some in the Administration are said to believe that Iraq might have had a

[8] Perlez, Jane. Powell Goes on the Road and Scores Some Points. *New York Times*, March 2, 2001.

[9] One account of Bush Administration internal debates on the strategy is found in, Hersh, Seymour. The Debate Within. *The New Yorker*, March 11, 2002.

[10] Sipress, Alan. Powell Defends Stand on Iraq. *Washington Post*, March 8, 2001.

[11] Sipress, Alan. U.S. Funds Satellite TV to Iraq. *Washington Post*, August 16, 2001

connection to the September 11 attacks or the subsequent anthrax mailings, although many press reports have downplayed such connections. Those who see a direct Iraqi connection tend to attach significance to official Czech accounts of a purported April 2001 meeting in Prague between September 11 hijacking leader Mohammad Atta and an Iraqi intelligence officer. Others point to a recent report that an Islamic group linked to Al Qaeda and which is operating in Northern Iraq, has links to the Iraqi government.[12] On the other hand, Baghdad does not control Northern Iraq and some U.S. officials, speaking on background, have said they cannot verify this report.[13]

Other U.S. officials reportedly maintain that Iraq's purported commitment to developing WMD - coupled with its support for terrorist groups to which Iraq might transfer WMD - constitute an unacceptable potential threat to the United States and that major U.S. military action could be justified. This view was represented in President Bush's January 29, 2002 State of the Union message, in which he named Iraq, along with North Korea and Iran, as part of an "axis of evil" against which, according to the President, the United States might act preemptively. In the aftermath of the speech, senior Administration officials said that the President's characterization was meant to identify the perceived threat, but did not necessarily imply that military action against any of the three states, including Iraq, was imminent.

In conjunction with the presidential and other statements on Iraq, press reports in early 2002, often quoting Administration sources, discussed numerous scenarios and purported U.S. planning to achieve a change of Iraq's regime. Several of the reports indicated that some in the Administration believe that successful U.S. military operations that brought down the Taliban in Afghanistan could easily be replicated in Iraq to depose Saddam Husayn.[14] Other U.S. defense officials were said to believe that the overthrow of Saddam Husayn by the U.S. military, while achievable, would require a robust U.S. military effort. Those who subscribe to this view believe that the Iraqi opposition is too weak to fully capitalize on a military campaign by U.S. airstrikes and special operations forces alone, particularly against an Iraqi military that is much larger than was that of the Taliban, and that direct U.S. ground combat would be required. Some defense experts speculated that a force of 200,000 or more U.S. troops would be needed to ensure success, although others feel that a smaller force could accomplish that mission, and with relatively few U.S. casualties.[15] A major issue in the debate over this scenario appears to be over whether Iraq's military would quickly unravel or rebel against Saddam Husayn in the face of U.S. military action, or whether it would fight hard to defend the regime.

The reports of Administration planning for military confrontation with Iraq prompted both support and criticism from outside experts. Several of the critics cite statements from several Arab leaders that a military attack on Iraq, in the absence of a clear Iraqi provocation, would lack regional support, and that a U.S. military move against Iraq could destabilize the region further in the context of ongoing Israeli-Palestinian violence. Several Arab leaders made public comments along these lines to Vice President Cheney during his March 2002 visit to the region, although aides to the Vice President told journalists that the Arab leaders were more supportive of the United States in private. Some experts say that Arab leaders

[12] Goldberg, Jeffrey. The Great Terror. The *New Yorker,* March 25, 2002.
[13] U.S. Uncertain About Northern Iraq Group's Link to Al Qaida. Dow Jones Newswire, March 18, 2002.
[14] Slavin, Barbara. U.S. Examining Options to Deal With Hussein. *USA Today,* February 12, 2002.
[15] Scarborough, Rowan. Military 'Leaning Forward' To Gird For War in Iraq. *Washington Times,* March 18, 2002.

would at least tacitly back a U.S. military effort to overthrow Saddam if the United States assures them it would complete that mission.

Some analysis suggested that the United States might be far from any decision to use military force to change Iraq's regime or reduce its WMD capabilities. Indicating that it was taking into account allied calls for diplomatic efforts to restart weapons inspections, the Administration publicly supported a March 7, 2002 meeting between Iraq and the U.K. Secretary-General to discuss the re-entry of U.N. weapons inspection teams to Iraq. Most experts believe negotiations on new inspections will likely be prolonged, and that these talks could push the horizon for any U.S. military action against Iraq well into the future. Others believe the Administration is likely at least informally, to set a deadline for Iraq's readmission of the inspectors.

Several press reports and Administration statements suggested that a U.S. confrontation of Iraq might not involve overt military action, but might be conducted covertly. Some believe the United States might pursue covert overthrow options prior to and independent of any decision to use military force against Iraq. A few press reports said that, in recent weeks, the Administration has stepped up planning for covert action to destabilize Iraq's regime.[16]

The INC appears to be a major factor in the purported U.S. planning efforts but it is also apparent that the Administration does not want to rely solely on promoting an INC-led insurgency. According to observers, the Administration believes the INC is making little progress in developing itself into a force that could challenge Iraq's regime, although others believe it could gain strength quickly if it were given a firm U.S. commitment and some lethal assistance.[17]

Increasing U.S. outreach to Iraqi former military officers suggests that the Administration might want to return to the strategy of promoting a coup d'etat, rather than an opposition insurgency, or perhaps that it is considering the pursuit of both plans simultaneously.[18] One press report said that the CIA had developed a plan, approved by President Bush, to arm the INC-related forces while also working to encourage defections within the Iraqi military.[19] On February 28, 2002, the State Department said it was discussing the possibility of a conference of former Iraqi military officers - a conference that might include but would not be limited to the INC - as part of a process of broadening the opposition coalition against Iraq.[20] Some observers say that the Administration is considering designated groups, notably on ex-military officers and tribes close to the regime, as eligible to receive assistance under the Iraq Liberation Act. At the same time, another report said that the Administration would finance the building of a broadcasting facility - either in northern Iraq or in Iran - run by the INC, as part of a stepped up program to undermine Iraq's regime.[21] In early 2001, the Bush Administration had granted the INC a license to open an office in Iran, a license made necessary by U.S. sanctions against Iran that ban any U.S. aid to that country.

Although the INC appears to continue to be a significant factor in Administration planning, there are signs of strain between the opposition group and Administration officials. In recent press interviews, Ahmad Chalabi has openly criticized the Administration for

---

[16] Scarborough, Rowan. White House Wants Saddam Out of Power by 2005. *Washington Times,* February 22, 2002.
[17] Gordon, Michael. Iraqis Seek to Oust Hussein With U.S. Military Training. *New York Times,* February 1, 2002.
[18] Nasrawi, Salah. Military Exiles Are Courted For Iraq Coup. *Washington Times,* March 13, 2002.
[19] Slavin, Barbara. U.S. Stirs Efforts to Oust Saddam. *USA Today,* February 28, 2002.
[20] Excerpt: U.S, Iraqi Opposition Discuss Broad Based Conference. *Washington File,* February 28, 2002.
[21] Gordon, Michael. Radio Transmitter to Oppose Hussein Wins U.S. Support. *New York Times,* February 28, 2002.

refusing to give the organization the lethal aid it wants, and he has expressed mistrust of the CIA. In September 2001, the State Department's Office of Inspector General issued an audit of the group's use of U.S. funds and found several examples of misuse, including expenditures for health club memberships, artwork, and household appliances.[22] As a result of the audit, the State Department temporarily suspended ESF grants to the INC, although funding resumed in late January 2002 on the grounds that the INC was taking steps to address the deficiencies noted in the audit.

Congressional Reactions

Congress, like the Administration, appears to have divergent views on the mechanisms for promoting regime change. Some Members have, at times, urged a more assertive U.S. regime change effort than that reportedly being considered within the Administration. On December 20, 2001, the House passed H.J.Res. 75, by a vote of 392-12, calling Iraq's refusal to readmit U.N. weapons inspectors a "mounting threat" to the United States. The resolution did not call for new U.S. steps to overthrow Saddam Husayn but a few Members, including Representative Benjamin Oilman and Representative Dana Rohrabacher, called for the overthrow of Saddam Husayn in their floor statements in support of the resolution. In a joint appearance with Senate Foreign Relations Committee Chairman Joseph Biden on Cable News Network on February 17, 2002, House International Relations Committee Chairman Henry Hyde said that "...supporting the underground, the opposition, the internal opposition, is to me the procedure of choice. That is an option that is being worked on. All of these options are under consideration."

Several Members have spoken strongly in favor of the INC and urged direct U.S. funding for that organization. In early December 2001, a bipartisan group of nine Members - Senators John McCain, Jesse Helms, Richard Shelby, Sam Brownback, Joseph Lieberman, and Trent Lott and Representatives Henry Hyde, Benjamin Oilman, and Harold Ford Jr. - wrote to President Bush to urge that U.S. assistance be provided to the INC for operations inside Iraq itself. According to the letter,

> Despite the express wishes of the Congress, the INC has been denied U.S. assistance for any operations inside any part of Iraq, including liberated Kurdish areas. Instead, successive Administrations have funded conferences, offices and other intellectual exercises that have done little more than expose the INC to accusations of being "limousine insurgents" and "armchair guerrillas."

Some Members have expressed concerns about the costs and risks of an all-out U.S. effort to achieve that result. On the CNN appearance noted above, Senator Biden said "...there is not a single, informed person I have ever spoken to, for or against moving into Iraq, that thinks you can move into Iraq now, take down Saddam Husayn, and have any real prospect that there will be a unified, central government that is able to maintain control of the Kurds in the north and the Shi'as in the south and the Sunnis in the middle, et cetera."

---

[22] Department of State. Office of Inspector General. Review of Awards to Iraqi National Congress Support Foundation. Report Number OI-FMA-R-092. September 2001.

Others have questioned the past U.S. reliance on the INC for its regime change strategy. In consideration of assistance to the opposition for FY2002, despite the support for the INC expressed by the nine Members in their letter to President Bush,

Congress criticized the INC. The criticism signaled doubts among many in Congress about the organization's viability and its role in me U.S. overthrow effort, and appears to have contributed to the decision by the Bush Administration to broaden its opposition contacts beyond the INC. The conference report on the FY2002 foreign aid appropriation (H.R. 2506/P.L. 107-115, H.Rept. 107-345) accepted Senate language referring to the critical State Department audit of the INC mentioned above, stating:

> [Conference] Managers are troubled by the recent audit by the State Department Inspector General on the use of prior year funds appropriated for this program. The managers also note that this section does not impose restrictions on which groups may receive those funds or on the use of funds for activities inside Iraq. As part of the consultation process regarding the use of these funds, the managers expect the Department to identify options for the transfer of funding to more appropriate sources.

Appendix. U.S. Assistance to the Opposition (Appropriated Economic Support Funds, E.S.F.)

(Figures in Millions of Dollars)

	INC	**War Crimes**	**Broadcasting**	**Unspecified Opposition Activities**	**Total**
FY1998 (P.L. 105-174)		2.0	5.0 (RFE/RL)	3.0	10.0
FY1999 (P.L. 105-277)	3.0	3.0		2.0	8.0
FY 2000 (P.L. 106-113)		2.0		8.0	10.0
FY 2001 (P.L. 106-429)	12.0 (aid distribution inside Iraq)	2.0	6.0 (INC radio)	5.0	25.0
FY2002 (P.L. 107-115)				25.0	25.0
Total (FY1998-FY2002)	15.0	9.0	11.0	43.0	78.0
FY2003 (request)				25.0	25.0

PART 2: HISTORICAL BACKGROUND

Chapter 10

IRAQ: A COUNTRY STUDY

Helen Chapin Metz

GEOGRAPHY

Size

Area of Iraq variously cited as between 433,970 (excluding Iraqi half of Iraq-Saudi Arabia Neutral Zone shared with Saudi Arabia, consisting of 3,522 square kilometers) and 437,393 square kilometers.

Topography

Country divided into four major regions: desert in west and southwest; rolling upland between upper Euphrates and Tigris rivers; highlands in north and northeast; and alluvial plain in central and southeast sections.

SOCIETY

Population

Preliminary 1987 census figures give total of 16,278,000, a 35 percent increase over 1977. Annual rate of growth 3.1 percent; about 57 percent of population in 1987 under twenty.

Religious and Ethnic Divisions

At least 95 percent of population adheres to some form of Islam. Government gives number of Shias (see Glossary) as 55 percent but probably 60 to 65 percent is reasonable figure. Most Iraqi Shias are Arabs. Almost all Kurds, approximately 19 percent of population, are Sunnis (see Glossary), together with about 13 percent Sunni Arabs. Total Arab population in 1987 given by government as 76 percent. Remainder of population small numbers of Turkomans, mostly Sunni Muslims; Assyrians and Armenians, predominantly Christians; Yazidis, of Kurdish stock with a syncretistic faith; and a few Jews.

Languages

Arabic official language and mother tongue of about 76 percent of population; understood by majority of others. Kurdish official language in As Sulaymaniyah, Dahuk, and Irbil governorates. Minorities speaking Turkic, Armenian, and Persian.

Education

Rapidly growing enrollment in tuition-free public schools. Six years of primary (elementary), three years of intermediate secondary, and three years of intermediate preparatory education. Six major universities, forty-four teacher training schools and institutes, and three colleges and technical institutes, all government owned and operated. Dramatic increases since 1977 in numbers of students in technical fields (300 percent rise) and numbers of female primary students (45 percent rise). Literacy variously estimated at about 40 percent by foreign observers and 70 percent by government. Academic year 1985-86: number of students in primary schools 2,812,516; secondary schools (general) 1,031,560; vocational schools 120,090; teacher training schools and institutions 34,187; universities, colleges, and technical institutes 53,037.

Health

High incidence of trachoma, influenza, measles, whooping cough, and tuberculosis. Considerable progress has been made in control of malaria. Continuing shortage of modern trained medical and paramedical personnel, especially in rural areas and probably in northern Kurdish areas.

INTRODUCTION

In the late 1980s, Iraq became a central actor in Middle Eastern affairs and a force to reckon with in the wider international community. Iraq's growing role resulted from the way in which it was adapting the principles of Baath (Arab Socialist Resurrection) Party socialism to meet the country's needs and from its somewhat unexpected success in compelling Iran in August 1988 to request a cease-fire in the eight-year-old Iran-Iraq War.

Iraq's reassertion in the 1980s of its role in the region and in the world community evoked its ancient history. At one time Mesopotamia ("the land between the rivers"), which encompassed much of present-day Iraq, formed the center not only of the Middle East but also of the civilized world. The people of the Tigris and Euphrates basin, the ancient

Sumerians, using the fertile land and the abundant water supply of the area, developed sophisticated irrigation systems and created what was probably the first cereal agriculture as well as the earliest writing, cuneiform. Their successors, the Akkadians, devised the most complete legal system of the period, the Code of Hammurabi. Located at a crossroads in the heart of the ancient Middle East, Mesopotamia was a plum sought by numerous foreign conquerors. Among them were the warlike Assyrians, from the tenth century through the seventh century B.C., and the Chaldeans, who in the sixth century B.C. created the Hanging Gardens of Babylon, one of the Seven Wonders of the Ancient World.

In 539 B.C., Semitic rule of the area ended with the conquest of Babylon by Cyrus the Great. The successors of Cyrus paid little attention to Mesopotamia, with the result that the infrastructure was allowed to fall into disrepair. Not until the Arab conquest and the coming of Islam did Mesopotamia begin to regain its glory, particularly when Baghdad was the seat of the Abbasid caliphate between 750 and 1258.

Iraq experienced various other foreign rulers, including the Mongols, the Ottoman Turks, and the British under a mandate established after World War I. The British placed Faisal, a Hashimite claiming descent from the Prophet Muhammad, on the throne in 1921. Popular discontent with the monarchy, which was regarded as a Western imposition, led in 1958 to a military revolution that overthrew the king.

Ultimately, the military regime installed a government ruled by the Baath's Revolutionary Command Council (RCC) and created the Provisional Constitution of July 16, 1970, that institutionalized the RCC's role. Within the Baath, power lay primarily in the hands of Baathists from the town of Tikrit, the birthplace of Saddam Husayn, who played an increasingly prominent role in the government in the 1970s. (Tikrit was also the hometown of his predecessor, Ahmad Hasan al Bakr, who formally resigned the leadership in 1979).

The Baathist government in 1970 granted the Kurdish minority a degree of autonomy, but not the complete self-rule the Kurds desired, in the predominantly Kurdish regions of Dahuk, Irbil, and As Sulaymaniyah. In the early 1970s, Iraqi casualties from the renewed warfare with the Kurds were such as to induce Saddam Husayn to sign an agreement with the shah of Iran in Algiers in March 1975 recognizing the thalweg, or the midpoint of the Shatt al Arab, as the boundary between the two countries. The agreement ended the shah's aid to the Kurds, thus eventually quelling the rebellion.

Saddam Husayn then turned his attention to domestic matters, particularly to the economy and to an industrial modernization program. He had notable success in distributing land, in improving the standard of living, and in increasing health and educational opportunities. Rural society was transformed as a result of large rural-to-urban migration and the decline of rural handicraft industries. Urban society witnessed the rise, particularly in the late 1970s and the 1980s, of a class of Baathist technocrats. In addition, the Shia (see Glossary) Muslims, who, although they constituted a majority, had been largely unrepresented in significant areas of Iraqi society, in which the minority Sunni (see Glossary) Muslims were the governing element, were integrated to a considerable degree into the government, into business, and into the professions.

Buoyed by domestic success, Saddam Husayn shifted his concentration to foreign affairs. Beginning in the late 1970s, Iraq sought to assume a more prominent regional role and to replace Egypt, which had been discredited from its position of Arab leadership because of signing the Camp David Accords in 1978. Iraq, therefore, gradually modified its somewhat hostile stance toward Saudi Arabia and the Persian Gulf states, seeking to win their support.

Relations with the Soviet Union, Iraq's major source of weapons, cooled, however, following the Soviet invasion and occupation of Afghanistan that began in December 1979. In contrast, Iraqi ties with France improved considerably, and France became Iraq's second most important arms supplier.

The overthrow of the monarchy in Iran and the coming to power in 1979 of Ayatollah Sayyid Ruhollah Musavi Khomeini--whom Saddam Husayn had expelled from Iraq in 1978, reportedly at the shah's request--revived the historic hostility between the two countries. Saddam Husayn feared the impact on Iraqi Shias of Khomeini's Islamic fundamentalism and resented Iran's attempted hegemony in the Persian Gulf region. Believing Iran's military forces to be unprepared as a result of the revolutionary purges, in September 1980, following a number of border skirmishes, Iraq invaded Iranian territory. Thus began a bitter, costly, eight- year-long war in which the strength and the revolutionary zeal of Iran were clearly demonstrated.

From late 1980 to 1988, the war took precedence over other matters. The Baath high command succeeded in controlling Iraq's military institution to a degree that surprised foreign observers. One of the major instruments for accomplishing this control was the People's Army, which served as the Baath Party's militia.

The Baath could do little, however, to counter Iran's superiority in manpower and materiel. At times when Iraq considered its situation particularly desperate--for example, when Iranian forces appeared to be gaining control of substantial areas of Iraqi territory, such as Al Faw Peninsula in the south and the northern mountainous Kurdish area--Iraq unleashed a barrage of missiles against Iranian cities. Further, reliable reports indicated that Iraq used chemical warfare against the enemy, possibly in the hope of bringing Iran to the negotiating table.

To prevent domestic unrest as a result of the war, Saddam Husayn adopted a "guns and butter" economic policy, bringing in foreign laborers to replace those called to military service and striving to keep casualties low. After drawing down its own reserves, Iraq needed the financial support of its Gulf neighbors. Of the latter, Kuwait, Qatar, Saudi Arabia, and the United Arab Emirates all provided Iraq with loans to help it prosecute the war. Relations with Egypt also improved significantly after the war's outbreak. Meanwhile Iraqi hostility toward Syria, its fellow Baathist government but traditional rival, increased as a result of Syria's strong support of Iran.

As part of his wartime economic policies, Saddam Husayn in 1987 returned agricultural collectives to the private sector, and in 1988 he took measures to privatize more than forty state-run factories because of the inefficiency and unprofitability of agriculture and industry when under state control. These privatizing steps reflected a desire for greater economic efficiency rather than a change in economic ideology. Government controls on the economy were decreased by cutting subsidies, by allowing partial foreign ownership, and by reducing bureaucratic regulation of enterprises, thus reducing labor costs.

Despite the introduction of more liberal economic policies in Iraq in the late 1980s, few indications suggested that the political system was becoming less rigid to any significant degree. Ultimate decisions in both the economic and the political realms apparently remained in the hands of Saddam Husayn rather than in those of the constitutionally designated RCC. According to a statement by Saddam Husayn to the Permanent Bureau of the Arab Jurists' Federation in Baghdad in November 1988, the Baath two years previously had approved steps toward democratization, but these had been delayed by the Iran-Iraq War. The measures included having a minimum of two candidates for each elective post, allowing non-Baathists to run for political office, and permitting the establishment of other political parties. In January 1989, following an RCC meeting chaired by Saddam Husayn, the formation of a special committee to draft a new constitution was reported; according to unconfirmed reports in November, the new constitution will abolish the RCC. Elections for the National Assembly were also announced, and this body was authorized to investigate government ministries and departments. The elections took place in early April and featured almost 1,000 candidates (among them 62 women, although none was elected) for the 250 seats; only 160 Baath Party members were elected. A number of Baathist candidates also were defeated in the September Kurdish regional assembly elections. The results of both elections indicated a gradual downgrading of the prominence of the Baath. The RCC, moreover, directed the minister of information to permit the public to voice complaints about government programs in the government-controlled press; and government officials were ordered to reply to such complaints. The role of Saddam Husayn's family in government affairs was somewhat muted as well. Following the helicopter crash in a sandstorm on May 5 that killed Saddam Husayn's brother-in-law and cousin, Minister of Defense Adnan Khayr Allah Talfah, a technocrat who did not come from Tikrit, replaced Talfah.

The internal security apparatus controlled by the Baath Party continued to keep a particularly close check on potential dissidents: these included Kurds, communists, and members of Shia revival movements. These movements, such as Ad Dawah al Islamiyah (the Islamic Call), commonly referred to as Ad Dawah, sought to propagate fundamentalist Islamic principles and were out of sympathy with Baath socialism. Furthermore, in 1988 in the final stages of the war, both before and after the cease-fire, Iraq was thought to have engaged in chemical warfare against the Kurds. Conceivably the regime saw an opportunity to instill such fear in the Kurds, a significant percentage of whom had cooperated with Iran during the war, that their dissidence would be discouraged. In the spring of 1989 the government announced it would depopulate a border strip thirty kilometers wide along the frontier with Turkey and Iran on the northeast, moving all inhabitants, mainly Kurds, from the area; it began this process in May.

In December 1988, reports surfaced of dissidence within the army, in which Saddam Husayn lacked a power base. The projected annual Army Day celebrations on January 6, 1989, were cancelled and allegedly a number of senior army officers and some civilian Baathists were executed. In February the regime announced that all units of the People's Army would be withdrawn from the front by late March; in July a further announcement disbanded the three-division strong 1st Special Army Corps, formed in June 1986, but apparently some time would elapse before soldiers actually returned to civilian status. Such measures were probably occasioned by the continued success of the cease-fire, initiated in August 1988. The cease-fire held, although a number of border incidents occurred, of which the most serious was the Iranian flooding of a sixty-four-kilometer frontier area northeast of Basra. Informed observers considered the flooding designed to put pressure on Iraq to return a strip of approximately 1,000 square kilometers of Iranian territory on the steppe beyond Baqubah. On October 27, Iran stopped flooding the area, probably as a prelude to a new United Nations (UN) and International Committee of the Red Cross (ICRC) mediation effort.

The peace talks under UN sponsorship, despite a score of face-to-face meetings, had made little progress as of mid- December. A few exchanges of prisoners of war (POWs), largely of those that were ill or wounded, had taken place, but both Iraq and Iran still held large numbers of each other's prisoners. Saddam Husayn, who had agreed on October 5, 1988, to the ICRC plan for prisoner repatriation, in March 1989 proposed in a letter to UN Secretary-General Javier Perez de Cuellar that the UN guarantee the return of the freed POWs to civilian life. Saddam Husayn made his proposal in the hope that this guarantee would reassure Iran, which held approximately 70,000 Iraqi POWs-- whereas Iraq held about half that number of Iranians--that the balance of power would not be disturbed. Iran has refused to exchange prisoners or to implement any of the ten points of UN Security Council Resolution 598 dealing with the dispute until Iraq returns all Iranian territory.

A major source of disagreement in the peace negotiations was Iraq's insistence on sovereignty over the Shatt al Arab, as opposed to the divided ownership created under the 1975 Algiers Agreement. Failing such a settlement, Iraq threatened to divert the waters of the Shatt al Arab above Basra so that it would rejoin the Gulf at Umm Qasr, a port that Iraq had announced it would deepen and widen. Iraq was eager to have Iran allow the UN to begin clearing sunken ships from the Shatt al Arab so as to permit Iraqi access to the sea.

Iraq, meanwhile, had launched a diplomatic campaign to improve its relations with other countries of the region, particularly with Jordan and Egypt. In the last half of 1988, beginning even before he accepted the cease-fire, Saddam Husayn met five times with King Hussein and three times with Egyptian president Husni Mubarak. These high-level meetings included symbolic elements, such as Saddam Husayn's accompanying Hussein on a visit in Baghdad to the graves of Faisal and Ghazi, the Hashimite kings of Iraq, an indication of a considerably more moderate Iraqi Baathist attitude toward monarchy than had been evident in the past. The meetings were designed to bolster political and economic support for Iraq (in December 1988 Iraq concluded a US$800 million trade agreement with Jordan for 1989), as well as to coordinate Arab policy toward the Palestine Liberation Organization and toward Israel, a revision of Iraq's previous rejection of any Arab-Israeli settlement. In addition, Saddam Husayn sought to reassure Saudi Arabia, from which Iraq had received substantial financial support during the Iran-Iraq War, that Iraq had no intention of dominating or of overthrowing the Persian Gulf monarchies.

In its relations with the Western world, Iraq also exhibited greater moderation than it had in the 1970s or early 1980s. For example, the United States Department of State indicated in late March 1989 that Iraq had agreed to pay US$27.3 million compensation to relatives of the thirty-seven American naval personnel killed in the 1987 Iraqi attack on the USS Stark. During the war with Iran, Iraq had borrowed extensively from France, Britain, Italy, and to a lesser extent from the Federal Republic of Germany (West Germany) and Japan. These countries would doubtless play significant roles in Iraq's reconstruction and rearmament; in view of their commercial interest, Iraq has succeeded in having its loan repayments rescheduled. For example, Iraq signed an agreement with France in September 1989 allowing it to repay its indebtedness, due in 1989, over a six- to nine-year period, and completing arrangements for Iraq's purchase of fifty Mirage 2000s.

Since the cease-fire in August 1988, Iraq has undertaken an extensive rearmament program involving foreign arms purchases and the intensified development of its domestic arms industry to generate export income as well as to meet domestic needs. The First Baghdad International Exhibition for Military Production took place from April 28 to May 2, 1989, featuring numerous types of Iraqi arms. Among weapons Iraq produced in 1989 were a T-74 tank, called the Lion of Baghdad, and an Iraqi version of the airborne early warning and control (AWACS) aircraft, developed from the Soviet Ilyushin Il-76. Iraq named the plane the

Adnan-1 after late Minister of Defense Adnan Khayr Allah Talfah. A military development that aroused considerable concern in Israel was Iraq's launching from its Al Anbar space research center in early December of a forty-eight ton, three-stage rocket capable of putting a satellite into space orbit. The minister of industry and military industrialization also announced that Iraq had developed two 2,000-kilometer range surface-to-surface missiles.

Apart from the need to replace lost armaments, the war imposed a heavy reconstruction burden on Iraq. To rebuild the infrastructure and to prevent disaffection among the population of the south who had suffered particularly, the government gave a high priority to the rebuilding of Basra. On June 25, Iraq published the completion of the basic reconstruction of Basra at a cost of approximately US$6 billion, stating that work was then beginning on rebuilding Al Faw, which prior to wartime evacuation had about 50,000 inhabitants. The government has also announced programs to create heavy industry, such as new iron and steel and aluminum works, to build another petrochemical complex, to upgrade fertilizer plants, and to reconstruct the offshore oil export terminals at Khor al Amaya and Mina al Bakr. In June 1989 Iraq reported its readiness to accommodate very large crude oil carriers at a new terminal at Mina al Bakr.

Iraq has taken other economic measures to stimulate oil production and to control inflation. Since the cease-fire, Iraq has pumped nearly its full OPEC quota of 2.8 billion barrels of oil per day. In September 1989, Iraq completed its second crude oil pipeline across Saudi Arabia, with a capacity of 1,650,000 barrels per day, terminating at the Red Sea just south of the Saudi port of Yanbu. These major economic ventures have led to inflation. To counter price rises, the regime has set weekly prices on fruit and vegetables and in late June instituted a price freeze for one year on state-produced goods and services. Concurrently it authorized an additional monthly salary of 25 Iraqi dinars (approximately $US80) for all civil servants and members of the police and military forces.

The negative economic consequences of the war extended beyond the reconstruction of cities and war-damaged infrastructure to include postponed development projects. For example, the massive rural-to-urban migration, particularly in southern Iraq, caused by the war had intensified a process begun before the war and had created an urgent need for housing, educational, and health facilities in urban areas. The war also had serious effects on Iraqi society, exacerbating the strained relations of Iraqi Arabs with the leading minority, the Kurds. The war, however, exerted a positive influence by promoting a greater sense of national unity, by diminishing differences between Shias and Sunnis, and by improving the role of women. The aftermath of the war permitted modification of traditional Baathist socialist doctrines so as to encourage greater privatization of the economy, although the degree to which the government would maintain its reduced interference in the economic sphere remained to be seen.

The end of the war left a number of unknown factors facing the Iraqi economy and society. One was the size of the postwar world petroleum demand and whether Iraq could sell its potential increased output on the international market. An important unanswered social question was whether women who had found employment during the war would return to domestic pursuits and help increase the birthrate as the government hoped. Although women might remain in the work force, presumably, work permits of most foreign workers brought in during the war would be terminated.

An immediate result of the war was an attempt by the government at political liberalization in allowing multiple candidates for elected posts and by offering an amnesty for political, but not for military, offenders. A test of this liberalization will be whether the reforms promised by the end of 1989--the new constitution, legalization of political parties other than the Baath, and freedom of the press-- occur. Measures taken as of mid-December reflected only minimal lessening of the personal control of President Saddam Husayn over the decision- making process in all spheres of the country's life.

The end of the war left many security issues unresolved. Although the regime had disbanded some armed forces units, would Iraq maintain a strong, well-trained army, posing a potential threat to its neighbors and to Israel? Also, what of the Iraqi POWs returning home after several years' indoctrination in POW camps in Iran--could the government of Saddam Husayn rely on their loyalty? Finally, Iraq faced the problem of its traditional Sunni-Shia dichotomy. The war had demonstrated the ability of Iraqi Shias to put nationalist commitment above sectarian differences, but the influence of fundamentalist Shia Islam in the area, represented by the Iranian regime, would continue to threaten that loyalty.

Historical Background

Iraq, a republic since the 1958 coup d'etat that ended the reign of King Faisal II, became a sovereign, independent state in 1932. Although the modern state, the Republic of Iraq, is quite young, the history of the land and its people dates back more than 5,000 years. Indeed, Iraq contains the world's richest known archaeological sites. Here, in ancient Mesopotamia (the land between the rivers), the first civilization--that of Sumer-- appeared in the Near East. Despite the millennium separating the two epochs, Iraqi history displays a continuity shaped by adaptation to the ebbings and flowings of the Tigris and Euphrates rivers (in Arabic, the Dijlis and Furat, respectively). Allowed to flow unchecked, the rivers wrought destruction in terrible floods that inundated whole towns. When the rivers were controlled by irrigation dikes and other waterworks, the land became extremely fertile.

The dual nature of the Tigris and the Euphrates--their potential to be destructive or productive--has resulted in two distinct legacies found throughout Iraqi history. On the one hand, Mesopotamia's plentiful water resources and lush river valleys allowed for the production of surplus food that served as the basis for the civilizing trend begun at Sumer and preserved by rulers such as Hammurabi (1792-1750 B.C.), Cyrus (550-530 B.C.), Darius (520-485 B.C.), Alexander (336-323 B.C.), and the Abbasids (750-1258). The ancient cities of Sumer, Babylon, and Assyria all were located in what is now Iraq. Surplus food production and joint irrigation and flood control efforts facilitated the growth of a powerful and expanding state.

Mesopotamia could also be an extremely threatening environment, however, driving its peoples to seek security from the vicissitudes of nature. Throughout Iraqi history, various groups have formed autonomous, self-contained social units. Allegiance to ancient religious deities at Ur and Eridu, membership in the Shiat Ali (or party of Ali, the small group of followers that supported Ali ibn Abu Talib as rightful leader of the Islamic community in the seventh century), residence in the asnaf (guilds) or the mahallat (city quarters) of Baghdad under the Ottoman Turks, membership in one of a multitude of tribes--such efforts to build autonomous security-providing structures have exerted a powerful centrifugal force on Iraqi culture.

Two other factors that have inhibited political centralization are the absence of stone and Iraq's geographic location as the eastern flank of the Arab world. For much of Iraqi history, the lack of stone has severely hindered the building of roads. As a result, many parts of the country have remained beyond government control. Also, because it borders nonArab Turkey and Iran and because of the great agricultural potential of its river valley, Iraq has attracted waves of ethnically diverse migrations. Although this influx of people has enriched Iraqi culture, it also has disrupted the country's internal balance and has led to deep-seated schisms.

Throughout Iraqi history, the conflict between political fragmentation and centralization has been reflected in the struggles among tribes and cities for the food-producing flatlands of the river valleys. When a central power neglected to keep the waterworks in repair, land fell into disuse, and tribes attacked settled peoples for precious and scarce agricultural commodities. For nearly 600 years, between the collapse of the Abbasid Empire in the thirteenth century and the waning years of the Ottoman era in the late nineteenth century, government authority was tenuous and tribal Iraq was, in effect, autonomous. At the beginning of the twentieth century, Iraq's disconnected, and often antagonistic, ethnic, religious, and tribal social groups professed little or no allegiance to the central government. As a result, the all-consuming concern of contemporary Iraqi history has been the forging of a nation-state out of this diverse and conflict-ridden social structure and the concomitant transformation of parochial loyalties, both tribal and ethnic, into a national identity.

Beginning in the middle of the nineteenth century, the tanzimat reforms (an administrative and legal reorganization of the Ottoman Empire), the emergence of private property, and the tying of Iraq to the world capitalist market severely altered Iraq's social structure. Tribal shaykhs (see Glossary) traditionally had provided both spiritual leadership and tribal security. Land reform and increasing links with the West transformed many shaykhs into profit-seeking landlords, whose tribesmen became impoverished sharecroppers. Moreover, as Western economic penetration increased, the products of Iraq's once-prosperous craftsmen were displaced by machine-made British textiles.

During the twentieth century, as the power of tribal Iraq waned, Baghdad benefited from the rise of a centralized governmental apparatus, a burgeoning bureaucracy, increased educational opportunities, and the growth of the oil industry. The transformation of the urban-tribal balance resulted in a massive rural-to-urban migration. The disruption of existing parochial loyalties and the rise of new class relations based on economics fueled frequent tribal rebellions and urban uprisings during much of the twentieth century.

Iraq's social fabric was in the throes of a destabilizing transition in the first half of the twentieth century. At the same time, because of its foreign roots, the Iraqi political system suffered from a severe legitimacy crisis. Beginning with its League of Nations Mandate in 1920, the British government had laid out the institutional framework for Iraqi government and politics. Britain imposed a Hashimite (also seen as Hashemite) monarchy, defined the territorial limits of Iraq with little correspondence to natural frontiers or traditional tribal and ethnic settlements, and influenced the writing of a constitution and the structure of parliament. The British also supported narrowly based groups--such as the tribal shaykhs--over the growing, urban-based nationalist movement, and resorted to military force when British interests were threatened, as in the 1941 Rashid Ali coup.

Between 1918 and 1958, British policy in Iraq had farreaching effects. The majority of Iraqis were divorced from the political process, and the process itself failed to develop procedures for resolving internal conflicts other than rule by decree and the frequent use of repressive measures. Also, because the formative experiences of Iraq's post-1958 political leadership centered around clandestine opposition activity, decision making and government activity in general have been veiled in secrecy. Furthermore, because the country lacks deeply rooted national political institutions, political power frequently has been monopolized by a small elite, the members of which are often bound by close family or tribal ties.

Between the overthrow of the monarchy in 1958 and the emergence of Saddam Husayn in the mid-1970s, Iraqi history was a chronicle of conspiracies, coups, countercoups, and fierce Kurdish uprisings. Beginning in 1975, however, with the signing of the Algiers Agreement--an agreement between Saddam Husayn and the shah of Iran that effectively ended Iranian military support for the Kurds in Iraq--Saddam Husayn was able to bring Iraq an unprecedented period of stability. He effectively used rising oil revenues to fund large-scale development projects, to increase public sector employment, and significantly to improve education and health care. This tied increasing numbers of Iraqis to the ruling Baath (Arab Socialist Resurrection) Party. As a result, for the first time in contemporary Iraqi history, an Iraqi leader successfully forged a national identity out of Iraq's diverse social structure. Saddam Husayn's achievements and Iraq's general prosperity, however, did not survive long. In September 1980, Iraqi troops crossed the border into Iran, embroiling the country in a costly war.

Ancient Mesopotamia

Sumer, Akkad, Babylon, and Assyria

Contemporary Iraq occupies the territory that historians traditionally have considered the site of the earliest civilizations of the ancient Near East. Geographically, modern Iraq corresponds to the Mesopotamia of the Old Testament and of other, older, Near Eastern texts. In Western mythology and religious tradition, the land of Mesopotamia in the ancient period was a land of lush vegetation, abundant wildlife, and copious if unpredictable water resources. As such, at a very early date it attracted people from neighboring, but less hospitable areas. By 6000 B.C., Mesopotamia had been settled, chiefly by migrants from the Turkish and Iranian highlands.

The civilized life that emerged at Sumer was shaped by two conflicting factors: the unpredictability of the Tigris and Euphrates rivers, which at any time could unleash devastating floods that wiped out entire peoples, and the extreme fecundity of the river valleys, caused by centuries-old deposits of soil. Thus, while the river valleys of southern Mesopotamia attracted migrations of neighboring peoples and made possible, for the first time in history, the growing of surplus food, the volatility of the rivers necessitated a form of collective management to protect the marshy, low-lying land from flooding. As surplus production increased and as collective management became more advanced, a process of urbanization evolved and Sumerian civilization took root.

Sumer is the ancient name for southern Mesopotamia. Historians are divided on when the Sumerians arrived in the area, but they agree that the population of Sumer was a mixture of linguistic and ethnic groups that included the earlier inhabitants of the region. Sumerian culture mixed foreign and local elements. The Sumerians were highly innovative people who responded creatively to the challenges of the changeable Tigris and Euphrates rivers. Many of the great Sumerian legacies, such as writing, irrigation, the wheel, astronomy, and literature, can be seen as adaptive responses to the great rivers.

The Sumerians were the first people known to have devised a scheme of written representation as a means of communication. From the earliest writings, which were pictograms (simplified pictures on clay tablets), the Sumerians gradually created cuneiform--a way of arranging impressions stamped on clay by the wedge-like section of a chopped-off reed. The use of combinations of the same basic wedge shape to stand for phonetic, and possibly for syllabic, elements provided more flexible communication than the pictogram. Through writing, the Sumerians were able to pass on complex agricultural techniques to successive generations; this led to marked improvements in agricultural production.

Another important Sumerian legacy was the recording of literature. The most famous Sumerian epic and the one that has survived in the most nearly complete form is the epic of Gilgamesh. The story of Gilgamesh, who actually was king of the city-state of Uruk in approximately 2700 B.C., is a moving story of the ruler's deep sorrow at the death of his friend and of his consequent search for immortality. Other central themes of the story are a devastating flood and the tenuous nature of man's existence. Laden with complex abstractions and emotional expressions, the epic of Gilgamesh reflects the intellectual sophistication of the Sumerians, and it has served as the prototype for all Near Eastern inundation stories.

The precariousness of existence in southern Mesopotamia also led to a highly developed sense of religion. Cult centers such as Eridu, dating back to 5000 B.C., served as important centers of pilgrimage and devotion even before the rise of Sumer. Many of the most important Mesopotamian cities emerged in areas surrounding the pre-Sumerian cult centers, thus reinforcing the close relationship between religion and government.

The Sumerians were pantheistic; their gods more or less personified local elements and natural forces. In exchange for sacrifice and adherence to an elaborate ritual, the gods of ancient Sumer were to provide the individual with security and prosperity. A powerful priesthood emerged to oversee ritual practices and to intervene with the gods. Sumerian religious beliefs also had important political aspects. Decisions relating to land rentals, agricultural questions, trade, commercial relations, and war were determined by the priesthood, because all property belonged to the gods. The priests ruled from their temples, called ziggurats, which were essentially artificial mountains of sunbaked brick, built with outside staircases that tapered toward a shrine at the top.

Because the well-being of the community depended upon close observation of natural phenomena, scientific or protoscientific activities occupied much of the priests' time. For example, the Sumerians believed that each of the gods was represented by a number. The number sixty, sacred to the god An, was their basic unit of calculation. The minutes of an hour and the notational degrees of a circle were Sumerian concepts. The highly developed agricultural system and the refined irrigation and water-control systems that enabled Sumer to achieve surplus production also led to the growth of large cities. The most important city-states were Uruk, Eridu, Kish, Lagash, Agade, Akshak, Larsa, and Ur (birthplace of the prophet Abraham). The emergence of urban life led to further technological advances. Lacking stone, the Sumerians made marked improvements in brick technology, making possible the construction of very large buildings such as the famous ziggurat of Ur. Sumer also pioneered advances in warfare technology. By the middle of the third millennium B.C., the Sumerians had developed the wheeled chariot. At approximately the same time, the Sumerians discovered that tin and copper when smelted together produced bronze--a new, more durable, and much harder metal. The wheeled chariot and bronze weapons became increasingly important as the Sumerians developed the institution of kingship and as individual city-states began to vie for supremacy.

Historians generally divide Sumerian history into three stages. In the first stage, which extended roughly from 3360 B.C. to 2400 B.C., the most important political development was the emergence of kings who, unlike the first priestly rulers, exercised distinct political rather than religious authority. Another important feature of this period was the emergence of warring Sumerian city-states, which fought for control of the river valleys in lower Mesopotamia. During the second phase, which lasted from 2400 B.C. to 2200 B.C., Sumer was conquered in approximately 2334 B.C. by Sargon I, king of the Semitic city of Akkad.

Sargon was the world's first empire-builder, sending his troops as far as Egypt and Ethiopia. He attempted to establish a unified empire and to end the hostilities among the city-states. Sargon's rule introduced a new level of political organization that was characterized by an even more clear-cut separation between religious authority and secular authority. To ensure his supremacy, Sargon created the first conscripted army, a development related to the need to mobilize large numbers of laborers for irrigation and flood-control works. Akkadian strength was boosted by the invention of the composite bow, a new weapon made of strips of wood and horn.

Despite their military prowess, Akkadian hegemony over southern Mesopotamia lasted only 200 years. Sargon's great- grandson was then overthrown by the Guti, a mountain people from the east. The fall of the Akkadians and the subsequent reemergence of Sumer under the king of Ur, who defeated the Guti, ushered in the third phase of Sumerian history. In this final phase, which was characterized by a synthesis of Sumerian and Akkadian cultures, the king of Ur established hegemony over much of Mesopotamia. Sumerian supremacy, however, was on the wane. By 2000 B.C. the combined attacks of the Amorites, a Semitic people from the west, and the Elamites, a Caucasian people from the east, had destroyed the Third Dynasty of Ur. The invaders nevertheless carried on the Sumero-Akkadian cultural legacy.

The Amorites established cities on the Tigris and the Euphrates rivers and made Babylon, a town to the north, their capital. During the time of their sixth ruler, King Hammurabi (1792-1750 B.C.), Babylonian rule encompassed a huge area covering most of the Tigris-Euphrates river valley from Sumer and the Persian Gulf in the south to Assyria in the north. To rule over such a large area, Hammurabi devised an elaborate administrative structure. His greatest achievement, however, was the issuance of a law code designed "to cause justice to prevail in the country, to destroy the wicked and the evil, that the strong may not oppress the weak." The Code of Hammurabi, not the earliest to appear in the Near East but certainly the most complete, dealt with land tenure, rent, the position of women, marriage, divorce, inheritance, contracts, control of public order, administration of justice, wages, and labor conditions.

In Hammurabi's legal code, the civilizing trend begun at Sumer had evolved to a new level of complexity. The sophisticated legal principles contained in the code reflect a highly advanced civilization in which social interaction extended far beyond the confines of kinship. The large number of laws pertaining to commerce reflect a diversified economic base and an extensive trading network. In politics, Hammurabi's code is evidence of a more pronounced separation between religious and secular authority than had existed in ancient Sumer. In addition to Hammurabi's legal code, the Babylonians made other important contributions, notably to the science of astronomy, and they increased the flexibility of cuneiform by developing the pictogram script so that it stood for a syllable rather than an individual word.

Beginning in approximately 1600 B.C., Indo-European-speaking tribes invaded India; other tribes settled in Iran and in Europe. One of these groups, the Hittites, allied itself with the Kassites, a people of unknown origins. Together, they conquered and destroyed Babylon. Hittite power subsequently waned, but, in the first half of the fourteenth century B.C., the Hittites reemerged, controlling an area that stretched from the Mediterranean Sea to the Persian Gulf. The military success of the Hittites has been attributed to their monopoly in iron production and to their use of the chariot. Nevertheless, in the twelfth century B.C., the Hittites were destroyed, and no great military power occupied Mesopotamia until the ninth century B.C.

One of the cities that flourished in the middle of the Tigris Valley during this period was that of Ashur, named after the sun-god of the Assyrians. The Assyrians were Semitic speakers who occupied Babylon for a brief period in the thirteenth century B.C. Invasions of iron-producing peoples into the Near East and into the Aegean region in approximately 1200 B.C. disrupted the indigenous empires of Mesopotamia, but eventually the Assyrians were able to capitalize on the new alignments of power in the region. Because of what has been called "the barbarous and unspeakable cruelty of the Assyrians," the names of such Assyrian kings as Ashurnasirpal (883-859 B.C.), Tiglath-Pileser III (745- 727 B.C.), Sennacherib (704-681 B.C.), and Ashurbanipal (669-626 B.C.) continue to evoke images of powerful, militarily brilliant, but brutally savage conquerors.

The Assyrians began to expand to the west in the early part of the ninth century B.C.; by 859 they had reached the Mediter- ranean Sea, where they occupied Phoenician cities. Damascus and Babylon fell to the next generations of Assyrian rulers. During the eighth century B.C., the Assyrians' control over their empire appeared tenuous, but Tiglath-Pileser III seized the throne and rapidly subdued Assyria's neighbors, captured Syria, and crowned himself king of Babylon. He developed a highly proficient war machine by creating a permanent standing army under the adminis- tration of a well-organized bureaucracy. Sennacherib built a new capital, Nineveh, on the Tigris River, destroyed Babylon (where citizens had risen in revolt), and made Judah a vassal state.

In 612 B.C., revolts of subject peoples combined with the allied forces of two new kingdoms, those of the Medes and the Chaldeans (Neo-Babylonians), effectively to extinguish Assyrian power. Nineveh was razed. The hatred that the Assyrians inspired, particularly for their policy of wholesale resettlement of subject peoples, was sufficiently great to ensure that few traces of Assyrian rule remained two years later. The Assyrians had used the visual arts to depict their many conquests, and Assyrian friezes, executed in minute detail, continue to be the best artifacts of Assyrian civilization.

The Chaldeans became heir to Assyrian power in 612 B.C., and they conquered formerly Assyrian-held lands in Syria and Palestine. King Nebuchadnezzar (605-562 B.C.) conquered the kingdom of Judah, and he destroyed Jerusalem in 586 B.C. Conscious of their ancient past, the Chaldeans sought to reestablish Babylon as the most magnificent city of the Near East. It was during the Chaldean period that the Hanging Gardens of Babylon, famed as one of the Seven Wonders of the Ancient World, were created. Because of an estrangement of the priesthood from the king, however, the monarchy was severely weakened, and it was unable to withstand the rising power of Achaemenid Iran. In 539 B.C., Babylon fell to Cyrus the Great (550-530 B.C.). In addition to incorporating Babylon into the Iranian empire, Cyrus the Great released the Jews who had been held in captivity there.

The Arab Conquest and the Coming of Islam

The power that toppled the Sassanids came from an unexpected source. The Iranians knew that the Arabs, a tribally oriented people, had never been organized under the rule of a single power and were at a primitive level of military development. The Iranians also knew of the Arabs through their mutual trading activities and because, for a brief period, Yemen, in southern Arabia, was an Iranian satrapy.

Events in Arabia changed rapidly and dramatically in the sixth century A.D. when Muhammad, a member of the Hashimite clan of the powerful Quraysh tribe of Mecca, claimed prophethood and began gathering adherents for the monotheistic faith of Islam that had been revealed to him (see Religious Life). The conversion of Arabia proved to be the most difficult of the Islamic conquests because of entrenched tribalism. Within one year of Muhammad's death in 632, however, Arabia was secure enough for the Prophet's secular successor, Abu Bakr (632-634), the first caliph and the father-in-law of Muhammad, to begin the campaign against the Byzantine Empire and the Sassanid Empire.

Islamic forays into Iraq began during the reign of Abu Bakr. In 634 an army of 18,000 Arab tribesmen, under the leadership of the brilliant general Khalid ibn al Walid (aptly nicknamed "The Sword of Islam"), reached the perimeter of the Euphrates delta. Although the occupying Iranian force was vastly superior in techniques and numbers, its soldiers were exhausted from their unremitting campaigns against the Byzantines. The Sassanid troops fought ineffectually, lacking sufficient reinforcement to do more. The first battle of the Arab campaign became known as the Battle of the Chains because Iranian soldiers were reputedly chained together so that they could not flee. Khalid offered the inhabitants of Iraq an ultimatum: "Accept the faith and you are safe; otherwise pay tribute. If you refuse to do either, you have only yourself to blame. A people is already upon you, loving death as you love life."

Most of the Iraqi tribes were Christian at the time of the Islamic conquest. They decided to pay the jizya, the tax required of non-Muslims living in Muslim-ruled areas, and were not further disturbed. The Iranians rallied briefly under their hero, Rustam, and attacked the Arabs at Al Hirah, west of the Euphrates. There, they were soundly defeated by the invading Arabs. The next year, in 635, the Arabs defeated the Iranians at the Battle of Buwayb. Finally, in May 636 at Al Qadisiyah, a village south of Baghdad on the Euphrates, Rustam was killed. The Iranians, who outnumbered the Arabs six to one, were decisively beaten. From Al Qadisiyah the Arabs pushed on to the Sassanid capital at Ctesiphon (Madain).

The Islamic conquest was made easier because both the Byzantine Empire and the Sassanid Empire were culturally and socially bankrupt; thus, the native populations had little to lose by cooperating with the conquering power. Because the Muslim warriors were fighting a jihad (holy war), they were regulated by religious law that strictly prohibited rape and the killing of women, children, religious leaders, or anyone who had not actually engaged in warfare. Further, the Muslim warriors had come to conquer and settle a land under Islamic law. It was not in their economic interest to destroy or pillage unnecessarily and indiscriminately.

The caliph Umar (634-44) ordered the founding of two garrisoned cities to protect the newly conquered territory: Kufah, named as the capital of Iraq, and Basra, which was also to be a port. Umar also organized the administration of the conquered Iranian lands. Acting on the advice of an Iranian, Umar continued the Sassanid office of the divan (Arabic form diwan). Essentially an institution to control income and expenditure through record keeping and the centralization of administration, the divan would be used henceforth throughout the lands of the Islamic conquest. Dihqans, minor revenue collection officials under the Sassanids, retained their function of assessing and collecting taxes. Tax collectors in Iraq had never enjoyed universal popularity, but the Arabs found them particularly noxious. Arabic replaced Persian as the official language, and it slowly filtered into common usage. Iraqis intermarried with Arabs and converted to Islam.

By 650 Muslim armies had reached the Amu Darya (Oxus River) and had conquered all the Sassanid domains, although some were more strongly held than others. Shortly thereafter, Arab expansion and conquest virtually ceased. Thereafter, the groups in power directed their energies to maintaining the status quo while those outside the major power structure devoted themselves to political and religious rebellion. The ideologies of the rebellions usually were couched in religious terms. Frequently, a difference in the interpretation of a point of doctrine was sufficient to spark armed warfare. More often, however, religious disputes were the rationalization for underlying nationalistic or cultural dissatisfactions.

The Ottoman Period, 1534-1918

From the sixteenth to the twentieth centuries, the course of Iraqi history was affected by the continuing conflicts between the Safavid Empire in Iran and the Ottoman Turks. The Safavids, who were the first to declare Shia Islam the official religion of Iran, sought to control Iraq both because of the Shia holy places at An Najaf and Karbala and because Baghdad, the seat of the old Abbasid Empire, had great symbolic value. The Ottomans, fearing that Shia Islam would spread to Anatolia (Asia Minor), sought to maintain Iraq as a Sunni-controlled buffer state. In 1509 the Safavids, led by Ismail Shah (1502-24), conquered Iraq, thereby initiating a series of protracted battles with the Ottomans. In 1514 Sultan Selim the Grim attacked Ismail's forces and in 1535 the Ottomans, led by Sultan Suleyman the Magnificent (1520-66), conquered Baghdad from the Safavids. The Safavids reconquered Baghdad in 1623 under the leadership of Shah Abbas (1587-1629), but they were expelled in 1638 after a series of brilliant military maneuvers by the dynamic Ottoman sultan, Murad IV.

The major impact of the Safavid-Ottoman conflict on Iraqi history was the deepening of the Shia-Sunni rift. Both the Ottomans and the Safavids used Sunni and Shia Islam respectively to mobilize domestic support. Thus, Iraq's Sunni population suffered immeasurably during the brief Safavid reign (1623-38), while Iraq's Shias were excluded from power altogether during the longer period of Ottoman supremacy (1638-1916). During the Ottoman period, the Sunnis gained the administrative experience that would allow them to monopolize political power in the twentieth century. The Sunnis were able to take advantage of new economic and educational opportunities while the Shias, frozen out of the political process, remained politically impotent and economically depressed. The Shia-Sunni rift continued as an important element of Iraqi social structure in the 1980s (see Religious Life).

By the seventeenth century, the frequent conflicts with the Safavids had sapped the strength of the Ottoman Empire and had weakened its control over its provinces. In Iraq, tribal authority once again dominated; the history of nineteenth-century Iraq is a chronicle of tribal migrations and of conflict. The nomadic population swelled with the influx of beduins from Najd, in the Arabian Peninsula. Beduin raids on settled areas became impossible to curb. In the interior, the large and powerful Muntafiq tribal confederation took shape under the leadership of the Sunni Saadun family of Mecca. In the desert southwest, the Shammar--one of the biggest tribal confederations of the Arabian Peninsula--entered the Syrian desert and clashed with the Anayzah confederation. On the lower Tigris near Al Amarah, a new tribal confederation, the Bani Lam, took root. In the north, the Kurdish Baban Dynasty emerged and organized Kurdish resistance. The resistance made it impossible for the Ottomans to maintain even nominal suzerainty over Iraqi Kurdistan (land of the Kurds). Between 1625 and 1668, and from 1694 to 1701, local shaykhs ruled Al Basrah and the marshlands, home of the Madan (Marsh Arabs). The powerful shaykhs basically ignored the Ottoman governor of Baghdad.

The cycle of tribal warfare and of deteriorating urban life that began in the thirteenth century with the Mongol invasions was temporarily reversed with the reemergence of the Mamluks. In the early eighteenth century, the Mamluks began asserting authority apart from the Ottomans. Extending their rule first over Basra, the Mamluks eventually controlled the Tigris and Euphrates river valleys from the Persian Gulf to the foothills of Kurdistan. For the most part, the Mamluks were able administrators, and their rule was marked by political stability and by economic revival. The greatest of the Mamluk leaders, Suleyman the II (1780-1802), made great strides in imposing the rule of law. The last Mamluk leader, Daud (1816-31), initiated important modernization programs that included clearing canals, establishing industries, training a 20,000-man army, and starting a printing press.

The Mamluk period ended in 1831, when a severe flood and plague devastated Baghdad, enabling the Ottoman sultan, Mahmud II, to reassert Ottoman sovereignty over Iraq. Ottoman rule was unstable; Baghdad, for example, had more than ten governors between 1831 and 1869. In 1869, however, the Ottomans regained authority when the reform-minded Midhat Pasha was appointed governor of Baghdad. Midhat immediately set out to modernize Iraq on the Western model. The primary objectives of Midhat's reforms, called the tanzimat, were to reorganize the army, to create codes of criminal and commercial law, to secularize the school system, and to improve provincial administration. He created provincial representative assemblies to assist the governor, and he set up elected municipal councils in the major cities. Staffed largely by Iraqi notables with no strong ties to the masses, the new offices nonetheless helped a group of Iraqis gain administrative experience.

By establishing government agencies in the cities and by attempting to settle the tribes, Midhat altered the tribal-urban balance of power, which since the thirteenth century had been largely in favor of the tribes. The most important element of Midhat's plan to extend Ottoman authority into the countryside was the 1858 TAPU land law (named after the initials of the government office issuing it). The new land reform replaced the feudal system of land holdings and tax farms with legally sanctioned property rights. It was designed both to induce tribal shaykhs to settle and to give them a stake in the existing political order. In practice, the TAPU laws enabled the tribal shaykhs to become large landowners; tribesmen, fearing that the new law was an attempt to collect taxes more effectively or to impose conscription, registered community-owned tribal lands in their shaykhs' names or sold them outright to urban speculators. As a result, tribal shaykhs gradually were transformed into profit-seeking landlords while their tribesmen were relegated to the role of impoverished sharecroppers.

Midhat also attempted to replace Iraq's clerically run Islamic school system with a more secular educational system. The new, secular schools provided a channel of upward social mobility to children of all classes, and they led slowly to the growth of an Iraqi intelligentsia. They also introduced students for the first time to Western languages and disciplines.

The introduction of Western disciplines in the schools accompanied a greater Western political and economic presence in Iraq. The British had established a consulate at Baghdad in 1802, and a French consulate followed shortly thereafter. European interest in modernizing Iraq to facilitate Western commercial interests coincided with the Ottoman reforms. Steamboats appeared on the rivers in 1836, the telegraph was introduced in 1861, and the Suez Canal was opened in 1869, providing Iraq with greater access to European markets. The landowning tribal shaykhs began to export cash crops to the capitalist markets of the West.

In 1908 a new ruling clique, the Young Turks, took power in Istanbul. The Young Turks aimed at making the Ottoman Empire a unified nation-state based on Western models. They stressed secular politics and patriotism over the pan-Islamic ideology preached by Sultan Abd al Hamid. They reintroduced the 1876 constitution (this Ottoman constitution set forth the rights of the ruler and the ruled, but it derived from the ruler and has been called as at best an "attenuated autocracy,"), held elections throughout the empire, and reopened parliament. Although the Iraqi delegates represented only the well- established families of Baghdad, their parliamentary experience in Istanbul proved to be an important introduction to self-government.

Most important to the history of Iraq, the Young Turks aggressively pursued a "Turkification" policy that alienated the nascent Iraqi intelligentsia and set in motion a fledgling Arab nationalist movement. Encouraged by the Young Turks' Revolution of 1908, nationalists in Iraq stepped up their political activity. Iraqi nationalists met in Cairo with the Ottoman Decentralization Party, and some Iraqis joined the Young Arab Society, which moved to Beirut in 1913. Because of its greater exposure to Westerners who encouraged the nationalists, Basra became the center from which Iraqi nationalists began to demand a measure of autonomy. After nearly 400 years under Ottoman rule, Iraq was ill-prepared to form a nation-state. The Ottomans had failed to control Iraq's rebellious tribal domains, and even in the cities their authority was tenuous. The Ottomans' inability to provide security led to the growth of autonomous, self- contained communities. As a result, Iraq entered the twentieth century beset by a complex web of social conflicts that seriously impeded the process of building a modern state.

The oldest and most deeply ingrained conflict was the competition between the tribes and the cities for control over the food-producing flatlands of the Tigris and the Euphrates rivers. The centralization policies of the Sublime Porte (Ottoman government), especially in the nineteenth century, constituted a direct threat to the nomadic structure and the fierce fighting spirit of the tribes. In addition to tribal-urban conflicts, the tribes fought among themselves, and there was a fairly rigid hierarchy between the most powerful tribes, the so-called "people of the camel," and the weaker tribes that included the "people of the sheep," marshdwellers, and peasants. The cities also were sharply divided, both according to occupation and along religious lines. The various guilds resided in distinct, autonomous areas, and Shia and Sunni Muslims rarely intermingled. The territory that eventually became the state of Iraq was beset, furthermore, by regional differences in orientation; Mosul in the north had historically looked to Syria and to Turkey, whereas Baghdad and the Shia holy cities had maintained close ties with Iran and with the people of the western and southwestern deserts.

Although Ottoman weakness had allowed Iraq's self-contained communities to grow stronger, the modernization initiated by the Sublime Porte tended to break down traditional autonomous groupings and to create a new social order. Beginning with the tanzimat reforms in 1869, Iraq's for the most part subsistence economy slowly was transformed into a market economy based on money and tied to the world capitalist market. Social status traditionally had been determined by noble lineage, by fighting prowess, and by knowledge of religion. With the advent of capitalism, social status increasingly was determined by property ownership and by the accumulation of wealth. Most disruptive in this regard was the TAPU land reform of 1858. Concomitantly, Western social and economic penetration increased; for example, Iraq's traditional crafts and craftsmen gradually were displaced by mass-produced British machine-made textiles.

The final Ottoman legacy in Iraq is related to the policies of the Young Turks and to the creation of a small but vocal Iraqi intelligentsia. Faced with the rapidly encroaching West, the

Young Turks attempted to centralize the empire by imposing upon it the Turkish language and culture and by clamping down on newly won political freedoms. These Turkification policies alienated many of the Ottoman-trained intelligentsia who had originally aligned themselves with the Young Turks in the hope of obtaining greater Arab autonomy. Despite its relatively small size, the nascent Iraqi intelligentsia formed several secret nationalist societies. The most important of these societies was Al Ahd (the Covenant), whose membership was drawn almost entirely from Iraqi officers in the Ottoman army. Membership in Al Ahd spread rapidly in Baghdad and in Mosul, growing to 4,000 by the outbreak of World War I. Despite the existence of Al Ahd and of other, smaller, nationalist societies, Iraqi nationalism was still mainly the concern of educated Arabs from the upper and the middle classes.

World War I and the British Mandate

By the beginning of the twentieth century, the Ottoman territories had become the focus of European power politics. During the previous century, enfeebled Ottoman rule had invited intense competition among European powers for commercial benefits and for spheres of influence. British interest in Iraq significantly increased when the Ottomans granted concessions to Germany to construct railroad lines from Konya in southwest Turkey to Baghdad in 1899 and from Baghdad to Basra in 1902. The British feared that a hostile German presence in the Fertile Crescent would threaten vital lines of communication to India via Iran and Afghanistan, menacing British oil interests in Iran and perhaps even India itself.

Entrance to the ruins of Babylon
Courtesy Ronald L. Kuipers

In 1914 when the British discovered that Turkey was entering the war on the side of the Germans, British forces from India landed at Al Faw on the Shatt al Arab and moved rapidly toward Basra. By the fall of 1915, when British forces were already well established in towns in the south, General Charles Townshend unsuccessfully attempted to take Baghdad. In retaliation, the Turks besieged the British garrison at Al Kut for 140 days; in April 1916, the garrison was forced to surrender unconditionally. The British quickly regrouped their forces, however, and resumed their advance under General Stanley Maude in December 1916. By March 1917 the British had captured Baghdad. Advancing northward in the spring of 1918, the British finally took Mosul in early November. As a result of the victory at Mosul, British authority was extended to all the Iraqi wilayat (sing., wilayah-province) with the exception of the Kurdish highlands bordering Turkey and Iran, the land alongside the Euphrates from Baghdad south to An Nasiriyah, and the Shia cities of Karbala and An Najaf.

On capturing Baghdad, General Maude proclaimed that Britain intended to return to Iraq some control of its own affairs. He stressed that this step would pave the way for ending the alien rule that the Iraqis had experienced since the latter days of the Abbasid caliphate. The proclamation was in accordance with the encouragement the British had given to Arab nationalists, such as Jafar al Askari; his brother-in-law, Nuri as Said; and Jamil al Midfai, who sought emancipation from Ottoman rule. The nationa- lists had supported the Allied powers in expectation of both the Ottoman defeat and the freedom many nationalists assumed would come with an Allied victory.

During the war, events in Iraq were greatly influenced by the Hashimite family of Husayn ibn Ali, sharif of Mecca, who claimed descent from the family of the Prophet Muhammad. Aspiring to become king of an independent Arab kingdom, Husayn had broken with the Ottomans, to whom he had been vassal, and had thrown in his lot with the British. Anxious for his support, the British gave Husayn reason to believe that he would have their endorsement when the war ended. Accordingly, Husayn and his sons led the June 1916 Arab Revolt, marching northward in conjunction with the British into Transjordan, Palestine, and Syria.

Anticipating the fulfillment of Allied pledges, Husayn's son, Prince Faisal (who was later to become modern Iraq's first king), arrived in Paris in 1919 as the chief spokesman for the Arab cause. Much to his disappointment, Faisal found that the Allied powers were less than enthusiastic about Arab independence.

At the 1919 Paris Peace Conference, under Article 22 of the League of Nations Covenant, Iraq was formally made a Class A mandate entrusted to Britain. This award was completed on April 25, 1920, at the San Remo Conference in Italy. Palestine also was placed under British mandate, and Syria was placed under French mandate. Faisal, who had been proclaimed king of Syria by a Syrian national congress in Damascus in March 1920, was ejected by the French in July of the same year.

The civil government of postwar Iraq was headed originally by the high commissioner, Sir Percy Cox, and his deputy, Colonel Arnold Talbot Wilson. The British were confronted with Iraq's age-old problems, compounded by some new ones. Villagers demanded that the tribes be restrained, and tribes demanded that their titles to tribal territories be extended and confirmed. Merchants demanded more effective legal procedures, courts, and laws to protect their activities and interests. Municipal authorities appealed for defined powers and grants-in-aid in addition to the establishment of public health and education facilities. Landlords pressed for grants of land, for the building of canals and roads, and for the provision of tested seeds and livestock.

The holy cities of An Najaf and Karbala and their satellite tribes were in a state of near anarchy. British reprisals after the murder of a British officer in An Najaf failed to restore order. The Anayzah, the Shammar, and the Jubur tribes of the western desert were beset by violent infighting. British adminis- tration had yet to be established in the mountains of Kurdistan. Meanwhile, from the Hakkari Mountains beyond Iraq's northern frontier and from the plains of Urmia in Iran, thousands of Assyrians began to pour into Iraqi territory seeking refuge from Turkish savagery. The most striking problem facing the British was the growing anger of the nationalists, who felt betrayed at being accorded mandate status. The nationalists soon came to view the mandate as a flimsy disguise for colonialism. The experienced Cox delegated governance of the country to Wilson while he served in Persia between April 1918 and October 1920. The younger man governed Iraq with the kind of paternalism that had characterized British rule in India. Impatient to establish an efficient administration, Wilson used experienced Indians to staff subordinate positions within his administration. The exclusion of Iraqis from administrative posts added humiliation to Iraqi discontent.

Three important anticolonial secret societies had been formed in Iraq during 1918 and 1919. At An Najaf, Jamiyat an Nahda al Islamiya (The League of the Islamic Awakening) was organized; its numerous and varied members included ulama (religious leaders), journalists, landlords, and tribal leaders. Members of the Jamiyat assassinated a British officer in the hope that the killing would act as a catalyst for a general rebellion at Iraq's other holy city, Karbala. Al Jamiya al Wataniya al Islamiya (The Muslim National League) was formed with the object of organizing and mobilizing the population for major resistance. In February 1919, in Baghdad, a coalition of Shia merchants, Sunni teachers and civil servants, Sunni and Shia ulama, and Iraqi officers formed the Haras al Istiqlal (The Guardians of Independence). The Istiqlal had member groups in Karbala, An Najaf, Al Kut, and Al Hillah.

Local outbreaks against British rule had occurred even before the news reached Iraq that the country had been given only mandate status. Upon the death of an important Shia mujtahid (religious scholar) in early May 1920, Sunni and Shia ulama temporarily put aside their differences as the memorial services metamorphosed into political rallies. Ramadan, the Islamic month of fasting, began later in that month; once again, through nationalistic poetry and oratory, religious leaders exhorted the people to throw off the bonds of imperialism. Violent demonstrations and strikes followed the British arrest of several leaders.

When the news of the mandate reached Iraq in late May, a group of Iraqi delegates met with Wilson and demanded independence. Wilson dismissed them as a "handful of ungrateful politicians." Nationalist political activity was stepped up, and the grand mujtahid of Karbala, Imam Shirazi, and his son, Mirza Muhammad Riza, began to organize the effort in earnest. Arab flags were made and distributed, and pamphlets were handed out urging the tribes to prepare for revolt. Muhammad Riza acted as liaison among insurgents in An Najaf and in Karbala, and the tribal confederations. Shirazi then issued a fatwa (religious ruling), pointing out that it was against Islamic law for Muslims to countenance being ruled by non-Muslims, and he called for a jihad against the British. By July 1920, Mosul was in rebellion against British rule, and the insurrection moved south down the Euphrates River valley. The southern tribes, who cherished their long-held political autonomy, needed little inducement to join in the fray. They did not cooperate in an organized effort against the British, however, which limited the effect of the revolt. The country was in a state of anarchy for three months; the

British restored order only with great difficulty and with the assistance of Royal Air Force bombers. British forces were obliged to send for reinforcements from India and from Iran.

Ath Thawra al Iraqiyya al Kubra, or The Great Iraqi Revolution (as the 1920 rebellion is called), was a watershed event in contemporary Iraqi history. For the first time, Sunnis and Shias, tribes and cities, were brought together in a common effort. In the opinion of Hanna Batatu, author of a seminal work on Iraq, the building of a nation-state in Iraq depended upon two major factors: the integration of Shias and Sunnis into the new body politic and the successful resolution of the age-old conflicts between the tribes and the riverine cities and among the tribes themselves over the food-producing flatlands of the Tigris and the Euphrates. The 1920 rebellion brought these groups together, if only briefly; this constituted an important first step in the long and arduous process of forging a nation-state out of Iraq's conflict-ridden social structure.

The 1920 revolt had been very costly to the British in both manpower and money. Whitehall was under domestic pressure to devise a formula that would provide the maximum control over Iraq at the least cost to the British taxpayer. The British replaced the military regime with a provisional Arab government, assisted by British advisers and answerable to the supreme authority of the high commissioner for Iraq, Cox. The new administration provided a channel of communication between the British and the restive population, and it gave Iraqi leaders an opportunity to prepare for eventual self-government. The provisional government was aided by the large number of trained Iraqi administrators who returned home when the French ejected Faisal from Syria. Like earlier Iraqi governments, however, the provisional government was composed chiefly of Sunni Arabs; once again the Shias were underrepresented.

At the Cairo Conference of 1921, the British set the parameters for Iraqi political life that were to continue until the 1958 revolution; they chose Faisal as Iraq's first King; they established an indigenous Iraqi army; and they proposed a new treaty. To confirm Faisal as Iraq's first monarch, a one-question plebiscite was carefully arranged that had a return of 96 percent in his favor. The British saw in Faisal a leader who possessed sufficient nationalist and Islamic credentials to have broad appeal, but who also was vulnerable enough to remain dependent on their support. Faisal traced his descent from the family of the Prophet Muhammad, and his ancestors had held political authority in the holy cities of Mecca and Medina since the tenth century. The British believed that these credentials would satisfy traditional Arab standards of political legitimacy; moreover, the British thought that Faisal would be accepted by the growing Iraqi nationalist movement because of his role in the 1916 revolt against the Turks, his achievements as a leader of the Arab emancipation movement, and his general leadership qualities.

As a counterforce to the nationalistic inclinations of the monarchy and as a means of insuring the king's dependence, the British cultivated the tribal shaykhs, whose power had been waning since the end of the nineteenth century. While the new king sought to create a national consciousness, to strengthen the institutions of the emerging state, and especially to create a national military, the tribal shaykhs supported a fragmented community and sought to weaken the coercive power of the state. A major goal of the British policy was to keep the monarchy stronger than any one tribe but weaker than a coalition of tribes so that British power would ultimately be decisive in arbitrating disputes between the two.

Ultimately, the British-created monarchy suffered from a chronic legitimacy crisis: the concept of a monarchy was alien to Iraq. Despite his Islamic and pan-Arab credentials, Faisal was not an Iraqi, and, no matter how effectively he ruled, Iraqis saw the monarchy as a British creation. The continuing inability of the government to gain the confidence of the people fueled political instability well into the 1970s.

The British decision at the Cairo Conference to establish an indigenous Iraqi army was significant. In Iraq, as in most of the developing world, the military establishment has been the best organized institution in an otherwise weak political system. Thus, while Iraq's body politic crumbled under immense political and economic pressure throughout the monarchic period, the military gained increasing power and influence; moreover, because the officers in the new army were by necessity Sunnis who had served under the Ottomans, while the lower ranks were predominantly filled by Shia tribal elements, Sunni dominance in the military was preserved.

The final major decision taken at the Cairo Conference related to the new Anglo-Iraqi Treaty. Faisal was under pressure from the nationalists and the anti-British mujtahids of An Najaf and Karbala to limit both British influence in Iraq and the duration of the treaty. Recognizing that the monarchy depended on British support--and wishing to avoid a repetition of his experience in Syria--Faisal maintained a moderate approach in dealing with Britain. The twenty-year treaty, which was ratified in October 1922, stated that the king would heed British advice on all matters affecting British interests and on fiscal policy as long as Iraq was in debt to Britain, and that British officials would be appointed to specified posts in eighteen departments to act as advisers and inspectors. A subsequent financial agreement, which significantly increased the financial burden on Iraq, required Iraq to pay half the cost of supporting British resident officials, among other expenses. British obligations under the new treaty included providing various kinds of aid, notably military assistance, and proposing Iraq for membership in the League of Nations at the earliest moment. In effect, the treaty ensured that Iraq would remain politically and economically dependent on Britain. While unable to prevent the treaty, Faisal clearly felt that the British had gone back on their promises to him.

After the treaty had been signed, Iraq readied itself for the country-wide elections that had been provided for in the May 1922 Electoral Law. There were important changes in the government at this time. Cox resigned his position as high commissioner and was replaced by Sir Henry Dobbs; Iraq's aging prime minister, Abd ar Rahman al Gailani, stepped down and was replaced by Abd al Muhsin as Saadun. In April 1923, Saadun signed a protocol that shortened the treaty period to four years. As a result of the elections, however, Saadun was replaced by Jafar al Askari, a veteran of the Arab Revolt and an early supporter of Faisal.

The elected Constituent Assembly met for the first time in March 1924, and it formally ratified the treaty despite strong (and sometimes physical) opposition on the part of many in the assembly. The assembly also accepted the Organic Law that declared Iraq to be a sovereign state with a representative system of government and a hereditary constitutional monarchy. The newly ratified constitution-- which, along with the treaty, had been hotly debated--legislated an important British role in Iraqi affairs. The major issue at stake in the constitutional debate revolved around the powers of the monarchy. In the final draft, British interests prevailed, and the monarchy was granted wide-ranging powers that included the right to confirm all laws, to call for a general election, to prorogue parliament, and to issue ordinances for the fulfillment of treaty obligations without parliamentary sanctions. Like the treaty, the constitution provided the British with a means of indirect control in Iraq.

After the Anglo-Iraqi Treaty was ratified, the most pressing issue confronting the newly established constitutional monarchy was the question of boundaries, especially in the former Ottoman wilayah of Mosul, now known as Mosul Province. The status of Mosul Province was complicated by two factors, the British desire to gain oil concessions and the existence of a majority Kurdish population that was seeking independence apart from either Iraq or Turkey. According to the Treaty of Sevres, concluded in 1920 with the Ottoman Sultan, Mosul was to be part of an autonomous Kurdish state. The treaty was scrapped, however, when nationalist leader Mustafa Kamal (1881-1938--also known as Atatürk) came to power in Turkey and established control over the Kurdish areas in eastern Turkey. In 1923, after two failed British attempts to establish an autonomous Kurdish province, London decided to include the Kurds in the new Iraqi state with the proviso that Kurds would hold government positions in Kurdish areas and that the Kurdish language would be preserved. The British decision to include Mosul in Iraq was based largely on their belief that the area contained large oil deposits.

Before the collapse of the Ottoman Empire, the British- controlled Turkish Petroleum Company (TPC) had held concessionary rights to the Mosul wilayah. Under the 1916 Sykes-Picot Agreement--an agreement in 1916 between Britain and France that delineated future control of the Middle East--the area would have fallen under French influence. In 1919, however, the French relinquished their claims to Mosul under the terms of the Long-Berenger Agreement. The 1919 agreement granted the French a 25 percent share in the TPC as compensation.

Beginning in 1923, British and Iraqi negotiators held acrimonious discussions over the new oil concession. The major obstacle was Iraq's insistence on a 20 percent equity participation in the company; this figure had been included in the original TPC concession to the Turks and had been agreed upon at San Remo for the Iraqis. In the end, despite strong nationalist sentiments against the concession agreement, the Iraqi negotiators acquiesced to it. The League of Nations was soon to vote on the disposition of Mosul, and the Iraqis feared that, without British support, Iraq would lose the area to Turkey. In March 1925, an agreement was concluded that contained none of the Iraqi demands. The TPC, now renamed the Iraq Petroleum Company (IPC), was granted a concession for a period of seventy-five years.

In 1925 the League of Nations decided that Mosul Province would be considered a part of Iraq, but it also suggested that the Anglo-Iraqi Treaty be extended from four to twenty-five years as a protection for the Kurdish minority, who intensely distrusted the Iraqi government. The Iraqis also were to give due regard to Kurdish sensibilities in matters of culture and of language. Although reluctant to do so, the Iraqi assembly ratified the treaty in January 1926. Turkey was eventually reconciled to the loss by being promised one-tenth of any oil revenues that might accrue in the area, and a tripartite Anglo-Turco-Iraqi treaty was signed in July 1926. This settlement was to have important repercussions, both positive and negative, for the future of Iraq. Vast oil revenues would accrue from the Mosul Province, but the inclusion of a large number of well-armed and restless Kurds in Iraqi territory would continue to plague Iraqi governments.

With the signing of the Anglo-Iraqi Treaty and the settling of the Mosul question, Iraqi politics took on a new dynamic. The emerging class of Sunni and Shia landowning tribal shaykhs vied for positions of power with wealthy and prestigious urban-based Sunni families and with Ottoman-trained army officers and bureaucrats. Because Iraq's newly established political institutions were the creation of a foreign power, and because the concept of democratic government had no precedent in Iraqi history, the politicians in Baghdad lacked legitimacy and never developed deeply rooted constituencies. Thus, despite a constitution and an elected assembly, Iraqi politics was more a shifting alliance of important personalities and cliques than a democracy in the Western sense. The absence of broadly based political institutions inhibited the early nationalist movement's ability to make deep inroads into Iraq's diverse social structure. Thus, despite the widely felt resentment at Iraq's mandate status, the burgeoning nationalist movement was largely ineffective.

Nonetheless, through the late 1920s, the nationalists persisted in opposing the Anglo-Iraqi Treaty and in demanding independence. A treaty more favorable to the Iraqis was presented in December 1927. It remained unratified, however, because of nationalist demands for an unconditional promise of independence. This promise eventually was made by the new high commissioner, Sir Gilbert Clayton, in 1929, but the confusion occasioned by the sudden death of Clayton and by the suicide of Abd al Muhsin as Saadun, the most powerful Iraqi advocate of the treaty, delayed the writing of a new treaty. In June 1929, the nationalists received their first positive response from London when a newly elected Labour Party government announced its intention to support Iraq's admission to the League of Nations in 1932 and to negotiate a new treaty recognizing Iraq's independence.

Faisal's closest adviser (and soon-to-be Iraqi strongman), Nuri as Said, carried out the treaty negotiations. Despite widespread opposition, Nuri as Said was able to force the treaty through parliament. The new Anglo-Iraqi Treaty was signed in June 1930. It provided for a "close alliance," for "full and frank consultations between the two countries in all matters of foreign policy," and for mutual assistance in case of war. Iraq granted the British the use of air bases near Basra and at Al Habbaniyah and the right to move troops across the country. The treaty, of twenty-five years' duration, was to come into force upon Iraq's admission to the League of Nations. The terms of the treaty gained Nuri as Said favor in British eyes but discredited him in the eyes of the Iraqi nationalists, who vehemently opposed its lengthy duration and the leasing of air bases. The Kurds and the Assyrians also opposed the treaty because it offered no guarantees for their status in the new country.

Iraq as an Independent Monarchy

On October 13, 1932, Iraq became a sovereign state, and it was admitted to the League of Nations. Iraq still was beset by a complex web of social, economic, ethnic, religious, and ideological conflicts, all of which retarded the process of state formation. The declaration of statehood and the imposition of fixed boundaries triggered an intense competition for power in the new entity. Sunnis and Shias, cities and tribes, shaykhs and tribesmen, Assyrians and Kurds, pan-Arabists and Iraqi nationalists--all fought vigorously for places in the emerging state structure. Ultimately, lacking legitimacy and unable to establish deep roots, the British-imposed political system was overwhelmed by these conflicting demands.

A statue of a lion at Babylon
Courtesy Ronald L. Kuipers

Bas relief, Babylon
Courtesy Ronald L. Kuipers

The Sunni-Shia conflict, a problem since the beginning of domination by the Umayyad caliphate in 661, continued to frustrate attempts to mold Iraq into a political community. The Shia tribes of the southern Euphrates, along with urban Shias, feared complete Sunni domination in the government. Their concern was well founded; a disproportionate number of

Sunnis occupied administrative positions. Favored by the Ottomans, the Sunnis historically had gained much more administrative experience. The Shias' depressed economic situation further widened the Sunni- Shia split, and it intensified Shia efforts to obtain a greater share of the new state's budget.

The arbitrary borders that divided Iraq and the other Arab lands of the old Ottoman Empire caused severe economic dislocations, frequent border disputes, and a debilitating ideological conflict. The cities of Mosul in the north and Basra in the south, separated from their traditional trading partners in Syria and in Iran, suffered severe commercial dislocations that led to economic depression. In the south, the British- created border (drawn through the desert on the understanding that the region was largely uninhabited) impeded migration patterns and led to great tribal unrest. Also in the south, uncertainty surrounding Iraq's new borders with Kuwait, with Saudi Arabia, and especially with Iran led to frequent border skirmishes. The new boundaries also contributed to the growth of competing nationalisms; Iraqi versus pan-Arab loyalties would severely strain Iraqi politics during the 1950s and the 1960s, when Egyptian leader Gamal Abdul Nasser held emotional sway over the Iraqi masses.

Ethnic groups such as the Kurds and the Assyrians, who had hoped for their own autonomous states, rebelled against inclusion within the Iraqi state. The Kurds, the majority of whom lived in the area around Mosul, had long been noted for their fierce spirit of independence and separatism. During the 1922 to 1924 period, the Kurds had engaged in a series of revolts in response to British encroachment in areas of traditional Kurdish autonomy; moreover, the Kurds preferred Turkish to Arab rule. When the League of Nations awarded Mosul to Iraq in 1925, Kurdish hostility thus increased. The Iraqi government maintained an uneasy peace with the Kurds in the first year of independence, but Kurdish hostility would remain an intractable problem for future governments.

From the start, the relationship of the Iraqi government with the Assyrians was openly hostile. Britain had resettled 20,000 Assyrians in northern Iraq around Zakhu and Dahuk after Turkey violently quelled a British-inspired Assyrian rebellion in 1918. As a result, approximately three-fourths of the Assyrians who had sided with the British during World War I now found themselves citizens of Iraq. The Assyrians found this situation both objectionable and dangerous. Thousands of Assyrians had been incorporated into the Iraqi Levies, a British-paid and British-officered force separate from the regular Iraqi army. They had been encouraged by the British to consider themselves superior to the majority of Arab Iraqis by virtue of their profession of Christianity. The British also had used them for retaliatory operations against the Kurds, in whose lands most of the Assyrians had settled. Pro-British, they had been apprehensive of Iraqi independence.

The Assyrians had hoped to form a nation-state in a region of their own. When no unoccupied area sufficiently large could be found, the Assyrians continued to insist that, at the very least, their patriarch, the Mar Shamun, be given some temporal authority. This demand was flatly refused by both the British and the Iraqis. In response, the Assyrians, who had been permitted by the British to retain their weapons after the dissolution of the Iraq Levies, flaunted their strength and refused to recognize the government. In retaliation the Iraqi authorities held the Mar Shamun under virtual house arrest in mid-1933, making his release contingent on his signing a document renouncing forever any claims to temporal authority. During July about 800 armed Assyrians headed for the Syrian border. For reasons that have never been explained, they were repelled by the Syrians. During this time, King

Faisal was outside the country for reasons of health. According to scholarly sources, Minister of Interior Hikmat Sulayman had adopted a policy aimed at the elimination of the Assyrians. This policy apparently was implemented by a Kurd, General Bakr Sidqi, who, after engaging in several clashes with the Assyrians, permitted his men to kill about 300 Assyrians, including women and children, at the Assyrian village of Simel (Sumayyil).

The Assyrian affair marked the military's entrance into Iraqi politics, setting a precedent that would be followed throughout the 1950s and the 1960s. It also paved the way for the passage of a conscription law that strengthened the army and, as increasing numbers of tribesmen were brought into military service, sapped strength from the tribal shaykhs. The Assyrian affair also set the stage for the increased prominence of Bakr Sidqi.

At the time of independence, tribal Iraq was experiencing a destabilizing realignment characterized by the waning role of the shaykhs in tribal society. The privatization of property rights, begun with the tanzimat reforms in the late 1860s, intensified when the British-supported Lazmah land reform of 1932 dispossessed even greater numbers of tribesmen. While the British were augmenting the economic power of the shaykhs, however, the tribal-urban balance was rapidly shifting in favor of the cities. The accelerated pace of modernization and the growth of a highly nationalistic intelligentsia, of a bureaucracy, and of a powerful military, all favored the cities. Thus, while the economic position of the shaykhs had improved significantly, their role in tribal society and their status in relation to the rapidly emerging urban elite had seriously eroded. These contradictory trends in tribal structure and authority pushed tribal Iraq into a major social revolution that would last for the next thirty years.

The ascendancy of the cities and the waning power of the tribes were most evident in the ease with which the military, led by Bakr Sidqi, put down tribal unrest. The tribal revolts themselves were set off by the government's decision in 1934 to allocate money for the new conscription plan rather than for a new dam, which would have improved agricultural productivity in the south.

The monarchy's ability to deal with tribal unrest suffered a major setback in September 1933, when King Faisal died while undergoing medical treatment in Switzerland. Faisal's death meant the loss of the main stabilizing personality in Iraqi politics. He was the one figure with sufficient prestige to draw the politicians together around a concept of national interest. Faisal was succeeded by his twenty-one-year-old son, Ghazi (1933- 39), an ardent but inexperienced Arab nationalist. Unlike his father, Ghazi was a product of Western education and had little experience with the complexities of Iraqi tribal life. Ghazi also was unable to balance nationalist and British pressures within the framework of the Anglo-Iraqi alliance; increasingly, the nationalist movement saw the monarchy as a British puppet. Iraqi politics during Ghazi's reign degenerated into a meaningless competition among narrowly based tribal shaykhs and urban notables that further eroded the legitimacy of the state and its constitutional structures.

In 1936 Iraq experienced its first military coup d'etat--the first coup d'etat in the modern Arab world. The agents of the coup, General Bakr Sidqi and two politicians (Hikmat Sulayman and Abu Timman, who were Turkoman and Shia respectively), represented a minority response to the pan-Arab Sunni government of Yasin al Hashimi. The eighteen-month Hashimi government was the most successful and the longest lived of the eight governments that came and went during the reign of King Ghazi. Hashimi's government was nationalistic and pan-Arab, but many Iraqis resented its authoritarianism and its supression of honest dissent. Sulayman, a reformer, sought to engineer an alliance of other reformers and minority elements within the army. The reformers included communists, orthodox and unorthodox socialists, and persons with more moderate positions. Most of the more moderate reformers were associated with the leftist-leaning Al Ahali newspaper, from which their group took its name.

The Sidqi coup marked a major turning point in Iraqi history; it made a crucial breach in the constitution, and it opened the door to further military involvement in politics. It also temporarily displaced the elite that had ruled since the state was founded; the new government contained few Arab Sunnis and not a single advocate of a pan-Arab cause. This configuration resulted in a foreign policy oriented toward Turkey and Iran instead of toward the Arab countries. The new government promptly signed an agreement with Iran, temporarily settling the question of boundary between Iraq and Iran in the Shatt al Arab. Iran maintained that it had agreed under British pressure to the international boundary's being set at the low water mark on the Iranian side rather than the usual international practice of the midpoint or thalweg.

After Bakr Sidqi moved against Baghdad, Sulayman formed an Ahali cabinet. Hashimi and Rashid Ali were banished, and Nuri as Said fled to Egypt. In the course of the assault on Baghdad, Nuri as Said's brother-in-law, Minister of Defense Jafar Askari, was killed.

Ghazi sanctioned Sulayman's government even though it had achieved power unconstitutionally; nevertheless, the coalition of forces that gained power in 1936 was beset by major contradictions. The Ahali group was interested in social reform whereas Sidqi and his supporters in the military were interested in expansion. Sidqi, moreover, alienated important sectors of the population: the nationalists in the army resented him because of his Kurdish background and because he encouraged Kurds to join the army; the Shias abhorred him because of his brutal suppression of a tribal revolt the previous year; and Nuri as Said sought revenge for the murder of his brother-in-law. Eventually, Sidqi's excesses alienated both his civilian and his military supporters, and he was murdered by a military group in August 1937.

In April 1939, Ghazi was killed in an automobile accident and was succeeded by his infant son, Faisal II. Ghazi's first cousin, Amir Abd al Ilah, was made regent. The death of Ghazi and the rise of Prince Abd al Ilah and Nuri as Said--the latter one of the Ottoman-trained officers who had fought with Sharif Husayn of Mecca--dramatically changed both the goals and the role of the monarchy. Whereas Faisal and Ghazi had been strong Arab nationalists and had opposed the British-supported tribal shaykhs, Abd al Ilah and Nuri as Said were Iraqi nationalists who relied on the tribal shaykhs as a counterforce against the growing urban nationalist movement. By the end of the 1930s, pan- Arabism had become a powerful ideological force in the Iraqi military, especially among younger officers who hailed from the northern provinces and who had suffered economically from the partition of the Ottoman Empire. The British role in quelling the Palestine revolt of 1936 to 1939 further intensified anti-British sentiments in the military and led a group of disgruntled officers to form the Free Officers' Movement, which aimed at overthrowing the monarchy.

As World War II approached, Nazi Germany attempted to capitalize on the anti-British sentiments in Iraq and to woo Baghdad to the Axis cause. In 1939 Iraq severed diplomatic relations with Germany--as it was obliged to do because of treaty obligations with Britain. In 1940, however, the Iraqi nationalist and ardent anglophobe Rashid Ali succeeded Nuri as Said as prime minister. The new prime minister was reluctant to break completely with the Axis powers, and he proposed restrictions on British troop movements in Iraq.

Abd al Ilah and Nuri as Said both were proponents of close cooperation with Britain. They opposed Rashid Ali's policies and pressed him to resign. In response, Rashid Ali and four generals led a military coup that ousted Nuri as Said and the regent, both of whom escaped to Transjordan. Shortly after seizing power in 1941, Rashid Ali appointed an ultranationalist civilian cabinet, which gave only conditional consent to British requests in April 1941 for troop landings in Iraq. The British quickly retaliated by landing forces at Basra, justifying this second occupation of Iraq by citing Rashid Ali's violation of the Anglo-Iraqi Treaty of 1930. Many Iraqis regarded the move as an attempt to restore British rule. They rallied to the support of the Iraqi army, which receiveda number of aircraft from the Axis powers. The Germans, however, were preoccupied with campaigns in Crete and with preparations for the invasion of the Soviet Union, and they could spare little assistance to Iraq. As the British steadily advanced, Rashid Ali and his government fled to Egypt. An armis- tice was signed on May 30. Abd al Ilah returned as regent, and Rashid Ali and the four generals were tried in absentia and were sentenced to death. The generals returned to Iraq and were subsequently executed, but Rashid Ali remained in exile.

The most important aspect of the Rashid Ali coup of 1941 was Britain's use of Transjordan's Arab Legion against the Iraqis and their reimposition by force of arms of Abd al Ilah as regent. Nothing contributed more to nationalist sentiment in Iraq, especially in the military, than the British invasion of 1941 and the reimposition of the monarchy. From then on, the monarchy was completely divorced from the powerful nationalist trend. Widely viewed as an anachronism that lacked popular legitimacy, the monarchy was perceived to be aligned with social forces that were retarding the country's development.

In January 1943, under the terms of the 1930 treaty with Britain, Iraq declared war on the Axis powers. Iraq cooperated completely with the British under the successive governments of Nuri as Said (1941-44) and Hamdi al Pachachi (1944-46). Iraq became a base for the military occupation of Iran and of the Levant (see Glossary). In March 1945, Iraq became a founding member of the British-supported League of Arab States (Arab League), which included Egypt, Transjordan, Lebanon, Saudi Arabia, Syria, and Yemen. Although the Arab League was ostensibly designed to foster Arab unity, many Arab nationalists viewed it as a British-dominated alignment of pro-Western Arab states. In December 1945, Iraq joined the United Nations (UN).

World War II exacerbated Iraq's social and economic problems. The spiraling prices and shortages brought on by the war increased the opportunity for exploitation and significantly widened the gap between rich and poor; thus, while wealthy landowners were enriching themselves through corruption, the salaried middle class, including teachers, civil servants, and army officers, saw their incomes depreciate daily. Even worse off were the peasants, who lived under the heavy burden of the 1932 land reform that permitted their landlords (shaykhs) to make huge profits selling cash crops to the British occupying force. The worsening economic situation of the mass of Iraqis during the 1950s and the 1960s enabled the Iraqi Communist Party (ICP) to establish deep roots during this period.

In addition to its festering socioeconomic problems, post- World War II Iraq was beset by a leadership crisis. After the 1941 Rashid Ali coup, Iraqi politics had been dominated by the pro-British Nuri as Said. The latter's British orientation and autocratic manner increasingly were at variance with the liberal, reformist philosophy of Iraq's new nationalists. Even before the end of the war, nationalists had demanded the restoration of political activity, which had been banned during the war in the interest of national security. Not until the government of Tawfiq Suwaidi (February-March 1946), however, were political parties allowed to organize. Within a short period, six parties were formed. The parties soon became so outspoken in their criticism of the government that the government closed or curtailed the activities of the more extreme leftist parties.

Accumulated grievances against Nuri as Said and the regent climaxed in the 1948 Wathbah (uprising). The Wathbah was a protest against the Portsmouth Treaty of January 1948 and its provision that a board of Iraqis and British be established to decide on defense matters of mutual interest. The treaty enraged Iraqi nationalists, who were still bitter over the Rashid Ali coup of 1941 and the continued influence of the British in Iraqi affairs. The uprising also was fueled by widespread popular discontent over rising prices, by an acute bread shortage, and by the regime's failure to liberalize the political system.

The Wathbah had three important effects on Iraqi politics. First, and most directly, it led Nuri as Said and the regent to repudiate the Portsmouth Treaty. Second, the success of the uprising led the opposition to intensify its campaign to discredit the regime. This activity not only weakened the monarchy but also seriously eroded the legitimacy of the political process. Finally, the uprising created a schism between Nuri as Said and Abd al Ilah. The former wanted to tighten political control and to deal harshly with the opposition; the regent advocated a more tempered approach. In response, the British increasingly mistrusted the regent and relied more and more on Nuri as Said.

Iraq bitterly objected to the 1947 UN decision to partition Palestine and sent several hundred recruits to the Palestine front when hostilities broke out on May 15, 1948. Iraq sent an additional 8,000 to 10,000 troops of the regular army during the course of the 1948 Arab-Israeli War; these troops were withdrawn in April 1949. The Iraqis had arrived at the Palestine front poorly equipped and undertrained because of the drastic reduction in defense expenditures imposed by Nuri as Said following the 1941 Rashid Ali coup. As a result, they fared very poorly in the fighting and returned to Iraq even more alienated from the regime. The war also had a negative impact on the Iraqi economy. The government allocated 40 percent of available funds for the army and for Palestinian refugees. Oil royalties paid to Iraq were halved when the pipeline to Haifa was cut off in 1948. The war and the hanging of a Jewish businessman led, moreover, to the departure of most of Iraq's prosperous Jewish community; about 120,000 Iraqi Jews emigrated to Israel between 1948 and 1952.

In 1952 the depressed economic situation, which had been exacerbated by a bad harvest and by the government's refusal to hold direct elections, triggered large-scale antiregime protests; the protests turned especially violent in Baghdad. In response, the government declared martial law, banned all political parties, suspended a number of newspapers, and imposed a curfew. The immense size of the protests showed how widespread dissatisfaction with the regime had become. The middle class, which had grown considerably as a result of the monarchy's expanded education system, had become increasingly alienated from the regime, in large part because they were unable to earn an income commensurate with their status. Nuri as Said's autocratic manner, his intolerance of dissent, and his heavy-handed treatment of the political opposition had further alienated the middle class, especially the army. Forced underground, the opposition had become more revolutionary.

By the early 1950s, government revenues began to improve with the growth of the oil industry. New pipelines were built to Tripoli, Lebanon, in 1949 and to Baniyas, Syria, in

1952. A new oil agreement, concluded in 1952, netted the government 50 percent of oil company profits before taxes. As a result, government oil revenues increased almost fourfold, from US$32 million in 1951 to US$112 million in 1952. The increased oil payments, however, did little for the masses. Corruption among high government officials increased; oil companies employed relatively few Iraqis; and the oil boom also had a severe inflationary effect on the economy. Inflation hurt in particular a growing number of urban poor and the salaried middle class. The increased economic power of the state further isolated Nuri as Said and the regent from Iraqi society and obscured from their view the tenuous nature of the monarchy's hold on power.

In the mid-1950s, the monarchy was embroiled in a series of foreign policy blunders that ultimately contributed to its overthrow. Following a 1949 military coup in Syria that brought to power Adib Shishakli, a military strongman who opposed union with Iraq, a split developed between Abd al Ilah, who had called for a Syrian-Iraqi union, and Nuri as Said, who opposed the union plan. Although Shishakli was overthrown with Iraqi help in 1954, the union plan never came to fruition. Instead, the schism between Nuri as Said and the regent widened. Sensing the regime's weakness, the opposition intensified its antiregime activity.

The monarchy's major foreign policy mistake occurred in 1955, when Nuri as Said announced that Iraq was joining a British- supported mutual defense pact with Iran, Pakistan, and Turkey. The Baghdad Pact constituted a direct challenge to Egyptian president Gamal Abdul Nasser. In response, Nasser launched a vituperative media campaign that challenged the legitimacy of the Iraqi monarchy and called on the officer corps to overthrow it. The 1956 British-French-Israeli attack on Sinai further alienated Nuri as Said's regime from the growing ranks of the opposition. In 1958 King Hussein of Jordan and Abd al Ilah proposed a union of Hashimite monarchies to counter the recently formed Egyptian- Syrian union. At this point, the monarchy found itself completely isolated. Nuri as Said was able to contain the rising discontent only by resorting to even greater oppression and to tighter control over the political process.

Republican Iraq

The Hashimite monarchy was overthrown on July 14, 1958, in a swift, predawn coup executed by officers of the Nineteenth Brigade under the leadership of Brigadier Abd al Karim Qasim and Colonel Abd as Salaam Arif. The coup was triggered when King Hussein, fearing that an anti-Western revolt in Lebanon might spread to Jordan, requested Iraqi assistance. Instead of moving toward Jordan, however, Colonel Arif led a battalion into Baghdad and immediately proclaimed a new republic and the end of the old regime. The July 14 Revolution met virtually no opposition and proclamations of the revolution brought crowds of people into the streets of Baghdad cheering for the deaths of Iraq's two "strong men," Nuri as Said and Abd al Ilah. King Faisal II and Abd al Ilah were executed, as were many others in the royal family. Nuri as Said also was killed after attempting to escape disguised as a veiled woman. In the ensuing mob demonstrations against the old order, angry crowds severely damaged the British embassy.

Put in its historical context, the July 14 Revolution was the culmination of a series of uprisings and coup attempts that began with the 1936 Bakr Sidqi coup and included the 1941 Rashid Ali military movement, the 1948 Wathbah Uprising, and the 1952 and 1956 protests.

The revolution radically altered Iraq's social structure, destroying the power of the landed shaykhs and the absentee landlords while enhancing the position of the urban workers, the peasants, and the middle class. In altering the old power structure, however, the revolution revived long-suppressed sectarian, tribal, and ethnic conflicts. The strongest of these conflicts were those between Kurds and Arabs and between Sunnis and Shias.

Despite a shared military background, the group of Free Officers (see Glossary) that carried out the July 14 Revolution was plagued by internal dissension. Its members lacked both a coherent ideology and an effective organizational structure. Many of the more senior officers resented having to take orders from Arif, their junior in rank. A power struggle developed between Qasim and Arif over joining the Egyptian-Syrian union. Arif's pro-Nasserite sympathies were supported by the Baath Party, while Qasim found support for his anti-union position in the ranks of the communists. Qasim, the more experienced and higher ranking of the two, eventually emerged victorious. Arif was first dismissed, then brought to trial for treason and condemned to death in January 1959; he was subsequently pardoned in December 1962.

Whereas he implemented many reforms that favored the poor, Qasim was primarily a centrist in outlook, proposing to improve the lot of the poor while not dispossessing the wealthy. In part, his ambiguous policies were a product of his lack of a solid base of support, especially in the military. Unlike the bulk of military officers, Qasim did not come from the Arab Sunni northwestern towns nor did he share their enthusiasm for pan- Arabism: he was of mixed Sunni-Shia parentage from southeastern Iraq. Qasim's ability to remain in power depended, therefore, on a skillful balancing of the communists and the pan-Arabists. For most of his tenure, Qasim sought to counterbalance the growing pan-Arab trend in the military by supporting the communists who controlled the streets. He authorized the formation of a communist-controlled militia, the People's Resistance Force, and he freed all communist prisoners.

Qasim's economic policies reflected his poor origins and his ties with the communists. He permitted trade unions, improved workers' conditions, and implemented land reform aimed at dismantling the old feudal structure of the countryside. Qasim also challenged the existing profit-sharing arrangements with the oil companies. On December 11, 1961, he passed Public Law 80, which dispossessed the IPC of 99.5 percent of its concession area, leaving it to operate only in those areas currently in production. The new arrangement significantly increased oil revenues accruing to the government. Qasim also announced the establishment of an Iraq National Oil Company (INOC) to exploit the new territory.

In March 1959, a group of disgruntled Free Officers, who came from conservative, well-known, Arab Sunni families and who opposed Qasim's increasing links with the communists, attempted a coup. Aware of the planned coup, Qasim had his communist allies mobilize 250,000 of their supporters in Mosul. The ill-planned coup attempt never really materialized and, in its aftermath, the communists massacred nationalists and some well-to-do Mosul families, leaving deep scars that proved to be very slow to heal.

Throughout 1959 the ranks of the ICP swelled as the party increased its presence in both the military and the government. In 1959 Qasim reestablished diplomatic relations between Iraq and Moscow, an extensive Iraqi-Soviet economic agreement was signed, and arms deliveries began. With communist fortunes riding high, another large-scale show of force was planned in Kirkuk, where a significant number of Kurds (many of them either members of, or sympathetic to, the ICP) lived in neighborhoods contiguous to a Turkoman upper class. In

Kirkuk, however, communist rallies got out of hand. A bloody battle ensued, and the Kurds looted and killed many Turkomans. The communist-initiated violence at Kirkuk led Qasim to crack down on the organization, by arresting some of the more unruly rank-and-file members and by temporarily suspending the People's Resistance Force. Following the events at Mosul and at Kirkuk, the Baath and its leader, Fuad Rikabi, decided that the only way to dislodge the Qasim regime would be to kill Qasim (see Coups, Coup Attempts, and Foreign Policy). The future president, Saddam Husayn, carried out the attempted assassination, which injured Qasim but failed to kill him. Qasim reacted by softening his stance on the communists and by suppressing the activities of the Baath and other nationalist parties. The renewed communist-Qasim relationship did not last long, however. Throughout 1960 and 1961, sensing that the communists had become too strong, Qasim again moved against the party by eliminating members from sensitive government positions, by cracking down on trade unions and on peasant associations, and by shutting down the communist press.

Qasim's divorce from the communists, his alienation from the nationalists, his aloof manner, and his monopoly of power--he was frequently referred to as the "sole leader"--isolated him from a domestic power base. In 1961 his tenuous hold on power was further weakened when the Kurds again took up arms against the central government.

The Kurds had ardently supported the 1958 revolution. Indeed, the new constitution put forth by Qasim and Arif had stipulated that the Kurds and the Arabs would be equal partners in the new state. Exiled Kurdish leaders, including Mullah Mustafa Barzani, were allowed to return. Mutual suspicions, however, soon soured the Barzani-Qasim relationship; in September 1961, full-scale fighting broke out between Kurdish guerrillas and the Iraqi army. The army did not fare well against the seasoned Kurdish guerrillas, many of whom had deserted from the army. By the spring of 1962, Qasim's inability to contain the Kurdish insurrection had further eroded his base of power. The growing opposition was now in a position to plot his overthrow.

Qasim's domestic problems were compounded by a number of foreign policy crises, the foremost of which was an escalating conflict with the shah of Iran. Although he had reined in the communists, Qasim's leftist sympathies aroused fears in the West and in neighboring Gulf states of an imminent communist takeover of Iraq. In April 1959, Allen Dulles, the director of the United States Central Intelligence Agency, described the situation in Iraq "as the most dangerous in the world." The pro-Western shah found Qasim's communist sympathies and his claims on Iranian Khuzestan (an area that stretched from Dezful to Ahvaz in Iran and that contained a majority of Iranians of Arab descent) to be anathema. In December 1959, Iraqi-Iranian relations rapidly deteriorated when Qasim, reacting to Iran's reopening of the Shatt al Arab dispute, nullified the 1937 agreement and claimed sovereignty over the anchorage area near Abadan. In July 1961, Qasim further alienated the West and pro-Western regional states by laying claim to the newly independent state of Kuwait. When the Arab League unanimously accepted Kuwait's membership, Iraq broke off diplomatic relations with its Arab neighbors. Qasim was completely isolated.

In February 1963, hemmed in by regional enemies and facing Kurdish insurrection in the north and a growing nationalist movement at home, Qasim was overthrown. Despite the long list of enemies who opposed him in his final days, Qasim was a hero to millions of urban poor and impoverished peasants, many of whom rushed to his defense.

The inability of the masses to stave off the nationalist onslaught attested to the near total divorce of the Iraqi people from the political process. From the days of the monarchy, the legitimacy of the political process had suffered repeated blows. The government's British legacy, Nuri as Said's authoritarianism, and the rapid encroachment of the military (who paid only scant homage to the institutions of state) had eroded the people's faith in the government; furthermore, Qasim's inability to stem the increasing ethnic, sectarian, and class-inspired violence reflected an even deeper malaise. The unraveling of Iraq's traditional social structure upset a precarious balance of social forces. Centuries-old religious and sectarian hatreds now combined with more recent class antagonisms in a volatile mix.

Coups, Coup Attempts, and Foreign Policy

The Baath Party that orchestrated the overthrow of Qasim was founded in the early 1940s by two Syrian students, Michel Aflaq and Salah ad Din al Bitar. Its ideological goals of socialism, freedom, and unity reflected the deeply felt sentiments of many Iraqis who, during the monarchy, had suffered from the economic dislocationa that followed the breakup of the old Ottoman domain, from an extremely skewed income distribution, and from the suppression of political freedoms. Beginning in 1952, under the leadership of Fuad Rikabi, the party grew rapidly, especially among the Iraqi intelligentsia. By 1958 the Baath had made some inroads into the military. The party went through a difficult period in 1959, however, after the Mosul and Kirkuk incidents, the failed attempt on Qasim's life, and disillusionment with Nasser. The Baath's major competitor throughout the Qasim period was the ICP; when Qasim was finally overthrown, strongly pitched battles between the two ensued. The Baath was able to consolidate its bid for power only with the emergence of Ali Salih as Saadi as leader.

King Faisal II inaugurating Parliament December 1956
Courtesy United States Information Agency

Upon assuming power, the Baath established the National Council of Revolutionary Command (NCRC) as the highest policy- making body and appointed Ahmad Hasan al Bakr, one of the Free Officers, as prime minister and Arif as president. The real power, however, was held by the party leader, Saadi. Despite the dominance of the newly established NCRC, the Baath's hold on power was extremely tenuous. The organization was small, with an active membership of fewer than 1,000, and it was not well represented in the officer corps or in the army at large. Its leadership was inexperienced, and its ideology was too vague to have any immediate relevance to the deep-seated problems besetting Iraq in the early 1960s. Its ambiguity of purpose had served the party well during the Qasim era, enabling it to attract a diverse membership sharing only a common aversion for "the sole leader." In the post-Qasim period, that ambiguity was tearing the party asunder.

The party's lack of cohesion and lack of a coherent program had two major effects on Baath policy. First, it led party strongman Saadi to establish a one-party state that showed little tolerance for opposing views. Second, in the absence of strong ideological ties, the Baath increasingly was pervaded by cliques from the same village, town, or tribe. This tendency became even more pronounced during the 1970s.

Troubled by internal dissension and unable to suppress a new wave of Kurdish unrest in the north, the Baath held power for less than a year. Most damaging was the foundering of unity talks with Nasser and the new Baathist regime in Syria. When the unity plan collapsed, Nasser launched a vituperative campaign challenging the legitimacy of the Baath in Iraq and in Syria. Nasser's attacks seriously eroded the legitimacy of a regime that had continually espoused pan-Arabism. Another factor contributing to the party's demise was Saadi's reliance on the National Guard- -a paramilitary force composed primarily of Baath sympathizers-- to counter the Baath's lack of support in the regular army. By bolstering the guard, Saadi alienated the regular army. Finally, the Baath was sharply divided between doctrinaire hard-liners, such as Saadi, and a more pragmatic moderate wing.

With its party ranks weakened, the Baath was overthrown by Arif and a coterie of military officers in a bloodless coup in November 1963. Upon assuming power, Arif immediately announced that the armed forces would manage the country. The governing core consisted of Arif; his brother, Abd ar Rahman Arif; and his trusted colleague, Colonel Said Slaibi. Arif was chairman of the NCRC, commander in chief of the armed forces, and president of the republic; his brother was acting chief of staff, and the colonel was commander of the Baghdad garrison. The Arif brothers, Slaibi, and the majority of Arif's Twentieth Brigade were united by a strong tribal bond as members of the Jumailah tribe.

Other groups who participated in the 1963 coup included Nasserites--an informal group of military officers and civilians who looked to Nasser for leadership and who desired some kind of unity with Egypt--and Baathists in the military. By the spring of 1964, Arif had adroitly outmaneuvered the military Baathists and had filled the top leadership posts with civilian Nasserites. Arif and the Nasserite officers took steps to integrate the military, economic, and political policies of Iraq with those of Egypt; this was expected to lead to the union of the two countries by 1966. (The United Arab Republic [UAR], which Iraq expected to join, existed from 1958 to 1961 and consisted of Egypt and Syria. Arif proposed that Iraq join [partly as an anticommunist measure] but this union never occurred.) In May 1964, the Joint Presidency Council was formed, and in December the Unified Political Command was established to expedite the ultimate constitutional union of the two countries. In July 1964, Arif announced that henceforth all political parties would coalesce to form the Iraqi Arab Socialist Union. Most important for the future, Arif adopted Nasser's socialist program, calling for the nationalization of insurance companies, banks, and such essential industries as steel, cement, and construction--along with the tobacco industry, tanneries, and flour mills. Arif's nationalization program proved to be one of the few legacies of the proposed Egyptian-Iraqi union.

By 1965 Arif had lost his enthusiasm for the proposed union, which had received only lukewarm support from Nasser. Arif began ousting Nasserite officers from the government. As a result, the newly appointed prime minister, Brigadier Arif Abd ar Razzaq, who was also a leading Nasserite, made an unsuccessful coup attempt on September 12, 1965. In response, President Arif curtailed Nasserite activities and appointed fellow tribal members to positions of power. Colonel Abd ar Razzaq an Nayif, a fellow Jumailah, became head of military intelligence. Arif also attempted to bring more civilians into the government. He appointed the first civilian prime minister since the days of the monarchy, Abd ar Rahman Bazzaz. Bazzaz strongly advocated the rule of law and was determined to end the erratic, military-dominated politics that had characterized Iraq since 1958. He also tried to implement the First Five-Year Economic Plan (1965-70) to streamline the bureaucracy and to encourage private and foreign investment.

In April 1966, Arif was killed in a helicopter crash and his brother, Major General Abd ar Rahman Arif, was installed in office with the approval of the National Defense Council and the cabinet. Abd ar Rahman Arif lacked the forcefulness and the political acumen of his brother; moreover, he was dominated by the ambitious military officers who were responsible for his appointment. The government's weak hold on the country thus became more apparent. The most pressing issue facing the new government was a renewed Kurdish rebellion.

The 1964 cease-fire signed by Kurdish leader Mustafa Barzani and Abd as Salaam Arif was short-lived; by April 1965, the two sides were again engaged in hostilities. This time military support provided by the shah of Iran helped the Kurds win important victories over the Iraqi army. Kurdish inroads in the north and escalating Iraqi-Iranian tensions prompted Iraq's prime minister Bazzaz to propose a more far-reaching settlement to the Kurdish problem. Some of the more salient points of Bazzaz's proposal included amnesty, use of the Kurdish language in Kurdish areas, Kurdish administration of their educational, health, and municipal institutions, and the promise of early elections by which the Kurds would gain proportional representation in national as well as in provincial assemblies. When Barzani indicated that he approved of these proposals, the Kurdish conflict appeared to have ended.

The army, however, which had opposed having Bazzaz as a civilian head of the cabinet, feared that he would reduce their pay and privileges; consequently, it strongly denounced reconciliation with the Kurds. President Arif yielded to pressure and asked for Bazzaz's resignation. This ended the rapprochement with the Kurds and led to a collapse of civilian rule. The new prime minister was General Naji Talib, a pro-Nasserite who had been instrumental in the 1958 Revolution and who strongly opposed the Kurdish peace plan.

Arif also sought to further the improved relations with Iran initiated by Bazzaz. This rapprochement was significant because it denied the Kurds access to their traditional place of asylum, which allowed recovery from Iraqi attacks. Arif visited Tehran in the spring of 1967; at the conclusion of his visit, it was announced that the countries would hold more meetings aimed at joint oil exploration in the Naft-e Shah and Naft Khaneh border regions. They also agreed to continue negotiations on toll collection and navigation rights on the Shatt al Arab and on the demarcation of the Persian Gulf's continental shelf.

During the winter of 1966-67, Arif faced a crisis emanating from a new source, Syria. The IPC transported oil from its northern fields to Mediterranean ports via pipelines in Syria.

In 1966 Damascus claimed that the IPC had been underpaying Syria, based on their 1955 agreement. Syria demanded back payments and immediately increased the transit fee it charged the IPC. When the IPC did not accede to Syrian demands, Syria cut off the flow of Iraqi oil to its Mediterranean ports. The loss of revenue threatened to cause a severe financial crisis. It also fueled anti-Talib forces and increased public clamor for his resignation. In response, Talib resigned, and Arif briefly headed an extremely unsteady group of military officers.

In the opinion of Phebe Marr, a leading authority on Iraq, on the eve of the June 1967 War between Israel and various Arab states, the Arif government had become little more than a collection of army officers balancing the special interests of various economic, political, ethnic, and sectarian groups. The non-intervention of Iraqi troops while Israel was overtaking the Egyptian, Syrian, and Jordanian armies and was conquering large tracts of Arab territory discredited the Arif regime in the eyes of the masses. To stave off rising discontent, Arif reappointed strongman Tahir Yahya as prime minister (he had first been appointed by Arif in November 1963). Yahya's only accomplishment was to lessen Iraq's economic dependence on the Western-owned IPC: on August 6, his government turned over all exploitation rights in the oil-rich North Rumailah field to the state- controlled INOC. The Arif government, however, had lost its base of power. Lacking a coherent political platform and facing increasing charges of corruption, the government was only hanging on.

Ultimately two disaffected Arif supporters--Colonel Abd ar Razzaq an Nayif and Ibrahim ad Daud--were able to stage a successful coup against Arif, and the Baath quickly capitalized on the situation. Nayif and Daud had been part of a small group of young officers, called the Arab Revolutionary Movement, that previously had been a major source of support for Arif. By July 1968, however, reports of corruption and Arif's increased reliance on the Nasserites (whom both Nayif and Daud opposed) had alienated the two officers. Nayif and Daud acted independently from the Baath in carrying out the coup, but lacked the organizational backing or the grass-roots support necessary to remain in power. In only a few weeks, the Baath had outmaneuvered Nayif and Daud, and, for the second time in five years, had taken over control of the government.

The Emergence of Saddam Husayn, 1968-79

The Baath of 1968 was more tightly organized and more determined to stay in power than the Baath of 1963. The demise of Nasserism following the June 1967 War and the emergence of a more parochially oriented Baath in Syria freed the Iraqi Baath from the debilitating aspects of pan-Arabism. In 1963 Nasser had been able to manipulate domestic Iraqi politics; by 1968 his ideological pull had waned, enabling the Iraqi Baath to focus on pressing domestic issues. The party also was aided by a 1967 reorganization that created a militia and an intelligence apparatus and set up local branches that gave the Baath broader support. In addition, by 1968 close family and tribal ties bound the Baath's ruling clique. Most notable in this regard was the emergence of Tikritis--Sunni Arabs from the northwest town of Tikrit--related to Ahmad Hasan al Bakr. Three of the five members of the Baath's Revolutionary Command Council (RCC) were Tikritis; two, Bakr and Hammad Shihab, were related to each other. The cabinet posts of president, prime minister, and defense minister went to Tikritis. Saddam Husayn, a key leader behind the scenes, also was a Tikriti and a relative of Bakr. Another distinguishing characteristic of the Baath in 1968 was that the top leadership consisted almost entirely of military men. Finally, Bakr was a much more seasoned politician in 1968 than he had been in 1963.

Less than two months after the formation of the Bakr government, a coalition of pro-Nasser elements, Arif supporters, and conservatives from the military attempted another coup. This event provided the rationale for numerous purges directed by Bakr and Saddam Husayn. Between 1968 and 1973, through a series of sham trials, executions, assassinations, and intimidations, the party ruthlessly eliminated any group or person suspected of challenging Baath rule. The Baath also institutionalized its rule by formally issuing a Provisional Constitution in July 1970. This document was a modification of an earlier constitution that had been issued in September 1968. The Provisional Constitution, which with some modifications is still in effect, granted the party-dominated RCC extensive powers and declared that new RCC members must belong to the party's Regional Command--the top policy-making and executive body of the Baathist organization (see Constitutional Framework).

Two men, Saddam Husayn and Bakr, increasingly dominated the party. Bakr, who had been associated with Arab nationalist causes for more than a decade, brought the party popular legitimacy. Even more important, he brought support from the army both among Baathist and non-Baathist officers, with whom he had cultivated ties for years. Saddam Husayn, on the other hand, was a consummate party politician whose formative experiences were in organizing clandestine opposition activity. He was adept at outmaneuvering--and at times ruthlessly eliminating--political opponents. Although Bakr was the older and more prestigious of the two, by 1969 Saddam Husayn clearly had become the moving force behind the party. He personally directed Baathist attempts to settle the Kurdish question and he organized the party's institutional structure.

In July 1973, after an unsuccessful coup attempt by a civilian faction within the Baath led by Nazim Kazzar, the party set out to reconsolidate its hold on power. First, the RCC amended the Provisional Constitution to give the president greater power. Second, in early 1974 the Regional Command was officially designated as the body responsible for making policy (see The Revolutionary Command Council). By September 1977, all Regional Command leaders had been appointed to the RCC. Third, the party created a more pervasive presence in Iraqi society by establishing a complex network of grass-roots and intelligence-gathering organizations. Finally, the party established its own militia, which in 1978 was reported to number close to 50,000 men.

Despite Baath attempts to institutionalize its rule, real power remained in the hands of a narrowly based elite, united by close family and tribal ties. By 1977 the most powerful men in the Baath thus were all somehow related to the triumvirate of Saddam Husayn, Bakr, and General Adnan Khayr Allah Talfah, Saddam Husayn's brother-in-law who became minister of defense in 1978. All were members of the party, the RCC, and the cabinet, and all were members of the Talfah family of Tikrit, headed by Khayr Allah Talfah. Khayr Allah Talfah was Saddam Husayn's uncle and guardian, Adnan Khayr Allah's father, and Bakr's cousin. Saddam Husayn was married to Adnan Khayr Allah's sister and Adnan Khayr Allah was married to Bakr's daughter. Increasingly, the most sensitive military posts were going to the Tikritis.

Beginning in the mid-1970s, Bakr was beset by illness and by a series of family tragedies. He increasingly turned over power to Saddam Husayn. By 1977 the party bureaus, the intelligence mechanisms, and even ministers who, according to the Provisional Constitution, should have reported to Bakr, reported to Saddam Husayn. Saddam Husayn, meanwhile, was less inclined to share power, and he viewed the cabinet and the RCC as rubber stamps. On July 16, 1979, President Bakr resigned, and Saddam Husayn officially replaced him as president of the republic, Secretary-General of the Baath Party Regional Command, chairman of the RCC, and commander in chief of the armed forces.

In foreign affairs, the Baath's pan-Arab and socialist leanings alienated both the pro-Western Arab Gulf states and the shah of Iran. The enmity between Iraq and Iran sharpened with the 1969 British announcement of a planned withdrawal from the Gulf in 1971. In February 1969, Iran announced that Iraq had not fulfilled its obligations under the 1937 treaty and demanded that the border in the Shatt al Arab waterway be set at the thalweg. Iraq's refusal to honor the Iranian demand led the shah to abrogate the 1937 treaty and to send Iranian ships through the Shatt al Arab without paying dues to Iraq. In response, Iraq aided anti-shah dissidents, while the shah renewed support for Kurdish rebels. Relations between the two countries soon deteriorated further. In November 1971, the shah occupied the islands of Abu Musa and the Greater and Lesser Tunbs, which previously had been under the sovereignty of Ras al Khaymah and Sharjah, both member states of the United Arab Emirates.

The Iraqi Baath also was involved in a confrontation with the conservative shaykhdoms of the Gulf over Iraq's support for the leftist People's Democratic Republic of Yemen (South Yemen) and the Popular Front for the Liberation of the Occupied Arabian Gulf. The major contention between Iraq and the conservative Gulf states, however, concerned the Kuwaiti islands of Bubiyan and Warbah that dominate the estuary leading to the southern Iraqi port of Umm Qasr. Beginning in the early 1970s, Iraq's desire to develop a deep-water port on the Gulf led to demands that the two islands be transferred or leased to Iraq. Kuwait refused, and in March 1973 Iraqi troops occupied As Samitah, a border post in the northeast corner of Kuwait. Saudi Arabia immediately came to Kuwait's aid and, together with the Arab League, obtained Iraq's withdrawal.

The most serious threat facing the Baath was a resurgence of Kurdish unrest in the north. In March 1970, the RCC and Mustafa Barzani announced agreement to a fifteen-article peace plan. This plan was almost identical to the previous Bazzaz-Kurdish settlement that had never been implemented. The Kurds were immediately pacified by the settlement, particularly because Barzani was permitted to retain his 15,000 Kurdish troops. Barzani's troops then became an official Iraqi frontier force called the Pesh Merga, meaning "Those Who Face Death." The plan, however, was not completely satisfactory because the legal status of the Kurdish territory remained unresolved. At the time of the signing of the peace plan, Barzani's forces controlled territory from Zakhu in the north to Halabjah in the southeast and already had established de facto Kurdish administration in most of the towns of the area. Barzani's group, the Kurdish Democratic Party (KDP), was granted official recognition as the legitimate representative of the Kurdish people.

The 1970 agreement unraveled throughout the early 1970s. After the March 1974 Baath attempt to assassinate Barzani and his son Idris, full-scale fighting broke out. In early 1974, it appeared that the Baath had finally succeeded in isolating Barzani and the KDP by coopting the ICP and by signing a treaty with the Soviet Union, both traditionally strong supporters of the KDP. Barzani, however, compensated for the loss of Soviet and ICP support by obtaining military aid from the shah of Iran and from the United States, both of which were alarmed by increasing Soviet influence in Iraq. When Iraqi forces reached Rawanduz, threatening to block the major Kurdish artery to Iran, the shah increased the flow of military supplies to the Kurdish rebels. Using antitank missiles and artillery obtained from Iran as well as military aid from Syria and Israel, the KDP inflicted heavy losses on the Iraqi forces. To avoid a costly stalemate like that which had weakened his predecessors, Saddam Husayn sought an agreement with the shah.

In Algiers on March 6, 1975, Saddam Husayn signed an agreement with the shah that recognized the thalweg as the boundary in the Shatt al Arab, legalized the shah's abrogation of the 1937 treaty in 1969, and dropped all Iraqi claims to Iranian Khuzestan and to the islands at the foot of the Gulf. In return, the shah agreed to prevent subversive elements from crossing the border. This agreement meant an end to Iranian assistance to the Kurds. Almost immediately after the signing of the Algiers Agreement, Iraqi forces went on the offensive and defeated the Pesh Merga, which was unable to hold out without Iranian support. Under an amnesty plan, about 70 percent of the Pesh Merga surrendered to the Iraqis. Some remained in the hills of Kurdistan to continue the fight, and about 30,000 crossed the border to Iran to join the civilian refugees, then estimated at between 100,000 and 200,000.

Even before the fighting broke out in March 1974, Saddam Husayn had offered the Kurds the most comprehensive autonomy plan ever proposed. The major provisions of the plan stated that Kurdistan would be an autonomous area governed by an elected legislative and an executive council, the president of which would be appointed by the Iraqi head of state. The Kurdish council would have control over local affairs except in the areas of defense and foreign relations, which would be controlled by the central government. The autonomous region did not include the oil-rich district of Kirkuk. To facilitate the autonomy plan, Saddam Husayn's administration helped form three progovernment Kurdish parties, allocated a special budget for development in Kurdish areas, and repatriated many Kurdish refugees then living in Iran.

In addition to the conciliatory measures offered to the Kurds, Saddam Husayn attempted to weaken Kurdish resistance by forcibly relocating many Kurds from the Kurdish heartland in the north, by introducing increasing numbers of Arabs into mixed Kurdish provinces, and by razing all Kurdish villages along a 1,300 kilometer stretch of the border with Iran. Saddam Husayn's combination of conciliation and severity failed to appease the Kurds, and renewed guerrilla attacks occurred as early as March 1976. At the same time, the failure of the KDP to obtain significant concessions from the Iraqi government caused a serious split within the Kurdish resistance. In June 1975, Jalal Talabani formed the Patriotic Union of Kurdistan (PUK). The PUK was urban-based and more leftist than the tribally based KDP. Following Barzani's death in 1975, Barzani's sons, Idris and Masud, took control of the KDP. In October 1979, Masud officially was elected KDP chairman. He issued a new platform calling for continued armed struggle against the Baath through guerrilla warfare. The effectiveness of the KDP, however, was blunted by its violent intra-Kurdish struggle with the PUK throughout 1978 and 1979.

Beginning in 1976, with the Baath firmly in power and after the Kurdish rebellion had been successfully quelled, Saddam Husayn set out to consolidate his position at home by strengthening the economy. He pursued a state-sponsored industrial modernization program that tied an increasing number of Iraqis to the Baath-controlled government. Saddam Husayn's economic policies were largely successful; they led to a wider distribution of wealth, to greater social mobility, to increased access to education and health care, and to the redistribution of land. The quadrupling of oil prices in 1973 and the subsequent oil price rises brought on by the 1979 Islamic Revolution in Iran greatly enhanced the success of Saddam Husayn's program. The more equitable distribution of income tied to the ruling party many Iraqis who had previously opposed the central government. For the first time in modern Iraqi history, a government--albeit at times a ruthless one, had thus achieved some success in forging a national community out of the country's disparate social elements.

Success on the economic front spurred Saddam Husayn to pursue an ambitious foreign policy aimed at pushing Iraq to the forefront of the Arab world. Between 1975 and 1979, a major plank of Saddam Husayn's bid for power in the region rested on improved relations with Iran, with Saudi Arabia, and with the smaller Gulf shaykhdoms. In 1975 Iraq established diplomatic relations with Sultan Qabus of Oman and extended several loans to him. In 1978 Iraq sharply reversed its support for the Marxist regime in South Yemen. The biggest boost to Saddam Husayn's quest for regional power, however, resulted from Egyptian President Anwar Sadat's signing the Camp David Accords in November 1978.

Saddam Husayn viewed Egypt's isolation within the Arab world as an opportunity for Iraq to play a leading role in Arab affairs. He was instrumental in convening an Arab summit in Baghdad that denounced Sadat's reconciliation with Israel and imposed sanctions on Egypt. He also attempted to end his long- standing feud with Syrian President Hafiz al Assad, and, in June 1979, Saddam Husayn became the first Iraqi head of state in twenty years to visit Jordan. In Amman, Saddam Husayn concluded a number of agreements with King Hussein, including one for the expansion of the port of Aqabah, regarded by Iraq as a potential replacement for ports in Lebanon and Syria.

The Iran-Iraq Conflict

In February 1979, Saddam Husayn's ambitious plans and the course of Iraqi history were drastically altered by the overthrow of the shah of Iran. Husayn viewed the 1979 Islamic Revolution in Iran as both a threat and an opportunity. The downfall of the shah and the confusion prevailing in postrevolutionary Iran suited Saddam Husayn's regional ambitions. A weakened Iran seemed to offer an opportunity to project Iraqi power over the Gulf, to regain control over the Shatt al Arab waterway, and to augment Iraqi claims to leadership of the Arab world. More ominously, the activist Shia Islam preached by the leader of the revolution in Iran, Ayatollah Sayyid Ruhollah Musavi Khomeini, threatened to upset the delicate Sunni-Shia balance in Iraq, and a hostile Iran would threaten Iraqi security in the Gulf. Furthermore, deepseated personal animosities separated the two leaders. The two men held widely divergent ideologies, and in 1978 Husayn had expelled Khomeini from Iraq--reportedly at the request of the shah--after he had lived thirteen years in exile in An Najaf.

For much of Iraqi history, the Shias have been both politically impotent and economically depressed. Beginning in the sixteenth century, when the Ottoman Sunnis favored their Iraqi coreligionists in the matter of educational and employment opportunities, the Shias consistently have been denied political power. Thus, although the Shias constitute more then 50 percent of the population, they occupy a relatively insignificant number of government posts. On the economic level, aside from a small number of wealthy landowners and merchants, the Shias historically were exploited as sharecropping peasants or menially employed slum dwellers. Even the prosperity brought by the oil boom of the 1970s only trickled down slowly to the Shias; however, beginning in the latter half of the 1970s,

Saddam's populist economic policies had a favorable impact on them, enabling many to join the ranks of a new Shia middle class.

Widespread Shia demonstrations took place in Iraq in February 1977, when the government, suspecting a bomb, closed Karbala to pilgrimage at the height of a religious ceremony. Violent clashes between police and Shia pilgrims spread from Karbala to An Najaf and lasted for several days before army troops were called in to quell the unrest. It was the 1979 Islamic Revolution in Iran, however, that transformed Shia dissatisfaction with the Baath into an organized religiously based opposition. The Baath leadership feared that the success of Iran's Islamic Revolution would serve as an inspiration to Iraqi Shias. These fears escalated in July 1979, when riots broke out in An Najaf and in Karbala after the government had refused Ayatollah Muhammad Baqir as Sadr's request to lead a procession to Iran to congratulate Khomeini. Even more worrisome to the Baath was the discovery of a clandestine Shia group headed by religious leaders having ties to Iran. Baqir as Sadr was the inspirational leader of the group, named Ad Dawah al Islamiyah (the Islamic Call), commonly referred to as Ad Dawah. He espoused a program similar to Khomeini's, which called for a return to Islamic precepts of government and for social justice.

Despite the Iraqi government's concern, the eruption of the 1979 Islamic Revolution in Iran did not immediately destroy the Iraqi-Iranian rapprochement that had prevailed since the 1975 Algiers Agreement. As a sign of Iraq's desire to maintain good relations with the new government in Tehran, President Bakr sent a personal message to Khomeini offering "his best wishes for the friendly Iranian people on the occasion of the establishment of the Islamic Republic." In addition, as late as the end of August 1979, Iraqi authorities extended an invitation to Mehdi Bazargan, the first president of the Islamic Republic of Iran, to visit Iraq with the aim of improving bilateral relations. The fall of the moderate Bazargan government in late 1979, however, and the rise of Islamic militants preaching an expansionist foreign policy soured Iraqi-Iranian relations.

The principal events that touched off the rapid deterioration in relations occurred during the spring of 1980. In April the Iranian-supported Ad Dawah attempted to assassinate Iraqi foreign minister Tariq Aziz. Shortly after the failed grenade attack on Tariq Aziz, Ad Dawah was suspected of attempting to assassinate another Iraqi leader, Minister of Culture and Information Latif Nayyif Jasim. In response, the Iraqis immediately rounded up members and supporters of Ad Dawah and deported to Iran thousands of Shias of Iranian origin. In the summer of 1980, Saddam Husayn ordered the executions of presumed Ad Dawah leader Ayatollah Sayyid Muhammad Baqr as Sadr and his sister.

In September 1980, border skirmishes erupted in the central sector near Qasr-e Shirin, with an exchange of artillery fire by both sides. A few weeks later, Saddam Husayn officially abrogated the 1975 treaty between Iraq and Iran and announced that the Shatt al Arab was returning to Iraqi sovereignty. Iran rejected this action and hostilities escalated as the two sides exchanged bombing raids deep into each other's territory. Finally, on September 23, Iraqi troops marched into Iranian territory, beginning what was to be a protracted and extremely costly war.

The Iran-Iraq War permanently altered the course of Iraqi history. It strained Iraqi political and social life, and led to severe economic dislocations. Viewed from a historical perspective, the outbreak of hostilities in 1980 was, in part, just another phase of the ancient Persian-Arab conflict that had been fueled by twentieth-century border disputes. Many observers, however, believe that Saddam Husayn's decision to invade Iran was a personal miscalculation based on ambition and a sense of vulnerability. Saddam Husayn, despite having made significant strides in forging an Iraqi nation-state, feared that Iran's new revolutionary leadership would threaten Iraq's delicate SunniShia balance and would exploit Iraq's geostrategic vulnerabilities--Iraq's minimal access to the Persian Gulf, for example. In this respect, Saddam Husayn's decision to invade Iran has historical precedent; the ancient rulers of Mesopotamia, fearing internal strife and foreign conquest, also engaged in frequent battles with the peoples of the highlands.

THE SOCIETY AND ITS ENVIRONMENT

Iraqi society is composed of sizable and distinct social groups whose differences and divisions have been only slowly and fitfully challenged by the emergence of a strong, centralized political regime and state apparatus. Moreover, there are regional and environmental differences between the scattered mountain villages whose economic base is rain-fed grain crops and the more densely populated riverine communities to the south that are dependent on intricate irrigation and drainage systems for their livelihood.

There are also linguistic and ethnic differences. The most important exception to the Arab character of Iraq is the large Kurdish minority, estimated at 19 percent of the population, or 3,092,820 in 1987. According to official government statistics, Turkomans and other Turkic-speaking peoples account for only 2 to 3 percent of the population. There was previously a large Iranian population settled around the Shia (see Glossary) holy cities of Karbala and An Najaf, and the southern port city of Basra; this element was largely expelled by government decree in 1971-72 and 1979-80, and in 1987 only an estimated 133,000 or 0.8 percent of the Iranian population remained.

Divisions along religious lines are deeprooted. Although upward of 95 percent of Iraq's population is Muslim, the community is split between Sunnis (see Glossary) and Shias; the latter group, a minority in the Arab world as a whole, constitutes a majority in Iraq. Numerous observers believe that the Shias make up between 60 and 65 percent of the inhabitants, although the data to support this figure are not firm (official government statistics set the number at only 55 percent). Of the non-Muslim communities, fragmented Christian sects cannot be more than 1 or 2 percent, concentrated mainly in the governorates of Nineveh and Dahuk. A formerly extensive Jewish community is to all practical purposes defunct. The establishment of the State of Israel in 1948 and the defeat of the Arab armies in 1948-49 rendered the situation of Iraqi Jews untenable and led to a mass exodus, both to Israel and to Iran in 1950.

Just before the Iran-Iraq War, the sharp cleavage between the rural and urban communities that formerly characterized Iraqi society had begun to break down as a result of policies instituted by the government. The war has accelerated this process. Large areas of the rural south have been devastated by continuous fighting, which in turn has triggered a massive rural migration to the capital. In the late 1980s, Iraqi and foreign observers agreed that for the nation's economic health this flight from the countryside would have to be reversed, and they anticipated that the government would undertake measures to accomplish this reversal once the war ended.

Geography and Population

Boundaries

The border with Iran has been a continuing source of conflict and was partially responsible for the outbreak in 1980 of the present war. The terms of a treaty negotiated in 1937 under British auspices provided that in one area of the Shatt al Arab the boundary would be at the low water mark on the Iranian side. Iran subsequently insisted that the 1937 treaty was imposed on it by "British imperialist pressures," and that the proper boundary throughout the Shatt was the thalweg. The matter came to a head in 1969 when Iraq, in effect, told the Iranian government that the Shatt was an integral part of Iraqi territory and that the waterway might be closed to Iranian shipping.

Through Algerian mediation, Iran and Iraq agreed in March 1975 to normalize their relations, and three months later they signed a treaty known as the Algiers Accord. The document defined the common border all along the Shatt estuary as the thalweg. To compensate Iraq for the loss of what formerly had been regarded as its territory, pockets of territory along the mountain border in the central sector of its common boundary with Iran were assigned to it. Nonetheless, in September 1980 Iraq went to war with Iran, citing among other complaints the fact that Iran had not turned over to it the land specified in the Algiers Accord. This problem has subsequently proved to be a stumbling block to a negotiated settlement of the ongoing conflict.

In 1988 the boundary with Kuwait was another outstanding problem. It was fixed in a 1913 treaty between the Ottoman Empire and British officials acting on behalf of Kuwait's ruling family, which in 1899 had ceded control over foreign affairs to Britain. The boundary was accepted by Iraq when it became independent in 1932, but in the 1960s and again in the mid-1970s, the Iraqi government advanced a claim to parts of Kuwait. Kuwait made several representations to the Iraqis during the war to fix the border once and for all but Baghdad has repeatedly demurred, claiming that the issue is a potentially divisive one that could enflame nationalist sentiment inside Iraq. Hence in 1988 it was likely that a solution would have to wait until the war ended.

In 1922 British officials concluded the Treaty of Mohammara with Abd al Aziz ibn Abd ar Rahman Al Saud, who in 1932 formed the Kingdom of Saudi Arabia. The treaty provided the basic agreement for the boundary between the eventually independent nations. Also in 1922 the two parties agreed to the creation of the diamond-shaped Neutral Zone of approximately 7,500 square kilometers adjacent to the western tip of Kuwait in which neither Iraq nor Saudi Arabia would build permanent dwellings or installations . Beduins from either country could utilize the limited water and seasonal grazing resources of the zone. In April 1975, an agreement signed in Baghdad fixed the borders of the countries. Despite a rumored agreement providing for the formal division of the Iraq-Saudi Arabia Neutral Zone, as of early 1988 such a document had not been published. Instead, Saudi Arabia was continuing to control oil wells in the offshore Neutral Zone and had been allocating proceeds from Neutral Zone oil sales to Iraq as a war payment.

Religious Life

Although members of the ruling Baath Party generally are ideologically committed to secularism, about 95 percent of Iraqis are Muslim and Islam is the officially recognized state religion. Islam came to the region with the victory of the Muslim armies under Caliph Umar over the Sassanians in A.D. 637 at the battle of Al Qadisiyah. The majority of inhabitants soon became Muslim, including the Kurds, although small communities of Christians and Jews remained intact in the area of present-day Iraq. Iraq has been the scene of many important events in the early history of Islam, including the schism over the rightful successor to the Prophet Muhammad.

Christian church, Baghdad
Courtesy Ronald L. Kuipers

Social Systems

The impact of Western penetration on the indigenous social and demographic structure in the nineteenth century was profound. Western influence took the initial form of transportation and trading links and the switch from tribal-based subsistence agriculture to cash crop production--mostly dates--for export. As this process accelerated, the nomadic population decreased both relatively and in absolute numbers and the rural sedentary population increased substantially, particularly in the southern region. This was accompanied by a pronounced transformation of tenurial relations: the tribal, communal character of subsistence production was transformed on a large scale into a landlord-tenant relationship; tribal shaykhs, urban merchants, and government officials took title under the open-ended terms of the newly promulgated Ottoman land codes. Incentives and pressures on this emerging landlord class to increase production (and thus exports and earnings) resulted in expanded cultivation, which brought more and more land under cultivation and simultaneously absorbed the "surplus" labor represented by the tribal, pastoral, and nomadic character of much of Iraqi society. This prolonged process of sedentarization was disrupted by the dismemberment of the Ottoman Empire during and after World War I, but it resumed with renewed intensity in the British Mandate period, when the political structure of independent Iraq was formed.

This threefold transformation of rural society--pastoral to agricultural, subsistence to commercial, tribal-communal to landlord-peasant--was accompanied by important shifts in urban society as well. There was a general increase in the number and size of marketing towns and their populations; but the destruction of handicraft industries, especially in Baghdad, by the import of cheap manufactured goods from the West, led to an absolute decline in the population of urban centers. It also indelibly stamped the subsequent urban growth with a mercantile and bureaucratic-administrative character that is still a strong feature of Iraqi society.

Thus, the general outline and history of Iraqi population dynamics in the modern era can be divided into a period extending from the middle of the nineteenth century to World War II, characterized chiefly by urbanization, with a steady and growing movement of people from the rural (especially southern) region to the urban (especially central) region. Furthermore, the basic trends of the 1980s are rooted in the particularly exploitive character of agricultural practices regarding both the land itself and the people who work it. Declining productivity of the land, stemming from the failure to develop drainage along the irrigation facilities and the wretched condition of the producers, has resulted in a potentially harmful demographic trajectory--the depopulation of the countryside--that in the late 1980s continued to bedevil government efforts to reverse the decades-long pattern of declining productivity in the agricultural sector.

The accelerated urbanization process since World War II is starkly illustrated in the shrinking proportion of the population living in rural areas: 61 percent in 1947, fillowed by 56 percent in 1965, then 36 percent in 1977, and an estimated 32 percent in 1987; concurrently between 1977 and 1987 the urban population rose from 7,646,054 to an estimated 11,078,000 (see table 1). The rural exodus has been most severe in Al Basrah and Al Qadisiyah governorates. The proportion of rural to urban population was lowest in the governorates of Al Basrah (37 percent in 1965, and 1 percent in 1987) and Baghdad (48 percent in 1965 and 19 percent in 1987). It was highest in Dhi Qar Governorate where it averaged 50 percent in 1987, followed closely by Al Muthanna and Diyala governorates with rural populations of 48 percent. Between 1957 and 1967, the population of Baghdad and Al Basrah governorates grew by 73 percent and 41 percent respectively. During the same years the city of Baghdad grew by 87 percent and the city of Basra by 64 percent.

Table 2. Population Distribution by Governorate, 1987 (in thousands)

Administrative Division	Female	Male	Urban	Rural	Total
Governorate					
Al Anbar	390	428	538	280	818
Al Basrah	438	434	782	90	872
Al Muthanna	160	153	163	150	313
Al Q adisiyah	280	281	321	240	561
An Najaf	362	361	568	155	723
At Tamim	255	338	473	120	593
Babylon	557	552	669	440	1,109
Baghdad	1,890	1,955	3,600	245	3,845
Dhi Qar	445	473	468	450	918
Diyala	445	455	465	435	900
Karbala	229	227	341	115	456
Maysan	244	256	275	225	500
Nineveh	745	762	982	525	1,507[1]
Salah ad Din	350	374	400	324	724
Wasit	225	235	260	200	460
Autonomous Region[2]					
As Sulaymaniyah	433	510	543	400	943
Dahuk	125	168	160	133	293
Irbil	340	403	475	268	743
TOTAL	7,913[1]	8,365[1]	11,483	4,795	16,278[1]

[1] From October 17, 1987, census; remaining figures are estimates.
[2] See Glossary.
Source: Based on information from Joint Publications Research Service, *Daily Report: Near East and South Asia*, October 20, 1987, 22, and October 21, 1987, 25.

Because of the war, the growth of Al Basrah Governorate has been reversed while that of Baghdad Governorate has accelerated alarmingly, with the 1987 census figure for urban Baghdad being 3,845,000. Iranian forces have mounted an offensive each year of the war since 1980, except for early 1988, seeking to capture Basra and the adjoining area and subjecting the city to regular bombardment. As a result, large numbers of the population fled northward from Basra and other southern areas, with many entering Baghdad, which was already experiencing overcrowding. The government has attempted to deal with this situation by moving war refugees out of the capital and resettling them in other smaller cities in the south, out of the range of the fighting.

Family and Society

Kinship groups are the fundamental social units, regulating many activities that in Westernized societies are the functions of political, economic, religious, or neighborhood groups. Rights and obligations center on the extended family and the lineage. The family remains the primary focus of loyalty; and it is in this context, rather than the broader one of corporate loyalties defined by sectarian, ethnic, or economic considerations, that the majority of Iraqis find the common denominators of their everyday lives. A mutually protective attitude among relatives is taken as a matter of course. Relatives tend to be preferred as business partners since they are believed to be more reliable than persons over whom one does not have the hold of kinship ties. On higher levels, deeply ingrained family loyalty manifests itself in business and public life.

The characteristic form of family organization involves a large group of kinsmen related to one another through descent and marriage, that is, an extended family usually consisting of three generations. Such an extended family may all live together, which is the more traditional pattern, or may reside separately like a nuclear family, but still share the values and functions of an extended family, such as depending upon one another and deferring to the older generation. As Iraqi society has become increasingly urbanized, however, the tendency toward nuclear family social organization, as opposed merely to residence, has become more prevalent. The status of an individual is traditionally determined by the position of his or her family in society and the individual's position within that group. The family transmits values and standards of behavior of the society to its members and holds them responsible for each other's conduct. It traditionally determines occupations and selects marriage partners. Kinsmen also cooperate in economic endeavors, such as farming or trade, and ownership in land and other assets frequently is vested in the group as a whole. The sharpest degree of divergence from these patterns occurs among educated urban Iraqis, an ever-increasing proportion of the society.

Until 1959 family life was subject to regulation only according to religious law and tradition. All Muslims were brought under a single body of family law for the first time in 1959 with the enactment of a secular law on personal status, based on sharia, statutes from other Islamic countries, and legal precedents established in Iraqi courts; a brief amendment was enacted in 1963. The law spells out provisions governing the right to contract marriage, the nature of the contract, economic rights of the partners, divorce and child custody, as well as bequests and inheritance.

The basic structural unit of the family consists of a senior couple, their sons, the sons' wives and children, and unmarried daughters. Other dependent relatives may also be attached to the group. The senior male is the head of the family; he manages its properties and has the final voice in decisions. Kinsmen are organized into still larger groups. The next level of organization is the lineage, composed of all persons, male and female, who trace their descent from a common ancestor. The number of generations by which this ancestor is removed from the oldest living one varies; a depth of four to six generations is usual.

Individuals or whole families of other descent sometimes attach themselves to a particular lineage in an arrangement of mutual advantage, becoming recognized after several generations as full members of the lineage on equal terms with those born into it. In small villages everyone is likely to belong to the same lineage; in larger ones there may be two or more lineages in common but tempered by economic cooperation, intermarriage, and the authority of the village leadership or elders. Also among nontribal Iraqis, kinship organization and traditions of common descent do not go beyond the lineage. Awareness of distant ties is keen among recent migrants to the cities and among the rural population.

In rural areas, new households are not usually set up until many years after the initial recognition of a marriage. In general, the wife moves in with her husband's parents, where the young couple remain for some time. Often this arrangement is maintained until the death of the father. Even when the father dies, the brothers sometimes stay together, forming joint family households that include themselves, their wives, and their children.

The actual number of persons who make up the household is determined by the family's economic circumstances, pattern of living, and mode of habitation. In an agricultural setting, as long as ownership of land and other possessions is vested in the family as a whole, the possibilities for a young man to set up an independent household are limited. In urban centers, on the other hand, young men can avail themselves of wage-earning employment.

Authority within the family is determined by seniority and sex. The father, in theory, has absolute authority over the activities of the members of the household, both within the confines of the house and outside. He decides what education his children will receive, what occupations his sons will enter, and, usually in consultation with his wife, whom his children will marry. These authority patterns also have been greatly weakened in the urban environment and by the shift of more and more responsibilities from the family to larger social institutions, such as the schools.

An even greater change in the traditional pattern of male dominance has been brought about by the war. Because Iraq is numerically a much smaller nation than Iran, it has experienced considerable difficulty maintaining an adequate defense on the battlefront. To field a sufficient force it has had to draw down the available labor pool on the home front, and to compensate has mobilized women. In the mid-1980s, observers reported that in many ministries the overwhelming proportion of employees were women. Foreign contractors have encountered women supervisors on huge construction projects, women doctors in the hospitals, and even women performing law enforcement roles. This emancipation--extraordinary for an Arab country--was sanctioned by the government, which expended a significant amount of propaganda publicizing the role of women in helping to win the war. The government further maintained that after the war women would be encouraged to retain their newfound work roles; this was doubtful, however, because in the same breath the government declared its determination to increase the birthrate.

The Muslim majority has traditionally regarded marriage as primarily a civil contract between two families, arranged by parents after negotiations, which may be prolonged and conducted by an intermediary. The arrangement of a marriage is a family matter in which the needs and position of the corporate kin group are primary considerations. Prospective partners are often known to each other, and they frequently come from the same village and the same kin group. Among educated urban dwellers, the traditional pattern of contracting marriage is giving way to a pattern in which the young persons make their own choices, but parents must still approve.

With regard to marriage and divorce, the 1959 Law of Personal Status, amended in 1963, liberalized various provisions that affected the status of women; in practice, however, the Iraqi judiciary up to the Revolution tended to be conservative in applying the provisions of the law. Specifically, Iraqi law required that divorce proceedings be initiated in a court of law, but the husband still had the controlling role in dissolving the marriage. Moreover, a man who wanted to marry a second wife was required first to get approval from the court. Provision was also made for the custody of children to be based on consideration of the welfare of the child.

Economic motivation and considerations of prestige and family strength all contribute to the high value placed on large families. The greater the number of children, especially sons, the greater the prestige of the father, and through him that of the family as a whole. Boys are especially welcome because they are the carriers of the family tradition, and because their economic contribution in an agricultural society is greater than that of girls.

Between the ages of three and six, children are given freedom to learn by imitating older siblings. Strong emphasis is then placed on conformity with elders' patterns and on loyalty and obedience. Family solidarity is stressed. The passage from adolescence to maturity is swift. Upon reaching puberty, there traditionally is a separation of sexes, and girls are excluded from male society except that of their close kin. Great emphasis is placed on premarital chastity, and this is one reason for early marriages. Boys have greater freedom during adolescence than girls and begin to be drawn into the company of their fathers and the world of men.

Education and Welfare

Education

The impact of government policies on the class structure and stratification patterns can be imputed from available statistics on education and training as well as employment and wage structures. Owing to the historic emphasis on the expansion of educational facilities, the leaders of the Baath Party and indeed much of Iraq's urban middle class were able to move from rural or urban lower-class origins to middle and even top positions in the state apparatus, the public sector, and the society at large.

This social history is confirmed in the efforts of the government to generalize opportunities for basic education throughout the country. Between 1976 and 1986, the number of primary-school students increased 30 percent; female students increased 45 percent, from 35 to 44 percent of the total. The number of primary-school teachers increased 40 percent over this period. At the secondary level, the number of students increased by 46 percent, and the number of female students increased by 55 percent, from 29 to 36 percent of the total. Baghdad, which had about 29 percent of the population, had 26 percent of the primary students, 27 percent of the female primary students, and 32 percent of the secondary students.

Education was provided by the government through a centrally organized school system. In the early 1980s, the system included a six-year primary (or elementary) level known as the first level. The second level, also of six years, consisted of an intermediate-secondary and an intermediate-preparatory, each of three years. Graduates of these schools could enroll in a vocational school, one of the teacher training schools or institutes, or one of the various colleges, universities, or technical institutes.

The number of students enrolled in primary and secondary schools was highest in the central region and lowest in the north, although the enrollment of the northern schools was only slightly lower than that of the south. Before the war, the government had made considerable gains in lessening the extreme concentration of primary and secondary educational facilities in the main cities, notably Baghdad. Vocational education, which had been notoriously inadequate in Iraq, received considerable official attention in the 1980s. The number of students in technical fields has increased threefold since 1977, to over 120,090 in 1986.

The Baath regime also seemed to have made progress since the late 1960s in reducing regional disparities, although they were far from eliminated and no doubt were more severe than statistics would suggest. Baghdad, for example, was the home of most educational facilities above the secondary level, since it was the site not only of Baghdad University, which in the academic year 1983-84 (the most recent year for which statistics were available in early 1988) had 34,555 students, but also of the Foundation of Technical Institutes with 34,277 students, Mustansiriya University with 11,686 students, and the University of Technology with 7,384 students. The universities in Basra, Mosul, and Irbil, taken together, enrolled 26 percent of all students in higher education in the academic year 1983-84.

The number of students seeking to pursue higher education in the 1980s increased dramatically. Accordingly, in the mid-1980s the government made plans to expand Salah ad Din University in Irbil in the north and to establish Ar Rashid University outside Baghdad. The latter was not yet in existence in early 1988 but both were designed ultimately to accommodate 50,000 students. In addition, at the end of December 1987, the government announced plans to create four more universities: one in Tikrit in the central area, one each at Al Kufah and Al Qadisiyah in the south, and one at Al Anbar in the west. Details of these universities were not known.

With the outbreak of the war, the government faced a difficult dilemma regarding education. Despite the shortage of wartime manpower, the regime was unwilling to tap the pool of available university students, arguing that these young people were Iraq's hope for the future. As of early 1988, therefore, the government routinely exempted students from military service until graduation, a policy it has adhered to rigorously. This policy, however, has likely caused resentment among the poorer classes and those forced to serve multiple tours at the front because of continuing manpower shortages.

THE ECONOMY

Following the 1968 Baath (Arab Socialist Resurrection) Party revolution, Iraq's government pursued a socialist economic policy. For more than a decade, the economy prospered, primarily because of massive infusions of cash from oil exports. Despite a quadrupling of imports between 1978 and 1980, Iraq continued to accrue current account surpluses in excess of US$10 billion per year. In 1980 on the eve of the outbreak of the Iran-Iraq War, Iraq held reserves estimated at US$35 billion. When Iraq launched the war against Iran in 1980, the Iraqis incorrectly calculated that they could force a quick Iranian capitulation and could annex Iranian territory at little cost in either men or money. Using a number of means, Iraq opted to keep the human costs of the war as low as possible, both on the battlefield and on the home front. In battle, Iraq attempted to keep casualties low by expending and by losing vast amounts of materiel. Behind the lines, Iraq attempted to insulate citizens from the effects of the war and to head off public protest in two ways. First, the government provided a benefits package worth tens of thousands of dollars to the surviving relatives of each soldier killed in action. The government also compensated property owners for the full value of property destroyed in the war. Second, the government adopted a "guns and butter" strategy. Along with the war, the government launched an economic development campaign of national scope, employing immigrant laborers to replace Iraqi fighting men.

In 1981, foreign expenditures not directly related to the war effort peaked at an all-time high of US$23.6 billion, as Iraq continued to import goods and services for the development effort, and construction continued unabated. Additionally, Iraq was paying an estimated US$25 million per day to wage the war. Although the Persian Gulf states contributed US$5 billion toward the war effort from 1980 to 1981, Iraq raised most of the money needed for war purposes by drawing down its reserves over several years. Iraq could not replenish its reserves because most of its oil terminals were destroyed by Iran in the opening days of the war. Iraqi exports dropped by 60 percent in 1981, and they were cut further in 1982 when Syria, acting in accord with Iran, closed the vital Iraqi oil export pipeline running through Syrian territory.

The total cost of the war to Iraq's economy was difficult to measure. A 1987 study by the Japanese Institute of Middle Eastern Economies estimated total Iraqi war losses from 1980 to 1985 at US$226 billion. This figure was disaggregated into US$120.8 billion in gross domestic product (GDP--see Glossary) lost in the oil sector, US$64 billion GDP lost in the nonoil sector, US$33 billion lost in destroyed materiel, and US$8.2 billion lost in damage to non-oil sector fixed capital investment. Included in the lost GDP was US$65.5 in lost oil revenues and US$43.4 billion in unrealized fixed capital investment.

As the 1980s progressed, the Iran-Iraq conflict evolved into a protracted war of attrition, in which Iran threatened to overwhelm Iraq by sheer economic weight and manpower. Although Iraq implemented some cost-cutting measures, the government feared that an austerity plan would threaten its stability, so it turned to outside sources to finance the war. Iraq's Persian Gulf neighbors assumed a larger share of the economic burden of the war, but as the price of oil skidded in the mid-1980s, this regional support of Iraq diminished. For the first time, Iraq turned to Western creditors to finance its deficit spending. Iraq's leadership calculated correctly that foreign lenders, both government and private, would be willing to provide loans and trade credit to preserve their access to the Iraqi economy, which would emerge as a major market and an oil supplier after the war. But the sustained slump in oil prices made foreign creditors more skeptical of Iraq's long-term economic prospects, and some lenders apparently concluded that providing more loans to Iraq amounted to throwing good money after bad. Some creditors were also wary of Iraq's postwar prospects because of Iranian demands for tens of billions of dollars in reparations as the price for any peace settlement. Although Iraq would probably pay only a fraction of the reparations demanded (and that, most likely, with the help of other Persian Gulf countries), a large settlement would nonetheless delay Iraq's postwar economic recovery.

In 1988, as the war entered its eighth year and Iraq's debt topped US$50 billion, the government was implementing comprehensive economic reforms it had announced in 1987. Iraq's new economic policy was designed to reverse twenty years of socialism by relinquishing considerable state control over the economy to the private sector. It was not immediately clear if this move would result in a fundamental and enduring restructuring of Iraq's economy, or if it was merely a stopgap measure to boost productivity, to cut costs, to tap private sector savings, and to reassure Western creditors.

Government and Politics

The political system in 1988 was in what was officially characterized as a "transitional" phase. This description meant that the current method of rule by decree, which had been in effect since 1968, would continue until the goal of a socialist, democratic republic with Islam as the state religion was attained. The end of the transition period was to be marked by the formal enactment of a permanent constitution. The timing and the specific circumstances that would terminate the transitional stage had not been specified as of early 1988.

The country remained under the regime of the Baath (Arab Socialist Resurrection) Party, which had seized power through a coup d'etat in July 1968. The legality of government institutions and actions was based on the Provisional Constitution of July 16, 1970, which embodied the basic principles of the Baath Party-- Arab unity, freedom, and socialism. These principles were in turn rooted in the pan-Arab aspirations of the party, aspirations sanctified through identification with the historic right and destiny of all Arabs to unite under the single leadership of "the Arab Nation."

The most powerful decision-making body in Iraq, the tenmember Revolutionary Command Council (RCC), which functioned as the top executive and legislative organ of the state, was for all practical purposes an arm of the Baath Party. All members of the RCC were also members of the party's Regional Command, or state apparatus. President Saddam Husayn was both the chairman of the RCC and the secretary general of the Baath's Regional Command. He was generally recognized as the most powerful political figure in the country.

From its earliest days, the Baath Party was beset by personality clashes and by factional infighting. These problems were a primary cause of the failure of the first Baath attempt to govern Iraq in 1963. After the Baath returned to power in 1968, intraparty fissures were generally held in check, albeit not eliminated, by President Ahmad Hasan al Bakr. When Saddam Husayn succeeded to the presidency in 1979, he also commanded the loyalty of the major elements of the Baath.

Saddam Husayn and other Baath leaders have always regarded the ability to balance endemic intraparty tensions--such as those between military and civilian elements and among personalities across boundaries of specialization--as the key to success in Baghdad. Above all, they perceived harmony in the militarycivilian coalition as pivotal. Although the Baath had begun recruiting within the Iraqi military as early as 1958, and within ten years military members constituted the backbone of the party's power, civilian Baath leaders maintained overall control of the party.

Iraqi politics under the Baath regime were generally geared toward mobilizing support for the regime. Loyal opposition had no place, and it was not recognized as legitimate. The party leaders believed competitive politics ill-suited to Iraq, at least during the indefinite transitional period. They condemned partisan political activity, which they insisted had had damaging consequences on national unity and integration. The Baath also invoked Iraq's unhappy legacy of ethnic and regional cleavages as justification for harsh curbs on political rights.

In 1988, twenty years after the Baath had come to power, it still was not possible to assess popular attitudes toward Saddam Husayn, toward the Baath Party, toward political institutions, or toward political issues because there had been insufficient field research in the country. Even though elections for a National Assembly had been held in 1980 and again in 1984, these had been carefully controlled by the government, and genuinely free elections had not been held for more than thirty years. Politicians or groups opposed to the principles of the 1968 Baath Revolution of July 17 to 30 were not permitted to operate openly. Those who aspired to be politically active had few choices: they could join the highly selective Baath Party, remain dormant, go underground or into exile, or join the Baath-sponsored Progressive National Front (PNF).

The PNF, which came into existence in 1974, was based on a national action charter that called for collaboration between the Baath and each of the other parties considered to be both progressive and nationalist. The PNF served as the only riskfree , non-Baath forum for political participation, although even this channel was denied to those whose loyalties to the regime were suspect. The Baath Party's objectives in establishing the front were to provide the semblance of broad popular support for the government as well as to provide the facade of alliance among the Baath and other parties. The Baath, however, held a dominant position within the front and therefore assumed sole responsibility for carrying out the decisions of the front's executive commission, which was composed of the Baath's most important members and sympathizers.

In early 1988, the war with Iran continued to preoccupy Saddam Husayn and his associates. Approximately 75,000 Iraqis had been killed in the war, and about 250,000 had been wounded; more than 50,000 Iraqis were being held as prisoners of war in Iran. Property damage was estimated in the tens of billions of dollars; destruction was especially severe in the southern part of the country

Constitutional Framework

The Provisional Constitution of July 16, 1970, upon which Iraq's governmental system was based in 1988, proclaims Iraq to be "a sovereign people's democratic republic" dedicated to the ultimate realization of a single Arab state and to the establishment of a socialist system. Islam is declared to be the state religion, but freedom of religion and of religious practices is guaranteed. Iraq is said to be formed of two principal nationalities, Arab and Kurd. A March 1974 amendment to the Constitution provides for autonomy for the Kurds in the region where they constitute a majority of the population. In this Autonomous Region (see Glossary) both Arabic and Kurdish are designated as official languages for administrative and educational purposes. The Constitution also prescribes, however, that the "national rights" of the Kurds as well as the "legitimate rights" of all minorities are to be exercised only within the framework of Iraqi unity, and the document stipulates that no part of Iraq can be relinquished.

The Constitution sets forth two basic aims, the establishment of a socialist system based on "scientific and revolutionary principles," and pan-Arab economic unity. The state is given an active role in "planning, directing, and guiding" the economy. National resources and the principal means of production are defined as "the property of the people" to be exploited by the state "directly in accordance with the requirements of the general planning of the national economy." The Constitution describes public properties and the properties of the public sector as inviolable.

The Constitution classifies the ownership of property as "a social function that shall be exercised within the limits of society's aims and the state's programs in accordance with the provisions of the law"; nevertheless, the Constitution also guarantees private ownership and individual economic freedom "within the limits of the law, provided that individual ownership will not contradict or be detrimental to general economic planning." The Constitution stipulates that private property may not be expropriated except for the public interest and then only with just compensation. The size of private agricultural land holdings is to be defined by law, and the excess is to be regarded as the property of the people. The Constitution also bars foreign ownership of real estate, although individuals may be granted a legal exemption from this prohibition.

Articles 19 through 36 of the Constitution spell out fundamental rights and duties in detail. The right to fair trial through due process, the inviolability of person and of residence, the privacy of correspondence, and the freedom to travel are guaranteed to all citizens. The Constitution also assures citizens of their right to religious freedom; to the freedom of speech, of publication, and of assembly; and to the freedom to form political parties, trade unions, and professional societies. The Constitution directs the state to eliminate illiteracy and to ensure the right of citizens to free education from elementary school through the university level. According to Article 28, the aims of education include instilling opposition to "the doctrines of capitalism, exploitation, reaction, Zionism, and colonialism" in order to ensure the achievement of the Baathist goals of Arab unity, freedom, and socialism. The Constitution also requires the state to provide every citizen with employment and with free medical care.

The Constitution defines the powers and the functions of the different government institutions. These include the RCC, the National Assembly, the presidency, the Council of Ministers, or cabinet, and the judiciary. According to Article 37, the RCC "is the supreme body in the State." Article 43 assigns to the RCC, by a vote of two-thirds of its members, authority to promulgate laws and regulations, to deal with national security, to declare war and conclude peace, and to approve the government's budget. Article 38 stipulates that all newly elected members of the RCC must be members of the Baath Party Regional Command. The Constitution also provides for an appointed Council of Ministers that has responsibility for carrying out the executive decisions of the RCC.

The chief executive of the RCC is the president, who serves as the commander in chief of the armed forces and as the head of both the government and the state. The powers of the president, according to the Constitution, include appointing, promoting, and dismissing personnel of the judiciary, civil service, and military. The president also has responsibility for preparing and approving the budget. The first president, Ahmad Hasan al Bakr, was in office from 1968 to 1979, when he resigned and was succeeded by Saddam Husayn.

Articles 47 through 56 of the Constitution provide for an elected National Assembly, but its powers are to be defined by the RCC. Elections for the Assembly took place for the first time in June 1980. Subsequent National assembly elections were held in October 1984.

The Constitution can be amended only by a two-thirds majority vote of the RCC. Although the 1970 Constitution is officially designated as provisional, it is to remain in force until a permanent constitution is promulgated.

Government

The Constitution provides for a governmental system that, in appearance, is divided into three mutually checking branches, the executive, the legislative, and the judicial. In practice, neither the legislature nor the judiciary has been independent of the executive.

The Revolutionary Command Council

In 1988 the Revolutionary Command Council (RCC) continued to be the top decision-making body of the state. The RCC was first formed in July 1968, and since then it has exercised both executive and legislative powers. The chairman of the RCC is the president of the republic. The number of RCC members has varied over time; in 1988 there were ten members.

According to the Constitution, the RCC is the supreme organ of the state, charged with the mission of carrying out the popular will by removing from power the reactionary, the dictatorial, and the corrupt elements of society and by returning power to the people. The RCC elects its chairman, who serves concurrently as president of the republic, by a two-thirds majority vote. In case of the chairman's official absence or incapacitation, his constitutional powers are to be exercised by the vice chairman, who also is elected by the RCC from among its members. Thus the vice chairman (in 1988 Izzat Ibrahim, who had served since 1979) is first in line of succession.

The members of the RCC, including both the chairman and the vice chairman, are answerable only to the RCC itself, which may dismiss any of its members by a two-thirds majority vote and may also charge and send to trial for wrongdoing any member of the council, any deputy to the president, or any cabinet minister. Since 1977 the Baath Party has regarded all members of the Baath Party Regional Command as members of the RCC. The interlocking leadership structure of the RCC and the Regional Command has served to emphasize the party's dominance in governmental affairs.

The RCC's constitutional powers are wide ranging. It may perform legislative functions, both in collaboration with, and independently of, the National Assembly; approve government recommendations concerning national defense and internal security; declare war, order general mobilization, conclude peace, and ratify treaties and international agreements; approve the state's general budget; lay down the rules for impeachment of its members and set up the special court to try those impeached; authorize the chairman or the vice chairman to exercise some of the council's powers except for legislative ones; and provide the internal regulations and working procedures of the council. The chairman is specifically empowered to preside over the council's closed sessions, to sign all laws and decrees issued by the council, and to supervise the work of cabinet ministers and the operation of the institutions of the state.

Politics

The Baath Party

In early 1988, the Baath Party continued to stress parallelism focused on "regional" (qutri) and "national" (qawmi) goals, following the Baath doctrine that the territorially and politically divided Arab countries were merely "regions" of a collective entity called "The Arab Nation." Hence the Baath movement in one country was considered merely an aspect of, or a phase leading to, "a unified democratic socialist Arab nation." That nation, when it materialized, would be under a single, unified Arab national leadership. Theoretically, therefore, success or failure at the regional level would have a corresponding effect on the movement toward that Arab nation. Moreover, the critical test of legitimacy for any Baath regime would necessarily be whether or not the regime's policies and actions were compatible with the basic aims of the revolution-- aims epitomized in the principles of "unity, freedom, and socialism."

The Baath Party in Iraq, like its counterparts in other Arab regions (states), derived from the official founding congress in Damascus in 1947. This conclave of pan-Arab intellectuals was inspired by the ideas of two Syrians, Michel Aflaq and Salah ad Din al Bitar, who are generally regarded as the fathers of the Baath movement. Several Iraqis, including Abd ar Rahman ad Damin and Abd al Khaliq al Khudayri, attended this congress and became members of the party. Upon their return to Baghdad, they formed the Iraqi branch of the Baath. Damin became the first secretary general of the Iraqi Baath.

Tahrir Square, Baghdad, showing the Monument of Liberty
Courtesy United Nations

From its early years, the Iraqi Baath recruited converts from a small number of college and high school students, intellectuals, and professionals--virtually all of whom were urban Sunni Arabs. A number of Baath high school members entered the Military College, where they influenced several classmates to join the party. Important military officers who became Baath members in the early 1950s included Ahmad Hasan al Bakr, Salih Mahdi Ammash, and Abd Allah Sultan, all of whom figured prominently in Iraqi political affairs in later years.

During the 1950s, the Baath was a clandestine party, and its members were subject to arrest if their identities were discovered. The Baath Party joined with other opposition parties to form the underground United National Front and participated in the activities that led to the 1958 revolution. The Baathists hoped that the new, republican government would favor pan-Arab causes, especially a union with Egypt, but instead the regime was dominated by non-Baathist military officers who did not support Arab unity or other Baath principles. Some younger members of the party, including Saddam Husayn, became convinced that Iraqi leader Abd al Karim Qasim had to be removed, and they plotted his assassination. The October 1959 attempt on Qasim's life, however, was bungled; Saddam Husayn fled Iraq, while other party members were arrested and tried for treason. The Baath was forced underground again, and it experienced a period of internal dissension as members debated over which tactics were appropriate to achieve their political objectives. The party's second attempt to overthrow Qasim, in February 1963, was successful, and it resulted in the formation of the country's first Baath government. The party, however, was more divided than ever between ideologues and more pragmatic members. Because of this lack of unity, the Baath's coup partners were able to outmaneuver it and, within nine months, to expel all Baathists from the government. It was not until 1965 that the Baath overcame the debilitating effects of ideological and of personal rivalries. The party then reorganized under the direction of General Bakr as secretary general with Saddam Husayn as his deputy. Both men were determined to return the Baath to power. In July 1968, the Baath finally staged a successful coup.

After the Baath takeover, Bakr became president of the regime, and he initiated programs aimed at the establishment of a "socialist, unionist, and democratic" Iraq. This was done, according to the National Action Charter, with scrupulous care for balancing the revolutionary requirements of Iraq on the one hand and the needs of the "Arab nation" on the other. According to a Baath Party pronouncement in January 1974, "Putting the regional above the national may lead to statism, and placing the national over the regional may lead to rash and childish action." This protestation notwithstanding, the government's primary concerns since 1968 have been domestic issues rather than pan- Arab ones.

In 1968 the Baath regime confronted a wide range of problems, such as ethnic and sectarian tensions, the stagnant condition of agriculture, commerce, and industry, the inefficiency and the corruption of government, and the lack of political consensus among the three main sociopolitical groups--the Shia Arabs, the Sunni Arabs, and the Kurds. The difficulties of consensus building were compounded by the pervasive apathy and mistrust at the grass-roots levels of all sects, by the shortage of qualified party cadres to serve as the standard-bearers of the Baath regime, and by the Kurdish armed insurgency. Rivalry with Syria and with Egypt for influence within the Arab world and the frontier dispute with Iran also complicated the regime's efforts to build the nation.

Since 1968 the Baath has attempted to create a strong and unified Iraq, through formal government channels and through political campaigns designed to eradicate what it called "harmful prerevolutionary values and practices," such as exploitation, social inequities, sectarian loyalties, apathy, and lack of civil spirit. Official statements called for abandonment of traditional ways in favor of a new life-style fashioned on the principles of patriotism, national loyalty, collectivism, participation, selflessness, love of labor, and civic responsibility. These "socialist principles and practices" would be instilled by the party's own example, through the state educational system, and through youth and other popular organizations. The Baath particularly emphasized "military training" for youth; such training was considered essential for creating "new men in the new society" and for defending the republic from the hostile forces of Zionism, imperialism, anti-Arab chauvinism (e.g., from Iran), rightists, opportunists, and reactionaries.

The Baath's major goal since 1968 has been to socialize the economy. By the late 1980s, the party had succeeded in socializing a significant part of the national economy, including agriculture, commerce, industry, and oil. Programs to collectivize agriculture were reversed in

1981, but government investment in industrial production remained important in the late 1980s. Large-scale industries such as iron, steel, and petrochemicals were fully owned and managed by the government, as were many medium-sized factories that manufactured textiles, processed food, and turned out construction materials.

The Baath's efforts to create a unified Arab nation have been more problematic. The party has not abandoned its goal of Arab unity. This goal, however, has become a long-term ideal rather than a short-term objective. President Saddam Husayn proclaimed the new view in 1982 by stating that Baathists now "believe that Arab unity must not take place through the elimination of the local and national characteristics of any Arab country. . . . but must be achieved through common fraternal opinion." In practice this meant that the Iraqi Baath Party had accepted unity of purpose among Arab leaders, rather than unification of Arab countries, as more important for the present.

As of early 1988, the Baath Party claimed about 10 percent of the population, a total of 1.5 million supporters and sympathizers; of this total, full party members, or cadres, were estimated at only 30,000, or 0.2 percent. The cadres were the nucleus of party organization, and they functioned as leaders, motivators, teachers, administrators, and watchdogs. Generally, party recruitment procedures emphasized selectivity rather than quantity, and those who desired to join the party had to pass successfully through several apprentice-like stages before being accepted into full membership. The Baath's elitist approach derived from the principle that the party's effectiveness could only be measured by its demonstrable ability to mobilize and to lead the people, and not by "size, number, or form." Participation in the party was virtually a requisite for social mobility.

The basic organizational unit of the Baath was the party cell or circle (halaqah). Composed of between three and seven members, cells functioned at the neighborhood or the village level, where members met to discuss and to carry out party directives. A minimum of two and a maximum of seven cells formed a party division (firqah). Divisions operated in urban quarters, larger villages, offices, factories, schools, and other organizations. Division units were spread throughout the bureaucracy and the military, where they functioned as the ears and eyes of the party. Two to five divisions formed a section (shabah). A section operated at the level of a large city quarter, a town, or a rural district. Above the section was the branch (fira), which was composed of at least two sections and which operated at the provincial level. There were twenty-one Baath Party branches in Iraq, one in each of the eighteen provinces and three in Baghdad. The union of all the branches formed the party's congress, which elected the Regional Command.

The Regional Command was both the core of party leadership and the top decision-making body. It had nine members, who were elected for five-year terms at regional congresses of the party. Its secretary general (also called the regional secretary) was the party's leader, and its deputy secretary general was second in rank and in power within the party hierarchy. The members of the command theoretically were responsible to the Regional Congress that, as a rule, was to convene annually to debate and to approve the party's policies and programs; actually, the members were chosen by Saddam Husayn and other senior party leaders to be "elected" by the Regional Congress, a formality seen as essential to the legitimation of party leadership.

Above the Regional Command was the National Command of the Baath Party, the highest policy-making and coordinating council for the Baath movement throughout the Arab world. The National Command consisted of representatives from all regional commands and was responsible to the National Congress, which convened periodically. It was vested with broad powers to guide, to coordinate, and to supervise the general direction of the movement, especially with respect to relationships among the regional Baath parties and with the outside world. These powers were to be exercised through a national secretariat that would direct policy-formulating bureaus.

In reality, the National Command did not oversee the Baath movement as a whole in 1988 because there continued to be no single command. In 1966 a major schism within the Baath movement had resulted in the creation of two rival National Commands, one based in Damascus and the other in Baghdad. Both commands claim to be the legitimate authority for the Baath, but since 1966 they have been mutually antagonistic. Michel Aflaq, one of the original cofounders of the Baath Party, was the secretary general of the Baghdad-based National Command, and Saddam Husayn was the vice-chairman. In practice, the Syrian Regional Command, under Hafiz al Assad, controlled the Damascus-based National Command of the Baath Party, while the Iraqi Regional Command controlled the Baghdad-based National Command.

Theoretically, the Iraqi Regional Command made decisions about Baath Party policy based on consensus. In practice, all decisions were made by the party's secretary general, Saddam Husayn, who since 1979 had also been chairman of the RCC and president of the republic. He worked closely with a small group of supporters, especially members of the Talfah family from the town of Tikrit (see The Emergence of Saddam Husayn, 1968-79); he also dealt ruthlessly with suspected opposition to his rule from within the party. In 1979 several high-ranking Baathists were tried and were executed for allegedly planning a coup; other prominent party members were forcibly retired in 1982. Saddam Husayn's detractors accused him of monopolizing power and of promoting a cult of personality.

Mass Media

In early 1988, all radio and television broadcasting in Iraq was controlled by the government. Radio Iraq had both domestic and foreign services. The domestic service broadcasted in Arabic, Kurdish, Syriac, and Turkoman; the foreign service, in English, French, German, Russian, Swahili, Turkish, and Urdu. Two radio stations based in Baghdad broadcasted all day, and they could be picked up by the overwhelming majority of the estimated 2.5 million radio receivers in the country. There were also separate radio stations with programs in Kurdish and Persian.

Baghdad Television was the main government television station. It broadcasted over two channels throughout the day. Government-owned commercial television stations also broadcasted from Basra, Kirkuk, Mosul, and nineteen other locations for an average of six hours a day. A Kurdish-language television station aired programs for eight hours each day. There were an estimated 750,000 privately owned television sets in the country in 1986, the latest year for which such statistics were available.

In 1988 there were six national daily newspapers, all of which were published in Baghdad. One of these papers, the Baghdad Observer, was published in English; it had an estimated circulation of 220,000. Another daily, Al-Iraq, with a circulation of abut 30,000, was published in Kurdish. The largest of the four Arabic-language dailies was Al Jumhuriya, which had a circulation of approximately 220,000. Ath Thawra, with a circulation of about

22,000, was the official organ of the Baath Party. There were also seven weekly papers, all published in Baghdad. The government's Iraqi News Agency (INA) distributed news to the foreign press based in, or passing through, Iraq.

Although Article 26 of the Provisional Constitution guarantees freedom of opinion and publication "within the limits of the law," newspapers, books, and other publications were subject to censorship. The Ministry of Guidance monitored published material to ensure that all writing was "in line with the nationalist and progressive line of the revolution." The Ministry of Culture and Information's National House for Publishing and Distributing Advertising had the sole authority to import and to distribute all foreign newspapers, magazines, and periodicals.

Foreign Policy

Iraq's relations with other countries and with international organizations are supervised by the Ministry of Foreign Affairs. In 1988 the minister of foreign affairs was Tariq Aziz, who had served in that post since 1983. Aziz was a member of the RCC and an influential leader of the Baath Party. Before becoming minister of foreign affairs, he had been director of the party's foreign affairs bureau. Aziz, Saddam Husayn, and the other members of the RCC formulated foreign policy, and the Ministry of Foreign Affairs bureaucracy implemented RCC directives. The Baath maintained control over the Ministry of Foreign Affairs and over all Iraqi diplomatic missions outside the country through its party cells that operated throughout the ministry and in all embassies abroad.

In 1988 Iraq's main foreign policy issue was the war with Iran. This war had begun in September 1980, when Saddam Husayn sent Iraqi forces across the Shatt al Arab into southwestern Iran (see The Iran-Iraq Conflict). Although the reasons for Saddam Husayn's decision to invade Iran were complicated, the leaders of the Baath Party had long resented Iranian hegemony in the Persian Gulf region and had especially resented the perceived Iranian interference in Iraq's internal affairs both before and after the 1979 Islamic Revolution. They may have thought that the revolutionary turmoil in Tehran would enable Iraq to achieve a quick victory. Their objectives were to halt any potential foreign assistance to the Shias and to the Kurdish opponents of the regime and to end Iranian domination of the area. The Baathists believed a weakened Iran would be incapable of posing a security threat and could not undermine Iraq's efforts to exercise the regional influence that had been blocked by non-Arab Iran since the mid-1960s. Although the Iraqis failed to obtain the expected easy victory, the war initially went well for them. By early 1982, however, the Iraqi occupation forces were on the defensive and were being forced to retreat from some of their forward lines. In June 1982, Saddam Husayn ordered most of the Iraqi units to withdraw from Iranian territory; after that time, the Baathist government tried to obtain a cease-fire based on a return of all armed personnel to the international borders that prevailed as of September 21, 1979.

Khalafa Street, Baghdad
Courtesy Ronald L. Kuipers

Iran did not accept Iraq's offer to negotiate an end to the war. Similarly, it rejected a July 1982 United Nations (UN) Security Council resolution calling for an immediate cease-fire. Subsequently, Iranian forces invaded Iraq by crossing the Shatt al Arab in the south and by capturing some mountain passes in the north. To discourage Iran's offensive, the Iraqi air force initiated bombing raids over several Iranian cities and towns. The air raids brought Iranian retaliation, which included the aerial bombing of Baghdad. Although Iraq eventually pushed back and contained the Iranian advances, it was not able to force Iranian troops completely out of Iraqi territory. The perceived threat to Iraq in the summer of 1982 thus was serious enough to force Saddam Husayn to request the Nonaligned Movement to change the venue of its scheduled September meeting from Baghdad to India; nevertheless, since the fall of 1982, the ground conflict has generally been a stalemated war of attrition--although Iran made small but demoralizing territorial advances as a result of its massive offensives in the reed marshes north of Basra in 1984 and in 1985, in Al Faw Peninsula in early 1986, and in the outskirts of Basra during January and February 1987. In addition, as of early 1988 the government had lost control of several mountainous districts in Kurdistan where, since 1983, dissident Kurds have cooperated militarily with Iran.

Rashid Hotel, Baghdad
Courtesy Ronald L. Kuipers

Saddam Husayn's government has maintained consistently since the summer of 1982 that Iraq wants a negotiated end to the war based upon the status quo ante. Iran's stated conditions for ceasing hostilities, namely the removal of Saddam Husayn and the Baath from power, however, have been unacceptable. The main objective of the regime became the extrication of the country from the war with as little additional damage as possible. To further this goal, Iraq has used various diplomatic, economic, and military strategies; none of these had been successful in bringing about a cease-fire as of early 1988 (see Introduction).

Although the war was a heavy burden on Iraq politically, economically, and socially, the most profound consequence of the war's prolongation was its impact on the patterns of Iraq's foreign relations. Whereas trends toward a moderation of the Baath Party's ideological approach to foreign affairs were evident before 1980, the war helped to accelerate these trends. Two of the most dramatic changes were in Iraq's relationships with the Soviet Union and with the United States. During the course of the war Iraq moved away from the close friendship with the Soviet Union that had persisted throughout the 1970s, and it initiated a rapprochement with the United States. Iraq also sought to ally itself with Kuwait and with Saudi Arabia, two neighboring countries with which there had been considerable friction during much of the 1970s. The alignment with these countries was accompanied by a more moderate Iraqi approach to other Arab countries, such as Egypt and Jordan, which previously Iraq had perceived as hostile.

NATIONAL SECURITY

Social upheavals have played a major role in Iraq's perception of its national security. Internal political instability, coupled with recurrent revolts by the Kurdish minority, mobilized the energies of successive regimes to crush opposition forces and to restore order. During the mid- and late 1970s, however, the Baath (Arab Socialist Resurrection) Party leaders succeeded in establishing a revolutionary government, which temporarily subdued the Kurdish revolt in northern Iraq and, using repressive measures, consolidated its power.

The higher prices of petroleum following the October 1973 Arab-Israeli War, and the Arab oil embargo, resulted in an accumulation of wealth that enabled Iraq to expand its armed forces in an attempt to match, in strength as well as in strategic importance, the capacity of its neighbor, Iran. Having signed a border treaty with Tehran in 1975, Baghdad assumed that its search for military parity would not result in conflict, in particular because the two states enjoyed economic prosperity; however, regional events, ranging from the Soviet Union's expulsion from Egypt in 1972 to Egypt's eventual expulsion from the League of Arab States (Arab League) in 1979, following the signing of the separate Israeli-Egyptian peace treaty, strengthened Baghdad's resolve to make a bid for regional leadership. Armed with modern weapons and with sophisticated equipment from the Soviet Union and France, Iraq gained a sense of invincibility and, when the opportunity arose, implemented its resolve. Threatened by the 1979 Islamic Revolution in Iran and by its potential influence on Iraq's majority Shia (see Glossary) population, Iraq attacked Iran on September 22, 1980.

For most of the 1980s, Iraq has been preoccupied with that war. In contrast to the first forty years of Iraqi independence, when the military participated in several coups, the Iraqi armed forces demonstrated growing professionalism in the 1980s by limiting their direct role in the country's political life. The armed forces' loyalty has also been assured by the Baath Party, however, which--after conducting purges against the military during the 1970s--continued to maintain a close eye on every aspect of military life and national security in the late 1980s.

Iraq invaded Kuwait in August 1990, but a U.S.-led coalition acting under United Nations (UN) resolutions expelled Iraq from Kuwait in February 1991. After the war, UN-mandated sanctions based on Security Council resolutions called for the regime to surrender its weapons of mass destruction and submit to UN inspections. The regime has refused to fully cooperate with the UN inspections and since 1998 has not allowed inspectors into Iraq. Iraq is allowed under the UN Oil-for-Food program to export unlimited quantities of oil with which to purchase food, medicine, and other humanitarian relief equipment and infrastructure support necessary to sustain the civilian population. The UN coalition enforces no-fly zones in southern and northern Iraq to protect Iraqi citizens from attack by the regime and a no-drive zone in southern Iraq to prevent the regime from massing forces to threaten or again invade Kuwait.

Source: U.S. Central Intelligence Agency, 1999.

GLOSSARY – IRAQ

Autonomous Region - Governorates of As Sulaymaniyah, Dahuk, and Irbil, the Kurdish majority area. In this region--popularly known as Kurdistan--Kurdish has status of official language, and residents enjoy limited autonomy from central government.

atabeg - Turkish word that during the period of the Ottoman Empire meant governor of a province.

barrels per day - Production of crude oil and petroleum products is frequently measured in barrels per day, often abbreviated bpd or bd. A barrel is a volume measure of forty-two United States gallons. Conversion of barrels to metric tons depends on the density of a specific product. About 7.3 barrels of average crude oil, or about 7 barrels of heavy crude oil, weigh 1 metric ton. Light products, such as gasoline and kerosene, average close to eight barrels per metric ton.

currency - See dinar.

dinar (ID) - Currency unit consisting of 1,000 fils or 20 dirhams. When officially introduced at the end of the British mandate (1932), the dinar was equal to, and was linked to, the British pound sterling, which at that time was equal to US$4.86. Iraqi dinar (ID) equaled US$4.86 between 1932 and 1949 and after devaluation in 1949, equaled US$2.80 between 1949 and 1971. Iraq officially uncoupled the dinar from the pound sterling as a gesture of independence in 1959, but the dinar remained at parity with the pound until the British unit of currency was again devalued in 1967. One Iraqi dinar remained equal to US$2.80 until December 1971, when major realignments of world currencies began. Upon the devaluation of the United States dollar in 1973, the Iraqi dinar appreciated to US$3.39. It remained at this level until the outbreak of the Iran-Iraq War in 1980. In 1982 Iraq devalued the dinar by 5 percent, to a value equal to US$3.22, and sustained this official exchange rate without additional devaluation despite mounting debt. In early 1988, the official dinar-dollar exchange rate was still ID1 to US$3.22; however, with estimates of the nation's inflation rate ranging from 25 percent to 50 percent per year in 1985 and 1986, the dinar's real transaction value, or black market exchange rate, was far lower-- only about half the 1986 official rate.

Free Officers - Term applied retroactively to the group of young military officers that planned and carried out the July 14 Revolution in 1958.

GDP (gross domestic product) - A value measure of the flow of domestic goods and services produced by an economy over a period of time, such as a year. Only output values of goods for final consumption and for intermediate production are assumed to be included in final prices. GDP is sometimes aggregated and shown at market prices, meaning that indirect taxes and subsidies are included; when these have been eliminated, the result is GDP at factor cost. The word gross indicates that deductions for depreciation of physical assets have not been made.

GNP (gross national product) - GDP (q.v.) plus the net income or loss stemming from transactions with foreign countries. GNP is the broadest measurement of the output of goods and services by an economy. It can be calculated at market prices, which include indirect taxes and subsidies. Because indirect taxes and subsidies are only transfer payments, GNP is often calculated at factor cost, removing indirect taxes and subsidies.

hadith - Tradition based on the precedent of Muhammad's nondivinely revealed words that serves as one of the sources of Islamic law (sharia).

hijra - Literally to migrate, to sever relations, to leave one's tribe. Throughout the Muslim world hijra refers to the migration of Muhammad and his followers to Medina. In this sense the word has come into European languages as hegira, and it is usually, and somewhat misleadingly, translated as flight.

ID - Iraqi dinar. See dinar.

Imam - A word used in several senses. In general use and in lower case, it means the leader of congregational prayers; as such it implies no ordination or special spiritual powers beyond sufficient education to carry out this function. It is also used figuratively by many Sunni (q.v.) Muslims to mean the leader of the Islamic community. Among Shias (q.v.) the word takes on many complex meanings; in general, it indicates that particular descendent of the House of Ali ibn Abu Talib, who is believed to have been God's designated repository of the spiritual authority inherent in that line. The identity of this individual and the means of ascertaining his identity have been major issues causing divisions among Shias.

International Monetary Fund (IMF) - Established along with the World Bank in 1945, the IMF is a specialized agency affiliated with the United Nations and is responsible for stabilizing international exchange rates and payments. The main business of the IMF is the provision of loans to its members (including industrialized and developing countries) when they experience balance of payments difficulties. These loans frequently carry conditions that require substantial internal economic adjustments by the recipients, most of which are developing countries.

Levant - Historically, the countries along the eastern shores of the Mediterranean.

shaykh - Leader or chief. Word of Arabic origin used to mean either a political leader or a learned religious leader. Also used as an honorific.

Shia, from Shiat Ali, the Party of Ali - A member of the smaller of the two great divisions of Islam. The Shias supported the claims of Ali and his line to presumptive right to the caliphate and to leadership of the Muslim community, and on this issue they divided from the Sunni (q.v.) in the great schism within Islam. Later schisms have produced further divisions among the Shias over the identity and the number of Imams (q.v.). Shias revere Twelve Imams, the last of whom is believed to be in hiding.

Shiite - See Shia.

Sunni (from sunna, orthodox) - A member of the larger of the two great divisions of Islam. The Sunnis supported the traditional method of election to the caliphate, and they accepted the Umayyad line that began with caliph Muawiyah in 661. On this issue they divided from the Shias (q.v.) in the great schism within Islam.

PART 3: BIBLIOGRAPHY

BIBLIOGRAPHY

"Chronology, July 16, 1982--October 15, 1982," Middle East Journal, 37, No. 1, Winter 1983, 65-88.

"Gulf War Moves Towards the Final Showdown," Middle East Economic Digest [London], 31, No. 51, December 19, 1987, 32-33.

"Interview With Saddam Husayn," Al Majallah [London], December 8, 1982.

"Iraq." Pages 432-42 in The Middle East and North Africa, 1987. London: Europa Publications, 1986.

"Syrians, Iraqis Bury Hatchet, but not in Iran," Iran Times, 17, No. 35, November 13, 1984, 15-16.

Abbas, A. "The Iraqi Armed Forces, Past and Present." Pages 203- 26 in Committee Against Repression and for Democratic Rights in Iraq (CARDRI), (ed.), Saddam's Iraq: Revolution or Reaction? London: Zed Books, 1986.

Abdulghani, Jasim M. Iraq and Iran: The Years of Crisis. Baltimore: Johns Hopkins University Press, 1984.

Abu Jaber, Kemal. The Arab Baath Socialist Party. Syracuse: Syracuse University Press, 1966.

Adams, Doris Goodrich. Iraq's People and Resources (University of California Publications in Economics, XVIII). Berkeley: University of California Press, 1958.

Adams, Martin E. "Lessons from Agrarian Reform in Iraq," Land Reform [Rome], No. 1, 1972, 56-64.

Adams, Robert McCormick. Irrigation's Impact on Society. Tucson: University of Arizona Press, 1974.

Al-Khafaji, Isam. "State Incubation of Iraqi Capitalism." Pages 4-12 in MERIP Middle East Report, No. 142. September-October 1986. Washington: Middle East Research and Information Project.

Alnasrawi, Abbas. Financing Economic Development in Iraq: The Role of Oil in a Middle Eastern Economy. New York: Praeger, 1967.

Arfa, Hassan. The Kurds: An Historical and Political Study. London: Oxford University Press, 1966.

Axelgard, Frederick W. (ed.) Iraq In Transition: A Political, Economic, and Strategic Perspective. Boulder, Colorado: Westview Press, 1986.

Baali, Fuad. "Relationships of Man to the Land in Iraq," Rural Sociology, 31, June 1966, 171-82.

Baali, Fuad. "Social Factors in Iraqi Rural-Urban Migrations," American Journal of Economic and Sociological Research, 25, October 1966, 359-64.

Baali, Fuad. Relation of the People to the Land in Southern Iraq (University of Florida Monographs, Social Sciences, No. 31). Gainesville: University of Florida Press, 1966.

Badre, Albert Y. "Economic Development of Iraq." Pages 281-328 in Charles A. Cooper and Sidney S. Alexander (eds.), Economic Development and Population Growth in the Middle East. New York: American Elsevier Publishing, 1972.

Baram, Amitzia. "The June 1980 Election to the National Assembly in Iraq," Orient, 27, No. 3, 1981.

Barth, Fredrik. Principles of Social Organization in Southern Kurdistan (University Ethnographic Museum Bulletin, No. 7). Oslo: Brodrene Jordensen, 1953.

Batatu, Hanna. "Iraq's Underground Shia Movements: Characteristics, Causes, and Prospects," Middle East Journal, 35, No. 4, Autumn 1981, 578-94.

Batatu, Hanna. "Shi'i Organizations in Iraq: Al-Da'wah al-Islamiyah and Al-Mujahidin." Pages 179-200 in Juan R.I. Cole and Nikki R. Keddie (eds.), Shi'ism and Social Protest. New Haven: Yale University Press, 1986.

Batatu, Hanna. The Old Social Classes and the Revolutionary Movements of Iraq: A Study of Iraq's Old Landed and Commercial Classes, and of Its Communists, Bathists, and Free Officers. Princeton, New Jersey: Princeton University Press, 1978.

Bigler, C.S. "Tensions Between International Law and Strategic Security-- Implications of Israel's Preemptive Raid on Iraq's Nuclear Reactor," Virginia Journal of International Law, 24, No. 2, 1984, 459-511.

Bill, James A. "Islam, Politics, and Shi'ism in the Gulf," Middle East Insight, 3, No. 3, January-February 1984, 3-12.

Brown, Michael E. "The Nationalization of the Iraqi Petroleum Company," International Journal of Middle East Studies, 10, No. 1, February 1979, 107-24.

Cook, M.A. (ed.) Studies in the Economic History of the Middle East. New York: Oxford University Press, 1970.

Cordesman, Anthony H. "Lessons of the Iran-Iraq War: Part Two--Tactics, Technology, and Training," Armed Forces Journal, 119, No. 10, June 1982, 68-85.

Cordesman, Anthony H. "Lessons of the Iran-Iraq War: The First Round," Armed Forces Journal, 119, No. 8, April 1982, 32- 47.

Cordesman, Anthony H. "The Attack on the USS Stark: The Tragic Cost of Human Error," Armed Forces [London], 6, No. 10, October 1987, 447-50.

Cordesman, Anthony H. "The Iran-Iraq War in 1984: An Escalating Threat to the Gulf and the West," Armed Forces Journal, 121, No. 8, March 1984, 22-30, 75.

Cordesman, Anthony H. "The Iran-Iraq War: Attrition Now, Chaos Later," Armed Forces Journal, 120, No. 10, May 1983, 36-42, 116-17.

Cordesman, Anthony H. The Iran-Iraq War: 1984-1986. Rosslyn, Virginia: Eaton Analytical Assessments Center, 1986.

Coulson, Noel, and Doreen Hinchcliffe. "Women and Law Reform in Contemporary Islam." Pages 37-51 in Lois Beck and Nikki Keddie (eds.), Women in the Muslim World. Cambridge: Harvard University Press, 1978.

Dann, Uriel. Iraq Under Qassem 1958-63. New York: Praeger, 1969.

Davidson, Roderic H. Turkey. Englewood Cliffs, New Jersey: Prentice Hall, 1968.

Dawisha, Adeed. "Iraq and the Arab World--The Gulf War and After," World Today [London], 37, No. 5, May 1981, 188-94.

Dawisha, Karen. "Moscow and the Gulf War," World Today [London], 37, No. 1, January 1981, 8-14.

Devlin, John. The Baath Party: A History from Its Origins to 1966. Stanford: Hoover Institution Press, 1976.

Drysdale, Alasdair and Gerald H. Blake. The Middle East and North Africa: A Political Geography. London: Oxford University Press, 1985.

Economist Intelligence Unit. Iraq: Country Report. (No. 1.) London: 1988.

El-Azhary, M.S. "The Attitudes of the Superpowers Towards the Gulf War," International Affairs [London], 59, No. 4, 1983, 609-20.

El-Azhary, M.S. The Iran-Iraq War: An Historical, Economic, and Political Analysis. New York: St. Martin's Press, 1984.

Entessar, Nader. "The Kurds in Post-Revolutionary Iran and Iraq," Third World Quarterly [London], 6, No. 4, October 1984, 911-33.

Evans, David and Richard Campany. "Iran-Iraq: Bloody Tomorrows," United States Naval Institute Proceedings, 111, No.1, January 1985, 33-43.

Feldman, Shai. "The Bombing of Osiraq--Revisited," International Security, 7, No. 1, Fall 1982, 114- 42.

Fernea, Elizabeth W. Guests of the Sheikh. New York: Doubleday, 1965.

Fernea, Robert A. Shaykh and Effendi: Changing Patterns of Authority among the Shabana of Southern Iraq. Cambridge: Harvard University Press, 1970.

Gabbay, Rony. Communism and Agrarian Reform in Iraq. London: Croom Helm, 1978.

Gallman, Waldemar. Iraq Under General Nuri. Baltimore: Johns Hopkins University Press, 1964.

Ghareeb, Edmund. "Iraq and Gulf Security." Pages 39-64 in Z. Michael Szaz (ed.), The Impact of the Iranian Events Upon Persian Gulf and United States Security. Washington: American Foreign Policy Institute, 1979.

Ghareeb, Edmund. "Iraq: Emergent Gulf Power." Pages 197-230 in Hossein Amirsadeghi (ed.), The Security of the Persian Gulf. New York: St. Martin's Press, 1981.

Ghareeb, Edmund. The Kurdish Question in Iraq. Syracuse: Syracuse University Press, 1981.

Gotlieb, Yosef. "Sectarianism and the Iraqi State." Pages 153-61 in Michael Curtis (ed.), Religion and Politics in the Middle East. Boulder, Colorado: Westview Press, 1981.

Gruemm, H. "Safeguards and Tamuz: Setting the Record Straight," International Atomic Energy Agency Bulletin [Vienna], 23, No. 4, December 1981, 10-14.

Grummond, Stephen. The Iran-Iraq War: Islam Embattled. New York: Praeger, 1982.

Halliday, Fred. "Gorbachev and the 'Arab Syndrome': Soviet Policy in the Middle East," World Policy Journal [London], 1987, 415-41.

Halliday, Fred. "The USSR and the Gulf War: Moscow's Growing Concern," Middle East Report, 148, September-October 1987, 10-11.

Heller, Mark. "Politics and the Military in Iraq and Jordan 1920- 1958: The British Influence," Armed Forces and Society, 4, No. 1, Fall 1977, 75-100.

Helms, Christine Moss. "The Iraqi Dilemma: Political Objectives Versus Military Strategy," American-Arab Affairs, No. 5, September 1983, 76-85.

Helms, Christine Moss. Iraq, Eastern Flank of the Arab World. Washington: Brookings Institution, 1984.

Hemphill, Paul P.J. "The Formation of the Iraqi Army, 1921-33." Pages 88-110 in Abbas Kelidar (ed.), The Integration of Modern Iraq. London: Croom Helm, 1979.

Hiro, Dilip. "Chronicle of the Gulf War." Pages 3-14 in MERIP Reports, No. 125-126. July-September 1984. Washington: Middle Easst Research and Information Project.

Hitti, Philip K. Makers of Arab History. New York: Harper and Row, 1968.

Hitti, Philip K. The Near East in Hitory. Princeton, New Jersey: Van Nostrand, 1961.

Hodgson, Marshall G.S. "How Did the Early Shia Become Sectarian?" Journal of the American Oriental Society, 75, No. 1, January-March 1955, 1-13.

International Institute for Strategic Studies. The Military Balance, 1977-78. London: 1977.

International Institute for Strategic Studies. The Military Balance, 1979-80. London: 1979.

International Institute for Strategic Studies. The Military Balance, 1981-82. London: 1981.

International Institute for Strategic Studies. The Military Balance, 1983-84. London: 1983.

International Institute for Strategic Studies. The Military Balance, 1985-86. London: 1985.

International Institute for Strategic Studies. The Military Balance, 1986-87. London: 1986.

International Institute for Strategic Studies. The Military Balance, 1987-88. London: 1987.

International Monetary Fund. Exchange Arrangements and Exchange Restrictions: Annual Report, 1987. Washington, 1987.

Iraq. Ministry of Planning. Central Statistial Organization. Annual Abstract of Statistics, 1985. Baghdad: n.d.

Iraq. Ministry of Planning. Central Statistical Organization. Economic and Social Progress Under the Revolution. Baghdad: July 1978.

Ireland, Philip. Iraq: A Study in Political Development. New York: Macmillan, 1938.

Ismael, Tareq Y. "Ideology in Recent Iraqi Foreign Policy." Pages 109-25 in Shirin Tahir-Kheli and Shaheen Ayubi (eds.), The Iran-Iraq War: New Weapons, Old Conflicts. New York: Praeger, 1983.

Ismael, Tareq Y. Iraq and Iran: Roots of Conflict. Syracuse: Syracuse University Press, 1982.

Issawi, Charles (ed.). The Economic History of the Middle East, 1800-1914. Chicago: University of Chicago Press, 1966.

Jalal, Ferhang. The Role of Government in the Industrialization of Iraq, 1950-65. London: Frank Cass, 1972.

Jansen, G.H. "Iraq: Bleak Outlook," Middle East International [London], February 4, 1983, 6.

Jawad, Saad. Iraq and the Kurdish Question, 1958-1970. London: Ithaca Press, 1981.

Kedourie, Elie. "Continuity and Change in Modern Iraqi History," Asian Affairs [London], June 1975, 140-146.

Kelidar, Abbas. "Iraq: The Search for Stability," Conflict Studies [London], 59, July 1975, 1-22.

Kelidar, Abbas. The Integration of Modern Iraq. New York: St. Martin's Press, 1979.

Kempe, Frederick. "Baghdad's Goal: Iraq's Aim in Gulf War Is No Longer to Win But to Avoid Losing," Wall Street Journal, August 28, 1987, 1, 14.

Kerr, Malcolm. The Arab Cold War. London: Oxford University Press, 1971.

Khadduri, Majid. "The Role of the Military in Iraqi Society." Pages 41-51 in Sydney Nettleton Fisher (ed.), The Military in the Middle East. Columbus: Ohio State University Press, 1963.

Khadduri, Majid. Independent Iraq, 1932-1958. London: Oxford University Press, 1970.

Khadduri, Majid. Republican Iraq. London: Oxford University Press, 1969.

Khadduri, Majid. Socialist Iraq: A Study in Iraqi Politics Since 1968. Washington: Middle East Institute, 1978.

Klieman, Aaron S. Foundations of British Policy in the World: The Cairo Conference of 1921. Baltimore: Johns Hopkins University Press, 1970.

Laffin, John. "The Gulf War." Pages 72-87 in John Laffin (ed.), War Annual, 1. London: Brassey's Defense Publishers, 1986.

Langley, Kathleen M. The Industrialization of Iraq (Harvard Middle Eastern Monograph Series, V). Cambridge: Harvard University Press, 1967.

Longrigg, Stephen Hemsley, and Frank Stoakes. Iraq (Nations of the Modern World series). London: Ernest Benn, 1958.

Longrigg, Stephen Hemsley. Four Centuries of Modern Iraq. London: Oxford University Press, 1925.

Longrigg, Stephen Hemsley. Iraq, 1900 to 1950. London: Oxford University Press, 1953.

Marr, Phebe. "Iraq's Leadership Dilemma: A Study in Leadership Trends, 1948-1968," Middle East Journal, 24, No. 3, Winter-Autumn 1970, 283-301.

Marr, Phebe. "The Political Elite in Iraq." Pages 109-49 in George Lenczowski (ed.), Political Elites in the Middle East. Washington: American Enterprise Institute, 1975.

Marr, Phebe. The Modern History of Iraq. Boulder, Colorado: Westview Press, 1985.

Momen, Moojan. An Introduction to Shii Islam. New Haven: Yale University Press, 1985.

Muhsin, Jabr. "The Gulf War." Pages 227-244 in Committee Against Repression and for Democratic Rights in Iraq (CARDRI), (ed.), Saddam's Iraq: Revolution or Reaction? London: Zed Books, 1986.

Niblock, Tim. Iraq: The Contemporary State. New York: St. Martin's Press, 1982.

Nonneman, Gerd. Iraq, the Gulf States, and the War: A Changing Relationship, 1980-1986 and Beyond. London: Ithaca Press, 1986.

O'Ballance, Edgar. The Kurdish Revolt, 1961-1970. Hamden, Connecticut: Archon Books, 1973.

Olson, William J. "Iraqi Policy and the Impact of the Iran-Iraq War." Pages 165-202 in Robert O. Freedman (ed.), The Middle East After the Israeli Invasion of Lebanon. Syracuse: Syracuse University Press, 1986.

Paxton, John. The Statesman's Yearbook, 1986-87. New York: St. Martin's Press, 1986.

Pelletiere, Stephen C. The Kurds: An Unstable Element in the Gulf. Boulder, Colorado: Westview Press, 1984.

Penrose, Edith and E.F. Penrose. Iraq: International Relations and National Development. Boulder, Colorado: Westview Press, 1978.

Petrossian, Vahe. "The Gulf War," World Today [London], 36, No. 11, November 1980, 415-17.

Quester, George H. "Nuclear Weapons and Israel," Middle East Journal, 37, No. 4, Autumn 1983, 547-64.

Ramazani, R.K. Revolutionary Iran: Challenge and Response in the Middle East. Baltimore: Johns Hopkins University Press, 1986.

Ramberg, Bennett. "Attacks on Nuclear Reactors: The Implications of Israel's Strike on Osiraq," Political Science Quarterly, 97, No. 4, Winter 1982-83, 653-69.

Renfrew, Nita M. "Who Started The War?" Foreign Policy, No. 66, Spring 1987, 98-108.

Roberts, J.M. The Pelican History of the World. New York: Penguin Books, 1980.

Roux, George. Ancient Iraq. Cleveland: World Publishing, 1965.

Sayigh, Yusuf Abd Allah. The Determinants of Arab Economic Development. New York: St. Martin's Press, 1978.

Sayigh, Yusuf Abd Allah. The Economics of the Arab World: Development since 1945. New York: St. Martin's Press, 1978.

Sciolino, Elaine. "The Big Brother: Iraq Under Saddam Hussein," New York Times Magazine, February 3, 1985, 16.

Seale, Patrick. The Struggle for Syria. New York: Oxford University Press, 1965.

Shwadran, Benjamin. The Power Struggle in Iraq. New York: Council for Middle Eastern Affairs Press, 1960.

Simon, Reeva. Iraq Between the Two World Wars. New York: Columbia University Press, 1986.

Sluglett, Peter and Marion Farouk-Sluglett. "Some Reflections on the Sunni/Shia Question in Iraq," British Society for Middle East Studies [London], 5, 1978, 79-87.

Sluglett, Peter. "The Kurds." Pages 177-202 in Committee Against Repression and for Democratic Rights in Iraq (CARDRI), (ed.), Saddam's Iraq: Revolution or Reaction? London: Zed Books, 1986.

Sluglett, Peter. Britain in Iraq, 1914-1932. London: Ithaca Press, 1976.

Snyder, Jed C. "The Road to Osiraq: Baghdad's Quest for the Bomb," Middle East Journal, 37, No. 4, Autumn 1983, 565-93.

Sourdel, D. "The Abbasid Caliphate." Pages 104-39 in P.M. Holt, Ann K.S. Lambton, and Bernard Lewis (eds.), The Cambridge History of Islam, I. Cambridge: Cambridge University Press, 1970.

Stafford, R.S. The Tragedy of the Assyrians. London: Allen and Unwin, 1935.

Sterner, Michael. "The Iran-Iraq War," Foreign Affairs, 63, No. 1, Fall 1984, 128-43.

Tahir-Kheli, Shirin, and Shaheen Ayubi (eds.) The Iran-Iraq War: New Weapons, Old Conflicts. New York: Praeger, 1983.

Tarbush, Mohammad A. The Role of the Military in Politics: A Case Study of Iraq to 1941. London: Kegan Paul International, 1982.

The Middle East and North Africa--1989. London: Europa Publications, 1988.

Thesiger, Wilfred. The Marsh Arabs. New York: Dutton, 1964.

United States. Department of Commerce. International Trade Administration. Foreign Economic Trends and Their Implications for the United States: Iraq. Washington: June 1986.

United States. Department of Defense. Soviet Military Power. Washington: 1987.

United States. Department of State. Country Reports on Human Rights Practices for 1985. (Report Submitted to 99th United States Congress, 1st Session. Committee on Foreign Affairs, House of Representatives, and Committee on Foreign Relations, Senate.) Washington: GPO, 1986.

Vandenbroucke, Lucien S. "The Israeli Strike Against Osiraq: The Dynamics of Fear and Proliferation in the Middle East," Air University Review, 35, No. 5, September-October 1984, 35-47.

Vanly, I.C. "Kurdistan in Iraq." Pages 192-203 in Gerard Chaliand (ed.), People Without a Country: The Kurds and Kurdistan. London: Zed Books, 1980.

Viorst, Milton. "A Reporter at Large: The View from the Mustansiriyah," New Yorker, Pt. 1, October 12, 1987, 92-114.

Viorst, Milton. "A Reporter at Large: The View from the Mustansiriyah," New Yorker, Pt. 2, October 19, 1987, 76-96.

Viorst, Milton. "Iraq at War," Foreign Affairs, 65, No. 2, Winter 1986-87, 349-65.

Warriner, Doreen. Land Reform and Development in the Middle East: A Study of Egypt, Syria, and Iraq. London: Oxford University Press for the Royal Institute of International Affairs, 1962.

World Armaments and Disarmament: SIPRI Yearbook, 1987. New York: Oxford University Press, 1987.

Wright, Claudia. "Iraq: New Power in the Middle East," Foreign Affairs, 58, Winter 1979-1980, 257-77.

Yodfat, Aryeh Y. The Soviet Union and the Arabian Peninsula: Soviet Policy Towards the Persian Gulf and Arabia. New York: St. Martin's Press, 1983.

Young, Gavin. Return to the Marshes: Life With the Marsh Arabs of Iraq. London: Collins, 1977.

Zaher, U. "Political Developments in Iraq, 1963-1980." Pages 30- 53 in Committee Against Repression and for Democratic Right in Iraq (CARDRI), (ed.), Saddam's Iraq: Revolution or Reaction? London: Zed Books, 1986.

Zaher, U. "The Opposition." Pages 138-76 in Committee Against Repression and for Democratic Rights in Iraq (CARDRI), (ed.) Saddam's Iraq: Revolution or Reaction? London: Zed Books, 1986.

INDEX

Y